W9-BVC-141

DATE DUE

MAY 0 3 2013	

MANAGING
ACROSS
CULTURES

MANAGING

ACROSS

CULTURES

The Seven Keys
to Doing Business
with a Global Mindset

CHARLENE M. SOLOMON
MICHAEL S. SCHELL

New York   Chicago   San Francisco
Lisbon   London   Madrid   Mexico City   Milan
New Delhi   San Juan   Seoul   Singapore
Sydney   Toronto

The *McGraw-Hill* Companies

1 2 3 4 5 6 7 8 9 0 DOC/DOC 0 1 0 9

ISBN: 978-0-07-160585-4
MHID: 0-07-160585-1

This publication is designed to provide accurate and authoritative information in regard to the subject matter covered. It is sold with the understanding that the publisher is engaged in rendering legal, accounting, or other professional service. If legal advice or other expert assistance is required, the services of a competent professional person should be sought.

—From a Declaration of Principles Jointly Adopted
by a Committee of the American Bar
Association and a Committee of Publishers and Associations

McGraw-Hill books are available at special quantity discounts to use as premiums and sales promotions, or for use in corporate training programs. To contact a representative, please visit the Contact Us pages at www.mhprofessional.com.

This book is printed on acid-free paper.

Library of Congress Cataloging-in-Publication Data

Solomon, Charlene Marmer.
    Managing across cultures : the seven keys to doing business with a global mindset / by Charlene M. Solomon and Michael S. Schell.
        p. cm.
    ISBN-13: 978-0-07-160585-4 (acid-free paper)
    ISBN-10: 0-07-160585-1 (acid-free paper) 1. International business enterprises–Management. 2. International business enterprises–Management–Cross-cultural studies. 3. Management–Cross-cultural studies. 4. Corporate culture–Cross-cultural studies. I. Schell, Michael S. II. Title.
    HD62.4.S6779 2009
    658'.049–dc22

                                                                                2009006676

Dedication

From Michael: To my wife, Lynne Schell, without whose love and forbearance nothing would be possible, and to my grandchildren, Adalai and Asher, whom I hope will one day enjoy this book. To the memory of the World's Doctor, Allan Rosenfield.

From Charlene: To Alan for your continuing love, amazing emotional support, and never-ending encouragement to follow my heart, and to Elizabeth, Andrew, and Chris, who inspire me to keep learning and who keep me laughing.

Contents

Acknowledgments

Over the last several years there have been innumerable friends, colleagues, and clients who have shared their wisdom, experiences, and insights with us. Those generous individuals have talked with us, debated issues with us, sent us resources, and generally stimulated our own thought process, and we thank them. All of that thinking made this book possible.

First we would like to acknowledge the contributions of our key staff members:

- Valerie Greenly, whose kind and positive perspective on everything that happens, coupled with her energy and attention to detail, have enriched lives and perfected our work. For the past 20 years, Valerie has helped make our work both fun and successful.

- Paul Bailey, whose efforts on the other side of the Atlantic have made our endeavors in Europe fruitful and wonderfully enriching.

- Joshua Sturtevant, who enthusiastically embraces new responsibilities and impresses us daily with his expertise and creative vision.

- Carrie Shearer, who has made an enormous contribution to this book, is largely responsible for Chapter 14, "Women Crossing Cultures," in which she shares her significant depth of experience and understanding of the international assignment experience. In addition, Carrie's tireless creative energy and remarkable resourcefulness have contributed significantly to the overall success of CultureWizard.

We'd also like to thank Annette Messler, who for the past 20 years has kept our financial lives in order, and to thank Sean Dubberke, Barbara Thorp, and Miranda Rowe, on whose unique energies we call everyday.

We give a special thank-you to Paula Caligiuri, Ph.D., Associate Professor of Human Resource Management at Rutgers University, School of Management and Labor Relations and Director of the Center for Human Resource Strategy. Paula, who is the creator of the SAGE (Self-Assessment for Global Endeavors), SAGE for Spouses, and SAGE for Global Business Leaders, has been a most valuable advisor and colleague for over the past decade. We've learned so much from her about global leadership development. Her contribution was a critical component of our work in Chapter 13. Paula's ongoing support and direction allows us to continue to do cutting-edge research and bring significantly greater value to our clients and to our online content and community.

Yang Zhang, PhD., also eagerly supported our research initiatives and gave us a deeper understanding of the generational and cultural differences in emerging China. She was extremely helpful in our work on intercultural global teams as well as a variety of other areas.

We would also like to thank the following individuals who helped us continue to develop our thoughts and perspectives: Michael Bruck, previously the head of Intel China, who generously shared his significant experiences in China that allowed us to gain wisdom on that critically important part of the world; Milton Ives of Mars, Inc., previously with HSBC Bank, whose gentle prodding and questioning kept us reaching for continuous improvement; Franck Andreutti of Motorola, who shared his own depth of cultural appreciation to enrich our understanding; Gerry Rausnitz, CEO of Meopta-Optika, who frequently shared his tactical business appreciation of Eastern Europe; Geremie Sawadogo of The World Bank, who gave us a new perspective and depth of awareness about Africa; and Jan Jung-Min Sunoo of the International Labor Organization, who generously offered wisdom and expertise about Southeast Asia.

As you'll see throughout the chapters in this book, we are indebted to culturally astute professionals who have allowed us to interview them and share their experiences: Franck Andreutti, Aaron Arun Baharani, Peter Bregman,

Liam Brown, Mark Burchell, Philip Durocher, Paul Grogan, Ed Hannibal, Jeri Hawthorne, Warren Heaps, Roger Herod, John Kovach, Dimitra Manis, Saira Mathews, Nazma Muhammad-Rosado, Anke Puscher, Geremie Sawadogo, Nancy Settle-Murphy, Jan Jung-Min Sunoo, Joyce Thorne, Dale Welcome, Ray Wilhelm, and Yang Zhang.

There are also other special friends and colleagues without whom we would not be where we are: David Abromovitz, Brenda Bellon, Andres Conde, Gary Dittrich, Ilene Dolins, Michael Elia, Sheri Gaster, Steve Gott, Johanna Johnson, Faye Lepp, Louis Lima, James Liu, Brian Lovell, Greg Nichols, Dave Nugent, Terry Paule, Jennifer Rowe, Seymour Siegel, Eric Stern, Ibraiz Tariq, Gina Teague, Rachelle Tobias, Igor Ulis, Rita Wagner, Patti Wilkie, and Katie Zaher. And personal thank-yous to Melinda Marmer, David Marmer, David Ben-Zur, Jon and Angela Schell, and Adam and Tracy Schell.

Editorially, Brenda Sunoo's cultural insights, sensitivity, and exceptional editing skills were instrumental in helping us achieve the kind of manuscript and tone we envisioned. Brenda has been a good friend and incisive editor of ours for over a decade, and she continues to urge us to stretch and explore new areas. We would also like to thank fellow writers Shari Caudron, Susan Golant, Samuel Greengard, and Allan Halcrow for their continued editorial input and encouragement. We would also like to thank Leah Spiro, our editor at McGraw-Hill, for her constant encouragement, enthusiasm, and support.

Preface

Why This Book? Why Now?

If we needed a reminder of how interconnected the world is as we finish writing this book, it was provided by the global financial markets continuing to slide downhill. Businesspeople in the United States watch the markets in Europe and Asia for indications of what will happen when the U.S. market opens. Eight hours later, Europe and Asia watch to see what impact the Dow Jones will have on the FTSE, Hang Seng, and Nikkei averages. Of course, these markets all prospered arm in arm, and that prosperity was built on the same interconnected global commerce that is bedeviling us now.

It's not only the financial markets that show clear signs of global interdependency. Americans watched with great interest along with Europeans as France elected a new president and the United Kingdom made the transition to a new prime minister. Yet those events were dwarfed as world citizens joined Americans who tuned in by the millions, anxiously awaiting the outcome of the American election to learn who would be the next president of the United States. This was a monumental event. It escaped no one's attention that the new U.S. president, Barack Obama, represents a dramatic recognition of the acceptance of diversity. He spent some of his formative years outside the United States and, as he campaigned for office, stressed the advantages of having global intercultural skills. Clearly, the world is becoming more interconnected, and the ability to move effectively between cultures has never been a more important skill.

Of course, the impetus for this book came to us well before these historic events. We already were well aware of the importance of these issues from our daily work lives, which involved bringing cultural skills to business managers through online and face-to-face cultural training programs. We often receive letters from clients who remind us of the value of cultural training when they tell us that they appreciate the skills they gained when they watch in dismay the serious mistakes that others make.

However, there's a barrier to what should be universal recognition of the importance of learning culture: You don't know you need it until you've had a problem or you're facing something that you can't understand. After all, doesn't everybody appreciate direct, candid communication? Doesn't everyone want to meet a deadline? Doesn't everyone want public recognition for his or her contributions?

Cultural values are instilled in us as "absolute truths," and many times we don't understand that others have a different perspective on those absolute truths. All too often, by the time people realize they need cultural training, they've made their first blunders and cost their companies and careers dearly.

It became obvious to us that a proactive resource, reaching out to people who were doing business anywhere in the world, was critically important. Therefore, we wrote *Managing Across Cultures: The Seven Keys to Doing Business with a Global Mindset* because a book that teaches culture in a practical, actionable business context is a much needed but missing resource.

When we wrote our first book, *Capitalizing on the Global Workforce: A Strategic Guide for Expatriate Managers*, in 1996, the primary audience for cultural training consisted of international assignees, because back then the only people who needed intercultural skills were those people who were going to live in another country. Since that time, cultural awareness has become a fundamental business prerequisite for all managers in global organizations. Inasmuch as nothing stays the same for very long in a rapidly changing business environment, our clients kept asking for a faster, more efficient way to bring cultural knowledge to this much larger cadre of employees.

Everyone Can Learn about Culture

The idea of creating an easy-to-understand cultural model came to us years ago after we had worked with a group of handpicked senior managers who were struggling. Having been chosen because of their excellent performance in the United States, Europe, and Asia, they were required to work together with no preparation. To their surprise, each of them found the experience profoundly frustrating.

As the Italians were trying to build relationships, the Germans were building schedules; as the Americans were creating stretch targets, the Japanese were trying to find consensus. As all this intergroup turmoil was taking place under the surface, the objectives for the project were neither uniformly understood nor universally implemented. All the while, the business mission wasn't being accomplished.

We became interested in creating a new cultural model because at that time culture was being taught through the academic models of Geert Hofstede and Edward T. Hall. Businesspeople were asking for a more tactical approach with terminology and situations that mirrored their work relationships. There was a need for a bridge between the research and tactical business applications.

The same impetus that brought about the creation of an actionable business model led us in 2001 to create RW[3] LLC (www.rw-3.com), which provides a practical online cultural learning solution. We knew we were witnessing another workplace transformation thanks to sophisticated software, widespread Internet access, and increasingly diverse, complex collaborative work. No longer were time zones and country borders a restriction to working together. *Workforce 2000*[1] was beginning to become a reality in which colleagues from widely different backgrounds were the norm, not the exception. All this requires us to understand different work styles and attitudes and be able to work across cultures.

---

[1] William B. Johnston and Arnold H. Packer, *Workforce 2000: Work and Workers for the 21st Century*, Hudson Institute, 1987.

What Will You Gain from This Book?

We provide you with a blueprint—a guideline—that enables you to translate and interpret behaviors so that you can respond in an effective way. We created the CultureWizard Model©, which is so easy to understand that you don't need a teacher. The CW Model© helps you identify seven key characteristics that are apparent in every society and gives you clues that will guide you as you do business and interact socially with people who have different backgrounds. After you learn the seven keys, you'll begin to understand what a global mindset is. Finally, you'll be able to see how individuals put the seven keys to work and the global mindset into action through the real-life case studies presented throughout the book.

To help you practice some of the skills you're going to learn, we've created a Web site and forum where you can interact with colleagues who are reading the book and have ideas, stories, and questions to share (our site can be found at http://book.culturewizard.com). In light of the nature of work and our interrelationship with people from all over the world, cross-cultural fluency is a critical business skill, and we want to help you develop it.

Thus, this book is intended for you if you are doing business in one of today's global organizations—whether large, small, multinational, or simply domestic and diverse. It will help you if you are a(n)

- Business leader and decision maker who must work across cultures

- Executive who creates strategies on the basis of international market conditions

- Manager who encounters serious international business opportunities and challenges, both travel-related and business-related

- Business manager who purchases goods from abroad and/or supervises people from different cultures and recruits and trains employees who have diverse backgrounds

- Woman manager who supervises global business initiatives and faces barriers different from those you face when managing domestically

- Business owner trying to use marketing and advertising to lure customers from other cultures to buy products and services

You will benefit as you become aware of the role culture plays in the thoughts and actions of others. We've set up this book in four sections so that it is easy to use and refer back to later:

1. Introduction: How we got here and why is it important to be able to manage across cultures with a global mindset

2. Culture Basics: What is culture and what is personal style?

3. The Seven Keys—the Seven CultureWizard Dimensions—to managing across cultures

4. Doing Business with a Global Mindset

People thank us all the time for helping them recognize why they have been having problems with work colleagues and helping them gain skills so that they can be more effective on their multicultural teams. This book grew out of a deep appreciation for those people who face and learn from enormous cross-cultural challenges every day, such as the following:

- The aeronautic quality control supervisor who lamented, "How am I ever going to be able to recognize when my Chinese colleagues are telling me the truth?"

- The publisher who sighed in frustration, "We keep misunderstanding our tech team from India—we're in our own little hell."

- The Texan who let his Saudi Arabian client hold his hand when he realized it was a sign of trust and friendship.

- The expat who wrote us, delighted, that every night after work he sat with his worried wife at the computer to pore over the details of their assignment and go through the culture program; this made her feel much more confident and made him feel he could take the assignment

We know that in today's global workplace, understanding your own culture, learning about the cultures of those you'll be interacting with, and then recognizing where you're similar and where it might be wise to adapt your behavior is a key skill to help you get over the barriers and smooth the way so that you can do your work and enjoy relationships with people who are different from you. This may happen when you're working or traveling abroad, but it may happen just as easily if you never leave your office because the world meets on your speakerphone—the one that's sitting in the middle of your conference table at work.

We hope that you will find this book valuable—not only in your cross-cultural endeavors, but in your interpersonal interactions with others. We hope that you develop the fluency to recognize behaviors and extrapolate from those actions to reach across differences in backgrounds and perspectives so that your everyday business dealings are rewarding and enriching.

Charlene Solomon
Michael Schell

PART

I

INTRODUCTION

How We Got Here

What you'll learn in this chapter:

- Culture and the Bottom Line: Doing It Right; Doing it Wrong

- The Global Century

- From the Twentieth to the Twenty-First Century

- What It Means to Manage across Cultures

- What Is a Global Mindset?

Culture and the Bottom Line: Doing It Right; Doing It Wrong

Can culture have an impact on the bottom line? We're about to show you how large that impact can be!

In May 2005, IBM sold its ThinkPad computer business to Lenovo Group Ltd., a Chinese manufacturer of personal computers that previously had sold only in China. Immediately upon the acquisition of the ThinkPad, Lenovo, which had purchased the business for over a billion dollars, was thrust into the global scene in a big way. Thinking it needed to address its new market to enhance sales, Lenovo brought in Western managers and tried to remake itself culturally overnight.

A quintessential Chinese company that led its workers in twice-daily calisthenics, Lenovo felt compelled to adopt English as the official company language and hired its new chief executive officer from Dell Computer Corporation. Regardless of the intent, instead of a confluence of cultures, there were immediate riptides and floods. The Americans were frustrated by the Chinese need for harmony and inability to make public statements that showed disagreement. The Americans misinterpreted this as lack of engagement and inability to add value. In an attempt to streamline operations, the American management cut 10 percent of the company's global workforce and shifted the marketing headquarters to Bangalore, India. This was especially threatening to Lenovo because it was a company that took great pride in being essentially Chinese. Then, because things weren't moving quickly enough, the American CEO replaced a popular Chinese executive with someone from the United States. That caused a tidal wave of discord, and other key Chinese executives quit in protest, saying that they could see they weren't valued.

Chen Shaopeng, president of Lenovo's China operations, said: "When we disagreed in meetings we kept silent, but Americans assumed we were agreeing."[1] The loquacious Americans talked so much that the Chinese felt the Americans didn't give them space to express themselves. What was the bottom-line impact? The company had serious problems that hurt it in the marketplace. Market share dropped from 7.8 percent to 7.3 percent at a time when the rest of the market was growing.[2]

However, the story doesn't end there. Bill Amelio, Lenovo's American CEO, pointed out in a 2008 interview, "Lenovo's Chinese heritage is a very strong part of our global DNA. . . . Our basic challenge is to take that diversity and make it work for us as a competitive weapon."[3]

To Lenovo's credit, the desire to make its global diversity a competitive advantage is reflected in the company's eschewal of a single headquarters. Amelio is based in Singapore; the company's chairman, a Chinese national, is based in Raleigh, North Carolina; and world headquarters are in Raleigh, Singapore, Paris, and Beijing with research and development labs scattered globally as well as in Yamato, Japan.

In other words, having learned from its earlier mistakes, Lenovo is in the process of making itself a truly global corporation that does what Amelio calls "worldsourcing—where we source talent, manufacturing, and markets from whichever location in the world it makes the most sense."[4]

As we will learn throughout this book, it takes more than sourcing to make global diversity a competitive advantage. It takes skill to enable that talent to overcome the cultural challenges it will encounter and elicit the special qualities each individual can contribute.

McDonald's in Europe is an excellent example of how an organization has used an appreciation of culture as a competitive business advantage. In October 2008, in the middle of a recession, McDonald's saw its sales from existing stores rise 8.2 percent globally, led by sales in Europe, Asia, and the Middle East.[5] That story stands in contrast to the blaring television images of a McDonald's fast-food restaurant being burned or bulldozed as French activists attempt to destroy a McDonald's under construction. The French are a nation for whom good food and quality dining are cultural icons akin to the Eiffel Tower.

Yet somehow McDonald's is thriving in France, with revenues second only to those in the United States. What's more, the French spend more than twice as much on their McMeals as Americans do, even though the cost of a Big Mac is about the same.

The company has about 950 restaurants in France, and in 2006 its sales in France grew by 8 percent, which is a pretty good growth for a country that treasures fine dining.[6] It makes one wonder what they're doing right.

The CEO, Denis Hennequin, mastered the concept of being global. He said, "Yes. . . . We were born in the USA, but we are made in France, made in Italy, made in Spain."[7] Hennequin respects cultures and has succeeded in harnessing culture to be a competitive advantage. While maintaining a global brand, he has adapted it to be respectful of local tastes and values. He's made the golden arches more discreet to blend in with their neighborhoods, banished Ronald McDonald, and adapted the restaurants so that they are more in keeping with the expectations of French diners. Some of the restaurants have leather upholstery, and some have fireplaces and candles.

He's adapted the menu to include *le petit moutarde* (a small burger on a ciabatta roll with a sophisticated mustard sauce). In addition to satisfying local tastes, McDonald's has developed relationships with local suppliers.[8] The bottom line is that McDonald's is thriving in Europe because it gets the culture right.

Throughout the rest of the book we show other examples, linked to lessons of do's and don'ts, which taken together underscore the importance of culture and will help you gain your own global mindset and develop your intercultural skills.

The Global Century

It simply can't be overstated: You will not succeed in global business today if you don't understand, appreciate, and know how to manage across cultures. No matter how smart you are, how innately talented, or how technically competent, without intercultural skills you will not achieve your potential.

Why? you ask.

Because in the twenty-first century, the whole world is your marketplace, and the people you work with come from every part of the globe. Indeed, global cultural diversity is not a slogan; it's an every-day fact of the workplace. It affects the way you interact with the people around you, conduct conference calls, set deadlines, and make presen-tations. Your customers, colleagues, and suppliers are probably from different cultures, and you need to understand their values and behaviors to manage them, sell to them, and satisfy their needs. In other words, in the twentieth century, you needed to be culturally adept to do business "over there," but now, in the twenty-first century, you need to understand culture to do business "over here."

Today, when you venture into the work world, you're entering a global marketplace with thousands of vendor booths, dozens of currencies, and myriad baffling behaviors.

Though it's much more subtle, when you telephone a foreign col-league, attend a meeting overseas, participate in a global team, or manage workers in an international office, you may find behaviors as perplexing as if you were trying to bargain for goods in an outdoor market in Bangkok or Bangalore. Indeed, understanding culture is as important as using the correct currency if you want to succeed in business today.

However, this can be surprising because people dress similarly, work in offices that are like your own, and may even share your tastes in cui-sine. Don't be fooled; the similarities are only on the surface. As you'll see throughout this book, products, services, and customer expectations are different in each culture, and organizations have to plan differently to succeed in various parts of the world. Look at the cultural faux pas com-mitted every day by well-meaning corporate executives who have been lulled into thinking that everyone is becoming the same and so are stunned when reminded of how confusing—and possibly divisive—cultural barriers can be. Stories abound: Starbucks, General Motors, Kentucky Fried Chicken, and Burger King all have made major cultural miscalculations that cost money and were potentially disastrous for the business.

Culture is important for an organization's success. It is also important for your individual success whether or not you work or travel internationally. Understanding culture is important for your success even if all your work takes place in your home headquarters. As you look at any leading multinational corporation, you'll see people from a variety of ethnicities, cultural backgrounds, and personal styles, all filling important slots as peers in the organization. The world has come to you, and in an environment where intellectual contribution is the key component people bring to work, the ability to interact effectively needs to be part of your core skill set.

From the Twentieth to the Twenty-First Century

How did we get here? In the early and middle twentieth century, businesses succeeded on the basis of financial resources, technology, and labor power. The business powerhouses of that time were U.S. Steel, American Can Company, General Motors, General Electric, and AT&T, all highly industrialized and heavily reliant on worker production. In many instances, individual workers were viewed as parts in a production cycle. Henry Ford's introduction of the modern assembly line, for example, meant that Ford Motor Company could mass-produce automobiles without regard to the individual talent of the people on the line. In other words, individuality wasn't a particularly important element in the success of the company and most employees were viewed as interchangeable parts. Perhaps in that environment worker individuality and uniqueness were even impediments to efficiency.

During that period, managers and executives needed skills related to efficiency that could ensure that their employees would deliver high-quality products on time; they needed to inspire organizational loyalty among their subordinates with the understanding that loyalty would be rewarded by promotions and longevity with the firm, and a manager's most coveted skills were those relating to productivity. Although individual judgment and creativity were valued, their use within the company generally was restricted to a select, small group of senior executives whose purview might be limited to a very small geographic area.

As the world moved into the information age, talent and individuality became increasingly important to the creation of the product as well as its production. Technology, ranging from sophisticated robotics to simple spell checkers, replaced the need for a significant amount of supervision to achieve quality control. In a technology-driven world, fewer line workers and supervisors were needed, and as a result lower-level production jobs began to disappear. Global competition also entered the marketplace, and organizations became more productive and began to cut jobs. Companies became flatter, workforces became leaner, and as the pace of change accelerated, companies were required to become ever more nimble.

As workers began acknowledging the shift from the traditional paternalistic or maternalistic system (AT&T was called "Ma Bell"), they also began to morph into a different type of resource—one that would thrive on individual talent. Individuals recognized that their long-term economic viability depended on their personal skill sets. In the new environment, promotions would be based on achievement and unique contributions rather than longevity. The personnel department changed its name to the human resources department, and the manager's role changed from being a production supervisor to being a talent manager.

At the beginning of the twenty-first century, the intellectual prowess of an organization's people often defines a company and what it produces. In fact, capital markets look to invest in firms that are endowed with an intellectual talent base. Not only did the huge multinational corporations of the mid-twentieth century trim their production workforces, but a new type of powerhouse emerged. Companies such as Google, Microsoft, Apple, and Cisco, among others, created products and services in which the firm's wealth resided in the intellectual capacity of its employees rather than in the production lines. Even venerable organizations such as General Electric and Siemens became as reliant on the intellectual contributions of their workers as they were on their production capability. Today, in most companies intellectual capital has become the ultimate resource necessary for success, and so nurturing and managing that capital has become a crucial business challenge.

As intellectual capital became an increasingly critical corporate asset, businesses realized that they had to seek out those talented individuals no matter where they resided in the world and be able to integrate them into a global talent pool. Technology responded to that need by developing a host of collaborative software products. By the end of the twentieth century, we had seen managers evolve from production supervisors to human resource developers. At the same time, the strength of the workforce evolved from valuing uniformity to valuing individuality and uniqueness. In other words, it became critical to value diversity whether it was domestic or intercultural.

What It Means to Manage Across Cultures

Today it's not at all uncommon to manage business functions in other countries with direct and matrixed reporting relationships to functional teams in many countries. It's also not unusual to interact with colleagues at home who have a variety of backgrounds and diverse personal styles, all of which respond to different management techniques. Learning these techniques and building an awareness of how to manage these diverse cultures is what this book is about.

In the following chapters you'll learn the seven key characteristics in the CultureWizard (CW) Model©, which are easy to understand

and will help you identify and translate behaviors so that you will be more effective as you do business (see page 53). You'll begin to learn the attributes of a global mindset, and through case studies you'll see how talented people manage business across cultures.

What Is a Global Mindset?

In all but the most local services, globalization has fundamentally changed the way we conduct work. Almost all business today is global or soon will be. Even your local restaurant may use a telephone-based reservation service half a world away, and when you put in an e-mail address, you're often unaware of where in the world it's going. A global mindset is the ability to recognize and adapt to cultural signals so that you intuitively see global opportunities and are effective in dealing with people from different backgrounds around the world.

Business leaders view the world as both a place to find resources—human and otherwise—and a place to locate and maximize markets. Obviously, the more able you are to identify cultural differences and the more capable you are at appreciating them, the better you'll be able to manage culturally distinct behaviors.

Why do you need a global mindset? A global mindset is the ability to see global opportunities intuitively. It enables those who have it to work effectively wherever they are in the world. To appreciate the importance of a global mindset, we think it's worthwhile to consider the confluence of the following phenomena in the global business community:

- *Global sourcing* refers to the procurement of everything from raw materials to human capital around the world.

- *Global mobility* refers to the flow of people and ideas around the world. Wherever you are in the world, you're likely to encounter people from other cultures.

○ *Global marketing* refers to the ability to develop products and services appropriate for the markets at which they're aimed. Organizations need to have people who understand cultural differences so that they can create products and services customized to local needs.

○ Finally, the phrase *global wisdom and collaboration* refers to the intellectual capital that fuels the contemporary marketplace. People need cultural skills to be able to collaborate, innovate, and maximize benefits and opportunities for themselves and their organizations.

Let's look at each of these phenomena in more depth.

Global Sourcing

Global sourcing is the worldwide search for human resources to provide an organization with the best people for the work regardless of their location. We used to want spice and silk from India and China, but today commodities go beyond natural and manufactured goods; we're looking for talented individuals. Global sourcing means that you're able to seek talent anywhere in the world, recognize it, and capitalize on it for your business. One prerequisite for making this effective is your ability to appreciate cultural differences and know enough so that you can interact with people from other countries.

Take, for example, the multinational Dutch firm that outsourced the development of a new global information technology service platform to an Indian company. When the Dutch head of the IT group met with the programming team in Bangalore to discuss the core platform on which to build the application, he casually suggested that the Indians use a well-known, commercially available platform. This was only one of many platforms that could be used but one with which the manager was familiar. He asked the lead on the Indian team if they could build the application on that platform.

"Yes," the team leader replied, "we can do it."

After six months of delay and cost overruns in excess of $10 million, the job was finished. The IT manager of the Dutch firm asked the Indian team why it had cost so much more and had taken so much longer than they'd originally estimated.

"You asked us to build it on a very unfriendly platform for this application," was the reply. "It would have been better doing it in a different way."

The Dutch technology manager was astonished. He hadn't told the team to build it a certain way; he simply had asked if it could be done! He had never questioned the way in which he communicated to the head of his technology group. In fact, he thought he had been asking simple questions, almost making idle conversation, and never considered that because he was the boss, his Indian employee would do as he asked. He expected that the technology design team would counter with another recommendation if his idea was inappropriate. He never realized that in the Indian culture such a challenge rarely is forthcoming.

The company had sourced world-class talent but was unable to translate those capabilities into effective work because cultural barriers got in the way. To take full advantage of the opportunities that the global environment offered, both the Dutch and the Indian teams needed to have a better understanding of the culturally based expectations of each group. In this case, the Dutch manager would have been more successful if he had asked, "What kind of platform do you suggest?" Rather than risking that his Indian employee would disagree with the suggestion he made, this approach would have allowed for a respectful dialogue. The Dutch manager should have known that Indians rarely disagree or say no because their communication style is indirect, and risking disharmony is considered unpleasant and unseemly. They could have saved millions of dollars and prevented months of frustration if the Dutch manager had been culturally astute enough to manage the multinational talent pool available to him.

By the same token, if the Indian senior manager had understood that a manager in an egalitarian culture such as the Dutch (unlike India's more hierarchal one) expects a collaborative effort from his employees, even if it requires disagreement, he would have avoided the problem as well.

Global Mobility

The second marketplace phenomenon we have been discussing is global mobility. Although national borders still exist, they have become more and more porous over the years, allowing people and ideas to migrate as never before. This is nothing new, of course. Throughout history, people have migrated for many reasons—to escape oppression and poverty and to find better opportunities, for example—but today one look at migration around the world will show you that it is more dramatic than ever. In the United States, one in eight workers is foreign-born (constituting over half the increase in the workforce from 1996 to 2000)[9]; the United Kingdom is experiencing the biggest immigration wave of workers in its history,[10] and Japan doubled the number of foreign workers coming to its shores between 1996 and 2006.[11] This migration has created a labor force that is not only more mobile but more diverse.

European countries, long bastions of homogeneity, now face foreign populations and ethnicities. Indeed, your coworkers, local customers, and suppliers come from many different cultures, and to interact with them effectively, you must understand their values and behaviors.

Moreover, not only could your colleague in the next cubicle come from Mumbai or Mexico City, but the person you are both working with on a virtual team may be physically located in Shanghai or SÇo Paulo. Globalization has made crossing borders an easier, more frequent occurrence both for immigration and for work-related tasks, but it has resulted in a greater, more complicated mixture of people from different backgrounds who need to work together.

Global Marketing

As a global manager, you know that organizations must be prepared to do business everywhere if they want to do business anywhere. In other words, it's getting more difficult to compete without a global reach and the benefits accrued from supplying consumers with goods and services around the globe. This isn't a new phenomenon. For decades, products and capital have not been limited by borders. From hamburgers to home electronics, from cosmetics to cars, you see products targeted to specific consumers outside the United States all the time. But that doesn't mean they're always successful. In fact, there are a significant number of examples in which cultural blunders have compromised the success of an initiative that could have succeeded if there had been greater cultural awareness at the outset.

Disneyland Paris, for example, struggled for years before it became profitable. This was the case partially because the park's promoters didn't understand several key culturally based buying and lifestyle habits of the French and neighboring Europeans. Disney wrongly assumed that European parkgoers would purchase Disney paraphernalia with the same relish as Americans and Japanese. However, they are not collectors of kitsch in the same way.

Equally problematic, Disney management was strongly committed to its own cultural biases and failed to recognize the need to customize its products to the local marketplace. Managers underestimated the importance of wine and wrongly assumed that French consumers would find wine interchangeable with Coke or iced tea. Of course that wasn't true. They didn't take into account the cultural importance of a meal in France and many other European countries, with all its social and relationship overtones. This not only lowered food consumption but dampened enthusiasm for park visits overall. Clearly, you need to understand your consumers, the modifications your products and services need, and the local business customs in the markets you target. You need to appreciate the unique cultural requirements of your marketplace and be agile enough to adapt to them. In the case of Disney, the company did learn from its mistakes and now offers visitors wine, beer, and the full meals they require. It rebounded and in 2008 turned a profit.[12]

Global Wisdom and Collaboration

Understanding how to work with people from diverse backgrounds and countries is an absolute necessity for an organization and a core competency for its employees and managers.

It's happening already—all over the globe. Countries such as Israel, India, and Ireland recognize that an educated populace is a resource equivalent to vast oil reserves. Look at Ireland, for example. Referred to as the Celtic Tiger, it has an educated workforce has that has changed Ireland from a resource-poor country (natural resources) to a resource-rich country (an educated workforce). As *The Economist* stated, "Surely no other country in the rich world has seen its image change so fast. Fifteen years ago Ireland was deemed an economic failure, a country that after years of mismanagement was suffering from an awful cocktail of high unemployment, slow growth, high inflation, heavy taxation and towering public debts. Yet within a few years it had become the 'Celtic Tiger,' a rare example of a developed country with a growth record to match East Asia's, as well as enviably low unemployment and inflation, a low tax burden and a tiny public debt."[13]

Israel is another example. With virtually no natural resources, that country has created the highest standard of living in the Middle East and is home to the highest number of NASDAQ-listed companies anywhere outside of the United States by harnessing the strength of its human capital.[14]

What does this mean for you as a global manager?

Having the smartest, best-educated, most competent people is only part of the equation. The other part is to create an environment and a corporate culture that allow those people to maximize their contribution. You do this by helping them work together effectively so that they can capitalize on and magnify one another's wisdom through collaboration. Research shows that diverse teams are more productive and creative than are homogeneous teams. We see on a daily basis how diversity of thought creates breakthrough products and services.

However, though technology has enabled people from all over the world to share their knowledge and work together, lack of cultural understanding can undo some of the advantages. Furthermore, global teams are ubiquitous throughout multinational organizations today, and for these multiregional, multicultural, and multifunctional teams to work, a variety of resources must be in place. Technology already allows those teams to assemble and work with a host of supporting technology software that enable teams to share work while their members are thousands of miles apart. These teams also need to understand how one another's cultures affect individuals' behaviors and perceptions.

Simply put, to be successful in the twenty-first century, you need to learn the seven keys and develop a global mindset. This requires you to reexamine deeply held values, suspend judgments, and question your biases so that you're able to read the cues and adjust to the subtle signals and messages being transmitted to you. It may sound complicated, but culture is learnable. This book is structured so that you can learn these new skills and put them into action right away:

Step 1: Recognize the impact of culture and how deeply rooted cultural values and ideas are. (You will learn this in Chapters 2 and 3.)

Step 2: Learn about your cultural roots and discover your Personal Cultural Profile. What makes you view the world the way you do? (See Chapter 3.)

Step 3: Recognize cultural differences in others and learn how to interpret behaviors and actions in the situations that you inevitably will encounter. (See Chapters 4 through 10.)

Step 4: Learn how to manage in multicultural situations by recognizing and managing behavior. (See Chapters 11 through 15.)

Cultural behaviors are the outward signs of deeply held values and beliefs that have built up in a society over time. In the following chapters, you will see the successes and failures of companies—great and small—and hear from CEOs, global managers, and business professionals about how they developed their cultural skills.

By understanding what culture is, how you've been shaped by your own culture, and how your cultural values differ from those of people in other parts of the world, you can become more perceptive and successful in this colorful global marketplace. Your exploration is beginning. If you stick with it, you'll learn the seven keys to doing business with a global mindset and learn to appreciate the cultural differences you encounter every day. Becoming culturally fluent may not be easy, but culture is learnable, and you're on your way.

DEFINITIONS FOR THIS CHAPTER

Culture: The visible behaviors and invisible values and beliefs that are unique for each society. These value systems are deeply rooted in the society and passed from generation to generation.

Global mindset: The ability to recognize and adapt to cultural signals so that you're effective in dealing with people from different backgrounds around the world.

Global collaboration: Technology has made it physically possible to work with people from around the world as easily as with colleagues next door. This makes it all the more important to understand how culture dictates people's behavior, values, and communication styles.

The seven keys: These are the seven cultural characteristics or dimensions: readily recognizable behaviors of people around the world that reflect their deeply held values and beliefs. The keys are available to everyone who learns how to use them (See page 53.)

Lessons Learned to Develop Your Cultural Skills

- Transition from the twentieth to the twenty-first century

- What culture is

- What it means to manage across cultures

- What a global mindset is

- Why understanding culture is more important now than ever before

  - Global sourcing, global mobility, global marketing, and global wisdom and collaboration

- The seven keys to doing business with a global mindset

Questions to Ponder

1. You've just arrived in Brazil with a challenging assignment and a tight time frame. You have a lot of appointments scheduled and an ambitious set of objectives. You want to get right down to business. You are frustrated because everyone is wasting time. No one seems to be moving on your timeline, and you are getting frustrated. What do you think is going on? Directions: Go to http://book.culturewizard.com and join the discussion.

2. You are in Spain on a sales trip for your organization. You've just had a very good meeting. The prospect you were calling on thought your product was great and saw how it could fit directly into his company's needs. Yet every time you call, there is general agreement but you cannot see any measurable progress toward a decision. What's going on? Directions: Go to http://book.culturewizard.com and join the discussion.

What Do You Think?

You have had your own experiences. Share them. Go to http://book .culturewizard.com and join the discussion.

Notes

[1] Jane Spencer and Loretta Chao, "Lenovo Goes Global, but Not Without Strife," *Wall Street Journal*, November 4, 2008.

[2] Ibid.

[3] CEO Forum Group, interview with Bill Amelio.

[4] Ibid.

5 MarketWatch.com.

6 Jacob Gershman, "McDonald's Takes Paris: Le Big Mac Booms in the Land of Haute Cuisine," *New York Sun*, July 2, 2007. http://www.nysun.com/article/57654.

7 Ibid.

8 "What's This? The French Love McDonald's?" *BusinessWeek*, January 23, 2003.

9 Abraham T. Moisisa, "The Role of Foreign-Born Workers in the U.S. Economy," *Monthly Labor Review*, May 2002.

10 "UK Migration Now at Its Highest," BBC News, July 21, 2006.

11 Bill Belew, "What Japan's Foreign Workers Are Doing," July 26, 2006. www.risingsunofnihon .com/category/doing-business-in-japan/page/79/.

12 Charles W. L. Hill, "Disney in France." In *International Business: Competing in the Global Marketplace*. Irwin/McGraw Hill, pp. 106–107. Financial stats from http://corporate. disneylandparis.com/investor-relations/financial-indicators/index.xhtml.

13 "The Luck of the Irish," *The Economist*, October 14, 2004.

14 http://www.finfacts.com/irelandbusinessnews/publish/article_10004428.shtml.

CHAPTER 2

Deal or Debacle? DaimlerChrysler and Cultural Lessons from the Big Guys

What you'll learn in this chapter:

- Perfect Deal or Debacle? The Case of DaimlerChrysler

- How a Global Mindset Translates to Bottom-Line Results

- What Is Culture?

Perfect Deal or Debacle? The Case of DaimlerChrysler

In July 1997, Bob Eaton, chief executive officer of the U.S. Chrysler Corporation, foresaw what he called "the perfect storm," in which global, environmental, and economic factors were about to put enormous pressure on the auto industry.

Up to that time, Chrysler Corporation was the most profitable car company in the United States. It had a 23 percent market share,[1] had 121,000 employees, and was valued at over $36 billion.[2]

Nevertheless, his foreboding about Chrysler's future led Eaton to believe that the best way to battle the coming hard times was to create a marriage with a perfectly matched partner.[3] Eaton, age 57 at the time, had been president of General Motors Europe when he came to Chrysler to be the vice chairman and chief operating officer in 1992. He had helped Lee Iacocca rebuild Chrysler to its robust current state and took great pride in its dynamic cowboy culture. Passionate, Eaton was confident that he knew what was right for his organization.

At about the same time in Germany, Jürgen Schrempp, the 53-year-old CEO of Daimler-Benz Corporation, assessed his company's business outlook and saw the need for a stronger, wider beachhead in the profitable American market. At that time, Mercedes was the dominant niche player in the luxury car market but had only 1 percent of the market in the United States.[4] In addition, he was finding it challenging to strengthen Daimler-Benz's position in the European economy car and SUV market and believed that a merger with Chrysler could help Daimler-Benz overcome those obstacles.

The cross-border merger in 1998 was called the deal of the century and promised to meet important strategic goals that each company's CEO was trying to achieve. It was hailed by many as a marriage made in heaven, and the management in both companies carefully studied and made detailed plans to address the financial and facilities integration of the organization, carefully negotiated management contracts, and planned the integration of business functions. Unfortunately, as in so many instances in business, they ignored the human element, which proved to be a key contributor to failure. They disregarded the impact of culture.

They Should Have Seen Trouble Brewing

Chrysler Corporation was the quintessential American company. Its corporate values reflected its American roots, and those values were what made the company successful. Chrysler had mastered the concept of speed from design to production and had the ability to read and adjust to the American consumer's taste and quickly design products appropriate for it. It valued innovation, risk taking, and rapid change. As a result, the company was thriving in the mid-1990s. It produced cars well suited for the U.S. marketplace: high on design, low-priced, and with frequent design changes to stay ahead of consumer tastes. It was an American company, producing cars for the American customer. Chrysler owners kept their cars an average of three years, and frequent change was an intrinsic part of the company's cultural values.

The company was rebuilt by Lee Iacocca, who put a strong personal imprint on the organization. He was a "regular guy," taking massive risks to achieve the American dream, and his personality was reflected in the corporation. Risk taking was one of the hallmarks of the Chrysler culture. It was also an egalitarian organization in which managers had access to all levels of the organization with little hierarchical protocol. In other words, from concept to manufacture to market, Chrysler embodied American culture, producing cars for the American Everyman with mass-market pricing from the low end to the middle range.

Daimler-Benz also was a company that reflected its national culture. Daimler was disciplined, structured, and formal. Its manufacturing process emphasized perfection, not speed. Its designs changed slowly through small modifications. Risk taking was eschewed. Change came slowly, and innovation had to be well documented, carefully designed, and meticulously produced. The company's success came from producing exceptionally well engineered, expensive cars that people owned for an average of nine years. In other words, Daimler was the quintessential German company, reflecting its German roots and cultural values in all aspects of its operations.

Its customers were not looking for rapid or cosmetic design changes but took pride in being able to recognize the Mercedes by the look of its lineage and the status they derived from being able to afford it. People bought it for its staid, substantive appeal. The company was as hierarchical as its marketing strategy. Its dealers reflected the elite status that the company strove for, and Daimler employees took great pride in their products and in the hierarchical, disciplined structure they were part of. Although Daimler sold fewer cars than Chrysler, its revenues were higher.[5] This search for perfection was reflected in the number of people it took to build a Mercedes.

In fact, both organizations were strong manifestations of their national cultures. The capacity for rapid change, innovation, and risk taking that made Chrysler successful was the antithesis of the meticulous detail that was synonymous with Daimler.

We See the World through Our Own Filter

Both companies' corporate values and cultural differences existed from the outset. They were obvious and readily visible. However, if you see only what you want to see, you choose not to recognize impending cultural land mines.

What was announced as a merger of equals to the world press was quietly called a takeover in Stuttgart's inner circles.[6] Equally revealing, stories about Mercedes dealers saying they wouldn't be caught dead driving a Chrysler illustrated the potential mismatch between the two companies.[7] Yet that might not have been fatal. Although the strategic marketing, the business positioning, and the deal's economics were worked out carefully, the different cultural perspectives of the people and work styles weren't taken seriously. Without adequate planning and attention, how could these hugely different corporate cultures and national cultures integrate well enough to take advantage of the economic opportunities?

Figure 2-1 shows how in regard to the seven key cultural values the Americans and Germans on the Chrysler and Daimler teams were dramatically different. The differences between the Germans and Americans, while appearing small on the scale shown here, translated into profound challenges.

Figure 2-1   American and German cultural characteristics

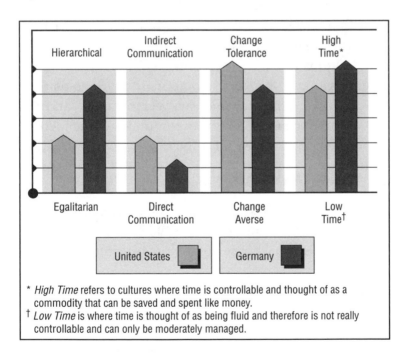

Culture is such a strong phenomenon that it comes out even when you think you've put a lid on it. It was clear to any observer that Daimler had emerged as the dominant partner in this merger of equals.

The new company was called DaimlerChrysler, not ChryslerDaimler, which would have been alphabetically correct. The headquarters were in Stuttgart, not in Auburn Hills, Michigan, or another neutral location (Amsterdam was considered). Shrempp emerged as the CEO of the combined company, and Eaton's tenure as vice chairman was defined as three years by contract.[8] Even the 13-member board was assigned 8 to 5 in favor of Daimler.[9]

The potential for cultural conflict was evident even during the negotiation and due-diligence stages. Chrysler employees, who were higher paid but came from a regular-guy company, were required to fly coach to their meetings in Germany, whereas their German counterparts traveled in the premium classes, reflective of the company's prestige brand.[10]

The two companies didn't just make different cars. They did everything differently—from the way they dressed, to the way they made decisions, to the way they worked together, to office manners. The Daimler and Chrysler organizations were dramatically different (see Figure 2-1). Whereas Daimler was hierarchical with many layers of approval and steps up the ladder for decision making, Chrysler was a relatively flat organization. In Stuttgart, everyone wore suits and ties; in Auburn Hills, employees dressed casually.

In spite of all those signs, there were no apparent efforts to develop a cultural integration plan. In light of the German penchant for exhaustive planning and attention to detail, this is particularly surprising. It's not as though no thought was given to cultural integration. The company had programs to teach Germans about American affirmative action, discrimination policies, and sexual harassment; there also was training to teach Americans about German dining etiquette.[11] However, in 1997, just after the merger was announced, American human resources managers at Chrysler recognized the need to address intercultural differences and proposed cultural awareness training. Those programs were rejected.[12]

It Only Got Worse

Culture is pervasive; it is palpable. All the people in the organization feel it even though they may not be able to describe it. Like manners and etiquette, some beliefs are visible, but other deeply held beliefs are invisible. Often we don't even know they exist. One of the reasons cultural attitudes are so powerful is that the distinguishing characteristics of deeply held beliefs are often invisible. Fons Trompenaars refers to these hidden layers of culture as being as natural as walking or breathing.[13] No one thinks about them; people just do things that way.

The impact of the invisible characteristics of the Daimler culture eventually became paralyzing to the Chrysler organization. At the outset, Shrempp, the chairman of the new entity, realized the value of not imposing Daimler's management on its counterpart and attempted in some ways to leave Chrysler alone. Nevertheless, after one year, a third of the senior managers at Chrysler had left the organization.[14] The vibrant, innovative executives who had elevated the car company to its heights in the mid-1990s began to feel somewhat unempowered, and defections to other companies began. Even though their jobs, reporting lines, and span of control hadn't changed, Chrysler managers sensed something about the dominant Daimler culture and felt it was time to leave. Even the dynamic, passionate CEO of Chrysler, Bob Eaton, found himself significantly less effective in the new environment and announced his intention to retire in three years.[15]

Chrysler's success had been based on a cowboy culture that allowed employees to accomplish things quickly in a freewheeling manner. Managers had to be empowered to make decisions, had to be comfortable with risk, and had to be able to operate in a relatively flat environment. Clearly, in the Daimler environment, precision was the value shared throughout the organization, and those two values were in direct conflict. How could one act with speed when speed might put precision at risk?

This became apparent in one incident after another.

Soon after the merger, Ray Wilhelm, a midlevel human resources manager from the previous Chrysler organization, was meeting with a group of American and German colleagues in Auburn Hills, Michigan, where Chrysler had been headquartered. They'd had a full day of meetings, had gone to dinner, and had planned to have a brainstorming session on expatriate medical benefits policies during the evening.

Energized to launch into the creative process with their German counterparts, the Americans were stopped in their tracks when they realized that their German counterparts had been preparing for the meeting since the night before. Rather than a blank slate (or blank whiteboard), the Daimler team had prepared a 50-slide PowerPoint presentation with detailed plans about how solutions could be implemented.

Perhaps what was most surprising was the sense of disapproval Ray and his team felt coming from their colleagues, who thought the Americans were unprepared. That rendered the U.S. team speechless and stymied the creative meeting.[16] Again, if anyone had been aware of the cultural differences between the two groups, this could have been predicted. The brainstorming session represented the different ways people become invested in a process. For the Germans, this kind of session is part of the decision-making process, part of a consensus-building experience. The incident brings into dramatic relief the different ways Germans and Americans make decisions. Germans make them as a group, trying to get as much buy-in as possible, and see that experience as a part of the chain of decision making, whereas Americans are comfortable without gaining consensus for a decision and believe that decisions can be changed easily.

Even though colleagues on both sides would say they enjoyed their social interactions, they ran into cultural roadblocks whenever they began to work together. The sense of collegiality that existed made the working conflicts all the more confounding. The ability to interact socially didn't automatically translate into workplace effectiveness.

As *The Economist* put it just before the divorce, economic conditions were also against the merger. "Since Daimler-Benz swallowed Chrysler in 1998, it has brought the struggling American carmaker to the verge of recovery three times, only to see the patient repeatedly relapse. This time the high price of petrol and raw materials turned the market against the big sport-utility vehicles, minivans and saloons around which Chrysler had built its latest plans for recovery. . . . Now Daimler, chafing at Chrysler's mounting losses and slumping market share, is contemplating divorce. Chrysler's managers also made mistakes. They kept production high, even as sales stalled. No one flying into Motown last year could miss the fields of unsold Jeeps and Ram pickups. It was the discounts offered to get this stock moving that caused the financial meltdown."[17]

In the final analysis, everyone except the company's automotive competitors ended up losing. Daimler sold Chrysler in 2007 for $6 billion, absorbing a $44 billion loss.[18] Chrysler went from the biggest winner in the U.S. auto market to the biggest loser. Mercedes was the subject of a humiliating report by J.D. Power and Associates in July 2003 that revealed "embarrassing quality deficiencies."[19] Careers in both organizations were severely damaged.

How could so many good intentions go awry? With so much at stake, how could management ignore the visible cultural clues? In the DaimlerChrysler deal, as in so many others, few people looked at the percolating cultural issues. They wanted to believe that because they had similar goals for the joint entity, their overriding intentions would ameliorate the debilitating differences.

In a stunning statement given in hindsight, Bob Lutz, former vice chairman of Chrysler, still didn't recognize that a cultural torpedo had sunk his deal. "There was a remarkable meeting of minds at the senior management level," Lutz said in an interview. "They look like us. They talk like us. They're focused on the same things. Their command of English is impeccable. There was definitely no culture clash there."[20]

In other words, everyone from the top executives to the guys in cubicles wanted to believe that everyone was the same. In reality, we're not all the same. We're quite different from one another. Given a chance, those differences can be enormously beneficial to a business endeavor, whether it is a cross-border merger, a multicultural team, or the insights of a manager from one country who is offering ideas to a manager in another country. Awareness of cultural differences can be a powerful tool.

However, unless they're recognized, addressed, and managed, cultural differences can become a bubbling cauldron. You can put a lid on the pot for a while and the differences will appear to subside, but unless you lower the flame or find a way to take the pot off the fire, it will blow the lid off.

The challenge faced by business is this: Unlike financial performance or facilities integration, cultural competence is not an easily measured component of the business. Therefore, it is neglected and often relegated to the back burner. But make no mistake: Creating cultural intelligence in the organization is as critical as having adequate working capital.

In the end, the DaimlerChrysler merger offered a profound lesson. Although economic factors played a large role and it is hard to say whether the merger would have succeeded even if the principals had had a greater appreciation of the role of culture, what can be said with certainty is that if the leadership had possessed a greater appreciation for deeply seated values and beliefs—if they had had a global mindset— they could have anticipated some of the events that blindsided them. In the end, that's what a global mindset provides—not the skill to solve the problem automatically but the wisdom to anticipate the cultural issues that may arise when one works across cultures.

The way you perceive and manage colleagues and employees, the way you approach the marketplace, and the way you deal with customers and vendors are culturally based. You cannot take the skills that made you successful in one culture and transplant them intact into another unless you're prepared to face the perfect corporate debacle.

How a Global Mindset Translates to Bottom-Line Results

So what is a global mindset? It's the ability to recognize, read, and adapt to cultural signals, both overt and subtle, comfortable and strange, so that your effectiveness is not compromised when you're dealing with people from different backgrounds. Based on the awareness that cultures are different from each other and that those differences matter, a global mindset allows you to survey the landscape with an eye to various opportunities that come in ways you normally might not anticipate.

This perspective requires acquiring information and reflecting on that new knowledge so that you can put it to work. Since we're all accustomed to our own ways of looking at the world, it's not always easy to decipher the cultural clues of other societies, but if you pay attention, you can develop that sense and create a global mindset.

A global mindset allows you to recognize marketplace opportunities, manage and motivate diverse employees, and tap into a range of alternative ideas about how to run your business so that cultural hurdles don't take you far off course. It gives you the ability to motivate people who may decline a promotion for reasons you ordinarily wouldn't understand, devise different schedules and methods for meeting deadlines, and develop a broad variety of approaches to communication and negotiations. It means you have to understand how people think, how they're motivated, and how to anticipate their reactions.

We believe the most effective way to start is with the seven keys or seven dimensions that we call the CultureWizard Model© (CW Model©). You'll learn about them in the next chapter. It presents you with a framework that defines *easily recognizable behaviors* that give visible clues to help you understand some of the invisible assumptions and underlying thoughts we all have. In this way, you know how to react. If you learn to identify behaviors that manifest themselves differently depending on the society and are able to plug them into a framework, you will have a better idea of how to respond. By developing an awareness of these behaviors, you will be in a better position to adjust your expectations, attitudes, and actions and significantly enhance your chance for success in the international business arena. This training process builds a foundation for:

• Recognizing cultural behaviors that are different

• Understanding how your cultural background colors the way you perceive the world

• Building awareness of ways to adjust your own behavior when you enter a new culture

The CW Model© is adapted from the Windham International Model (created by Michael S. Schell and Marian Stoltz-Loike, Ph.D.) and the Intercultural Awareness Model, ICAM© (developed by Paula Caligiuri, Ph.D., of Rutgers University's Center for Human Resource Strategy and Caligiuri & Associates). It also is grounded in the work of respected sociologists and anthropologists, including Fons Trompenaars, Geert Hofstede, and Edward T. Hall, who are considered pioneers in the field.[21] This preparation helps people become multiculturally fluent and capable of functioning in a multiplicity of environments with a global mindset.

What Is Culture?

What, then, is "culture"?

• Is it the way people act?

• Is it what they think?

• Is it what they believe?

The answer to all three questions is yes. Culture is everything you see around you: the words people use, the food they eat, their clothes, the pace of their lives. But that's only the surface: what is called "visible" culture. It's the stuff of travel guides and first impressions.

Figure 2-2 illustrates that the part of a society that can be seen—visible culture—is far smaller than what lies beneath the surface.

Figure 2-2   Traditional iceberg model of visible and invisible culture

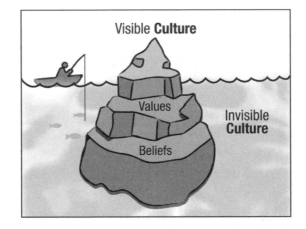

Experts use the iceberg analogy to describe this phenomenon. The part of the iceberg that's below the surface—what's termed invisible culture—is far more powerful than the area of visible culture because you don't know what is there. The only way to deal successfully with people from a different country is to be aware of what's going on beneath the surface and use that knowledge to shape your own behavior and expectations. If you don't understand that what's below the surface is far more powerful and potentially dangerous than what you can see, you run the risk of hitting the invisible part of the iceberg.

How can you begin to recognize cultural differences? The CW Model© provides seven keys to help you navigate, which you'll discover in Chapter 3.

DEFINITIONS FOR
THIS CHAPTER

Culture: The visible and invisible values and beliefs that underlie behaviors and are unique to each society.

Global mindset: The ability to recognize and adapt to cultural signals so that you intuitively see global opportunities and are effective in dealing with people from different backgrounds around the world.

Lessons Learned to Develop Your Cultural Skills

- The importance of creating a cultural integration plan as part of due diligence

- The ability to recognize the potential for cultural challenges before they materialize

- How culture defines work styles and priorities

- How the seven key dimensions contribute to a global mindset

- How the subtle and visible cultural signs are indicative of profound belief systems

Questions to Ponder

1. You just finished a meeting with your German colleagues and cannot understand why they have scheduled three more planning sessions when you were ready to begin tackling the task at hand. What do you think is going on?

Directions: Go to http://book.culturewizard.com and join the discussion.

2. Within the context of the DaimlerChrysler situation, do you think that the corporate cultures or the national cultures played a bigger role?
Directions: Go to http://book.culturewizard.com and join the discussion.

What Do You Think?

You have had your own experiences. Share them. Go to http://book .culturewizard.com and join the discussion.

Notes

[1] "The DaimlerChrysler Merger," Tuck School of Business at Dartmouth, No. 1-0071, 2002.

[2] Paul Ingrassia, "Chrysler, Daimler Agree to Merge in Deal That Will Reshape Industry," *The Wall Street Journal*, http://online.wsj.com, May 6, 1998.

[3] "The DaimlerChrysler Merger."

[4] "Daimler-Benz AG," Standard & Poors Stock Reports, New York: Standard & Poors, Inc., July 21, 1997, cited in Tuck School of Business case study.

[5] Ingrassia, chart on page 2.

[6] Jürgen Shrempp, quoted in *Financial Times*, October 2000.

[7] "The DaimlerChrysler Merger."

[8] Donald L. Bates and Jeff Badrtalei, "Effect of Organizational Cultures on Mergers and Acquisitions: The Case of DaimlerChrysler," *International Journal of Management*, 2007.

[9] Ibid.

[10] Ibid.

[11] "The DaimlerChrysler Merger."

[12] Michael Schell, meeting with Libby Siliberty and Ray Wilhelm, 1998.

[13] Fons Trompenaars, *Riding the Waves of Culture: Understanding Diversity in Global Business*, Irwin Professional Publishing, 1993 and 1994.

[14] Bates and Badrtalei, "Effect of Organizational Cultures on Mergers and Acquisitions."

[15] Ibid.

[16] Interview with Ray Wilhelm, January 2008.

[17] "Dis-Assembly," *The Economist*, February 15, 2007.

[18] Steve Rosenbush, "When Big Deals Go Bad—and Why," *BusinessWeek*, October 4, 2007.

[19] "DaimlerChrysler: Stalled," *BusinessWeek* International European Cover Story, September 29, 2003.

[20] Interview with Robert Lutz, Tuck School of Business, February 23, 2001.

[21] Edward T. Hall, *Anthropology of Everyday Life*, Doubleday, 1993; *Dance of Life*, Doubleday, 1984; *The Hidden Dimension*, Doubleday, 1966; *The Silent Language*, Doubleday, 1959; E. H. and Mildred Reed Hall, *Understanding Cultural Differences*, Intercultural Press, 1990; Geert Hofstede and Gert Jan Hofstede, *Cultures and Organizations: Software of the Mind*, McGraw-Hill, 2004.

PART

II

CULTURE BASICS: HOW CULTURE AND A GLOBAL MINDSET WORK

3

What Is Culture and What Is Personal Style?

What you'll learn in this chapter:

- The Fable of the White Elephant of Siam

- Culture's Core

- Culture Is Layered

- The Layers of Culture

- The CW Model©

- The Need to Generalize and the Risk of Stereotyping

- Using the CW Model©

- Personal Cultural Style

The Fable of the White Elephant of Siam

In ancient Thailand, white elephants were considered sacred. All the white elephants in the kingdom belonged to the king, who would bestow them on his favored noblemen as a sign of honor. White elephants were considered sacred and therefore could not be worked. Since the noblemen had enough money and didn't have to worry about the cost of caring for the animals, they were greatly honored.

Thailand is a very hierarchical society in which people know their place and respect authority and power. In ancient times, there were many practices that reinforced the hierarchical structure of the society.

The fable goes that when people reached beyond their station and pretended to have wealth and power they didn't really have, the king would bestow on them a white elephant, a gift they couldn't reject. However, they couldn't afford to own it. The white elephant would eat them out of house and home.

Thus, the white elephant—a symbol of status and power—was also a way of maintaining the hierarchical cultural values of the country. It was used to recognize status and keep people in their place lest they attempt to exceed their rightful status. (Of course, in the United States "white elephant" has a very different meaning: something that squanders energy and resources while producing nothing.)

The cultural value of hierarchy and knowing one's place in society that affected the entire quality of life in Siam still exists in modern Thailand. Although there are no princes distributing white elephants, there are many signals of culturally appropriate behaviors. Those signals are flashed to everyone but are read only by those who are alert to them.

Similar fables exist in every society. You face similar symbolism whenever you interact with people from other cultures because they understand the symbols' meaning and you don't. You must learn the meaning of those metaphors. The journey begins when you recognize how deeply pervasive cultural values are.

Culture's Core

Learned and absorbed during the earliest stages of childhood; reinforced by literature, history, and religion; embodied by heroes; and expressed in instinctive values and views, culture is a powerful force that shapes thoughts and perceptions. At the core is a nation's geography, its climate, its mythology—elements that have fashioned its history and religious choices. Rising up out of those fundamentals is a complex web of values and beliefs, multilayered and intersecting, possibly woven with issues of race and class, and shaped by personality. Finally, on the surface, there is the product of those influences: the way people actually behave. This affects the way you perceive and judge events, the way you respond to and interpret them, and the way you communicate in both spoken and unspoken language. Culture, with all its implications, differs in each society. The differences may be profound or subtle; they may be obvious or invisible. Ever-present yet constantly changing, culture permeates the world and molds the way people construct reality.

Businesses can't be separated from people and their cultural milieu. Understanding culture—being sensitive to nuances and differences in people from country to country—is fundamental for success in the international marketplace. As important as any other aspects of the business experience, an understanding of culture develops credibility, nurtures goodwill, inspires a workforce, and helps companies develop marketable products. It affects the way you develop and maintain relationships and plays a significant role in determining the characteristics to look for in selecting people, how to develop global talent, how to conduct meetings, how to manage employees, and how to work with teams. Understanding culture fundamentally affects how you run your business, and that directly translates to bottom-line results.

Culture Is Layered

Culture is at the same time visible, hidden, and invisible (see the figures on pages 48–50). What makes culture learnable is that in many cases, the visible culture is a manifestation of the invisible and hidden values. For example, bowing in Japan is indicative of hierarchical beliefs and the importance of good manners and protocol. At the other end of the spectrum, looking someone in the eye in the United States is a manifestation of an egalitarian mindset that sees everyone as equal, deserving the same level of respect as everyone else.

Another visible sign of culture is the way people relate to time. The fact that someone is late to a meeting is a visible sign. In many societies, it connotes a deeper sense of fluidity regarding time that indicates a belief that time is not under your control because other factors, such as interpersonal relationships, weather, and traffic, may prevent you from being on time. It is impractical to try to control all those elements.

The Layers of Culture

Imagine culture as a cross-section of the earth. Figures 3-1 and 3-2 illustrate the different layers. Visible culture (Figure 3-1) includes dress, food, and customs, along with what people say and do, how they dress, how they speak, their architecture, their offices, and their behavioral customs. Hidden culture (Figure 3-2) includes the values, beliefs, and philosophy that define the culture, such as attitudes toward time, communication, and religion and notions about good and evil.

Figure 3-1   The outer layer, or visible culture

ON THE SURFACE
- What People Say and Do
- How They Speak
- How They Dress
- How They Treat One Another

The hidden layer is where you find the attitudes and values that have grown over time. Here, hidden from view, is where you find the clues to the behavior you see around you: common attitudes and emotions that sit on top of long-standing beliefs and social codes that overlay deeper standards of thought and conduct. Getting to understand the hidden layers takes time, study, and observation.

Core culture is the invisible layer: the principles people take for granted (see Figure 3-3). Core or invisible culture harkens back to the essence of innermost beliefs about universal, nonnegotiable truths. Core culture is so deeply embedded that it is difficult to recognize. Here are the influences absorbed since childhood: religious ideas and ideals,

Figure 3-2   The middle layer, or hidden culture

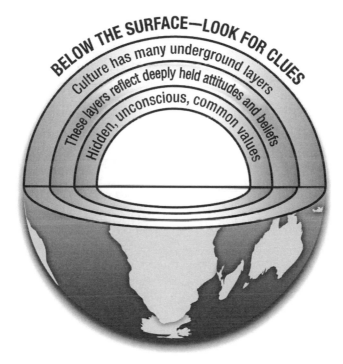

the nation's history and mythology, its heroes, its landscape, and stories handed down and retold generation after generation.

Culture is created by myriad factors such as history, religion, mythology, and the climate and geography of a country; it is made up of shared values and beliefs and forms the fundamental assumptions on which the whole society is built. Since no two countries have exactly the same influences, national cultures always vary. Geert Hofstede, the cultural anthropologist who first studied the impact of cultural differences on business behavior, said that if the brain is the hardware, culture is "the software of the mind."[1] Because it is so natural, you never think about it, and it is only when you encounter other cultures that

Figure 3-3   The invisible layer or core culture: the principles people take for granted and universal truths

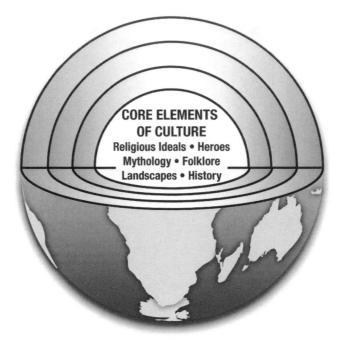

CORE ELEMENTS OF CULTURE
Religious Ideals • Heroes
Mythology • Folklore
Landscapes • History

you are aware of the differences. Cultural anthropologists have described culture as a shared way of viewing the world or processing ideas.[2]

The visible layers may change, but these changes are superficial and shouldn't delude you into thinking that deep alterations in culture have been made. The rules and protocols of everyday life may fluster you at first, but these are things you'll become fluent in quickly.

The CW Model©

Keep in mind the image of multilayered culture as you continue. At the core are a nation's geography, climate, and mythology—elements that have fashioned its history and religious choices. Rising from this foundation is a complex web of values and beliefs that result in behaviors and attitudes that you need to be able to read and understand. These values bubble to the surface to influence all kinds of behavior, from making eye contact to giving gifts, from the treatment of women and minorities to the size of the nameplate on your office door.

But how does that help you? Are you going to have to learn a long list of do's and don'ts that seem random and unrelated? Do you need to look up every potential situation in the index of a cultural rule book for every nationality?

No, because culture *isn't* random. It consists of distinct and logical behavior patterns that you can identify and even measure. These patterns form the framework for analyzing culture, and once you understand that framework, you can use it to predict the way people will respond in a variety of situations. For example, if you know that maintaining harmony is an important virtue in India and some of your team members are from India, you can make educated guesses about how to bring up difficult subjects with them. If you have a colleague who is Swiss—a society in which communication is very direct and extremely brief—you'll be less likely to take offense when that colleague is blunt with you.

Anthropologists have studied contemporary cultures in work-life settings. They've enabled us to make relatively reliable research-based conclusions about the behaviors we observe and what they mean as we move between cultures. Sometimes the models consist of several pairs of opposite characteristics that describe a continuum; other models measure a society as being high, medium, or low in certain dimensions. To study behavior and attitudes, researchers have measured all societies and come up with guidelines; thus, every society falls somewhere on the continuum. For example, if direct communication is at one end of the dimension and indirect communication is at the other end, you will find some cultures clustered at either end (for example, Germany, Switzerland, and the Netherlands at one extreme and Japan, Thailand, and India at the other) and other countries dispersed between the extremes.[3]

As was mentioned in Chapter 2, the CW Model© is adapted from the Windham International and ICAM© models and also is steeped in the work of world-renowned thinkers, including Geert Hofstede, Fons Trompenaars, and Edward T. Hall.[4] The CW Model© defines seven key characteristics and is an easy to-understand cultural template that takes this amorphous subject and concretizes it, giving it distinct definitions, or what are referred to commonly as *cultural dimensions.* The CW Model© is a tool for businesspeople who need to understand their own behaviors as well as the people with whom they are working. Tailored to be easy to learn, it builds on familiar terms and experiences and is intended to be used in a mobile, ever-changing business world where global professionals travel from culture to culture, work on multicultural teams, and need a readily understandable working model. It has been used as a core component in cross-cultural training and counseling programs for hundreds of expatriates and thousands of CultureWizard© Web site users who need to understand and adjust to behavioral differences. Having a grasp of the CW Model© is the master key to developing a global mindset.

The Need to Generalize and the Risk of Stereotyping

We all have colleagues and friends who may have similar backgrounds but who behave differently from us. For example, you may show up at a meeting exactly on time, pen in hand and ready to get right down to business, whereas your partner may stand outside the door chatting with others and ignoring the clock on the wall. You're both from the same culture and the same organization and even live in the same neighborhood, but you know—and frequently can see—that you are different from each other. (More about this later in the chapter.)

We need to create cultural generalizations to teach and learn culture, but keep this individuality in mind as you are reading this material. However, although two people from the same culture may have a different sense of building relationships (versus being on time to a meeting in this example), there still is an accepted national norm. Although you may see yourself as being different from your partner, to people from other cultures both of you appear to approach things in a similar way. In other words, if they are to learn about your culture, they have to generalize about your behaviors.

Furthermore, there are subcultures within each national culture that have their own distinct values and beliefs. For example, a Texan and a New Yorker see themselves as extremely different from each other (and in fact, when working together, they need to be aware of the cultural differences between them), but someone from another culture will see them as being quite similar and representative of American cultural values.

Using the CW Model©: The Seven Keys

This model defines seven key characteristics or dimensions:

1. Hierarchy and egalitarianism

2. Group focus

3. Relationships

4. Communication styles

5. Time orientation

6. Change tolerance

7. Motivation—work-life balance.

The following chapters (4–10) will examine these seven cultural dimensions by identifying the surface behaviors you can see as well as what they mean to you. Using real-life business case studies, you'll see the power of culture and the ability to make use of the understanding you'll gain when you can decipher interrelated and complex cultural characteristics. Taken together, these dimensions account for almost the entire spectrum of the behavior you'll encounter (see Figure 3-4).

Figure 3-4 Recognizing cultural differences through a global mindset filter

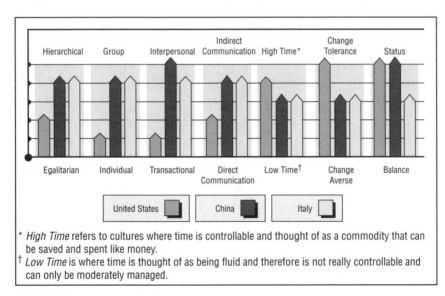

| | | | Indirect | | Change | |
| Hierarchical | Group | Interpersonal | Communication | High Time* | Tolerance | Status |

| Egalitarian | Individual | Transactional | Direct Communication | Low Time† | Change Averse | Balance |

| United States ■ | China ■ | Italy □ |

* *High Time* refers to cultures where time is controllable and thought of as a commodity that can be saved and spent like money.
† *Low Time* is where time is thought of as being fluid and therefore is not really controllable and can only be moderately managed.

What makes this process even more complicated is the fact that cultural behaviors are layered in multidimensional ways. On one level, you can look at culture's layers by nationality, but within any country there are subcultures that have distinguishably different values and behaviors. Also, there are also personality differences and personal styles.

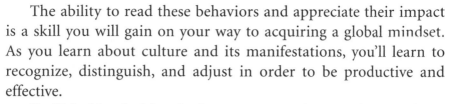

The ability to read these behaviors and appreciate their impact is a skill you will gain on your way to acquiring a global mindset. As you learn about culture and its manifestations, you'll learn to recognize, distinguish, and adjust in order to be productive and effective.

You'll find it valuable to look at your own culture to give you a basis for comparison and make it easier to understand other cultures. One word of caution: As we describe these dimensions, they will seem distinct from each other, but as you'll see from the case studies, many of the dimensions are interdependent. For example, a hierarchical culture such as Japan's is more likely to be formal than informal and may show more of a tendency toward group interests than toward individual ones.

Finally, as you go through this section, remember that to be able to describe these traits, we make many generalizations, but as we cautioned before, beware. Everyone is an individual, and stereotypes can be misleading, let alone unfair and counterproductive.

Personal Cultural Style

No two people from a culture are exactly the same, so recognizing national characteristics isn't enough. You know from your own experience that individuals can be quite different from their national culture. Within every culture, individuals have their own personal styles and behavioral preferences that represent the diversity in that culture. Therefore, although you need to make generalizations about behaviors in a specific country to learn about them, all people are different.

To appreciate culture and diversity fully, it's important to begin with an understanding of your own personal cultural style. (You'll soon discover your Personal Cultural Profile.) As you think about your personal preferences, you will see how your culture has influenced you. You also will recognize how people who share your cultural framework have their own personal preferences that are slightly different from yours. For example, you and your business partner may both come from a high-time culture in which being late is inconsiderate, but you don't have the same anxiety about being on time.

Personal cultural preferences are introduced into our lives by our families' background, expectations, and behaviors. Fundamentally, they're transmitted to us in the same way that societies transmit values: through the earliest childhood experiences and through the reactions people have to those experiences.

For example, if you come from a family that was very relationship-focused and built long-lasting and long-standing relationships in which your parents had friends you knew for most of your life and people discussed at home how well they knew each other and how well they trusted each other, that becomes part of your intrinsic value system. You are relationship-oriented regardless of the society in which you grew up. These principles become part of your cultural value system and stay with you through adulthood. You intuitively integrate your personal cultural style into your daily interactions. To add to the diversity, you and your siblings may have slightly different perceptions of the importance of relationships.

In today's workplace, in which an intellectual contribution is the most important attribute people bring to work, it's not just how fast you can type but how much wisdom you can communicate. Being able to develop a way for people with diverse personal styles and cultural backgrounds to make a maximum contribution is critical. Similarly, if you want to be able to adapt to your colleagues and make the greatest contribution you can, it is extremely helpful to understand your personal cultural preferences and the influence of your cultural background.

Diversity is all about understanding and appreciating personal styles. An additional value of learning culture is that it enables you to transfer the knowledge you've gained about multicultural differences to your domestic workplace. There are three major requirements in this area:

1. You need to be nonjudgmental about behavioral styles and preferences. (In other words, your way is not necessarily the only way.)

2. You need to be aware that your preferences are culturally based.

3. You need to be open to learning from your colleagues and environment and appreciating their potential contribution.

Learning culture starts with learning about yourself, understanding that not everyone is like you, and realizing how those differences affect interpersonal interactions. The first step is to discover your personal cultural style. We call it your Personal Cultural Profile. It consists of 35 questions in seven parts (Figures 3-5a through 3-5g) and will give you the opportunity to start discovering more about yourself. In later chapters, you'll be able to see a picture of your personal tendencies compared with the cultural attributes of your home country.

To use these figures, answer each set of questions, giving each one a rank (1 = disagree strongly and 5 = agree strongly), and enter that number in the box on the right. Then calculate a total score by adding up your answers to all the questions. Next, check the box that corresponds to your score on the scale below. This will be a reflection of your personal profile on that cultural dimension. You will be using these numbers in the following chapters and compiling your complete Personal Cultural Profile in Chapter 11.

Figure 3-5a   Egalitarian/hierarchical questionnaire

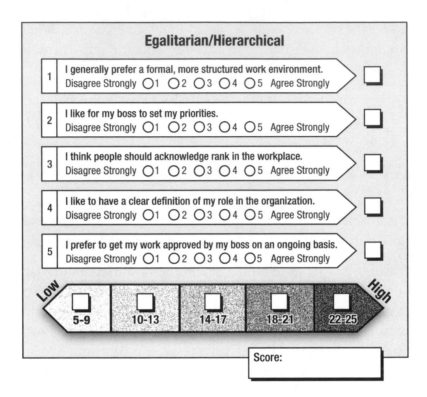

Figure 3-5b   Group focus questionnaire

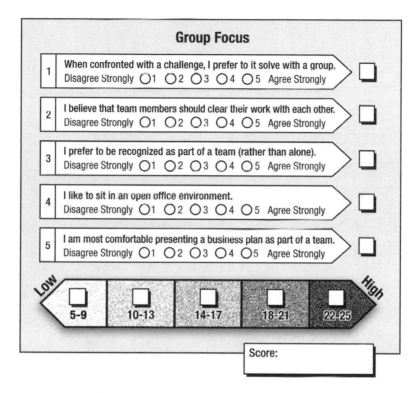

Group Focus

1. When confronted with a challenge, I prefer to it solve with a group.
Disagree Strongly ○1 ○2 ○3 ○4 ○5 Agree Strongly

2. I believe that team members should clear their work with each other.
Disagree Strongly ○1 ○2 ○3 ○4 ○5 Agree Strongly

3. I prefer to be recognized as part of a team (rather than alone).
Disagree Strongly ○1 ○2 ○3 ○4 ○5 Agree Strongly

4. I like to sit in an open office environment.
Disagree Strongly ○1 ○2 ○3 ○4 ○5 Agree Strongly

5. I am most comfortable presenting a business plan as part of a team.
Disagree Strongly ○1 ○2 ○3 ○4 ○5 Agree Strongly

Low 5-9   10-13   14-17   18-21   22-25 High

Score:

Figure 3-5c   Relationships questionnaire

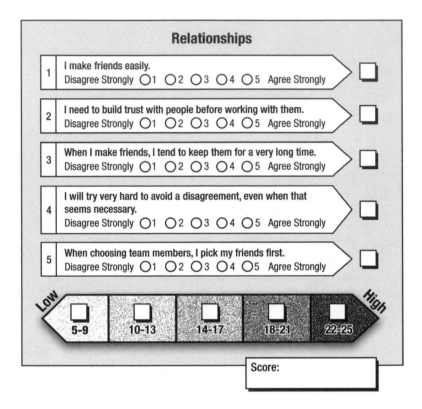

Figure 3-5d Communication styles questionnaire

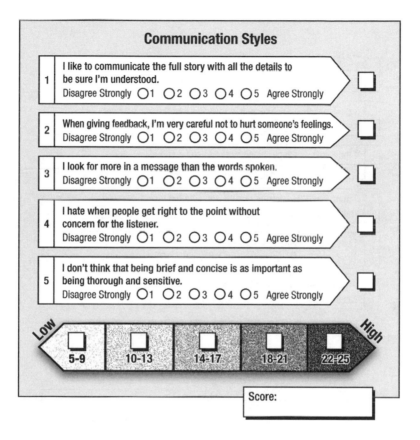

Figure 3-5e   Time orientation questionnaire

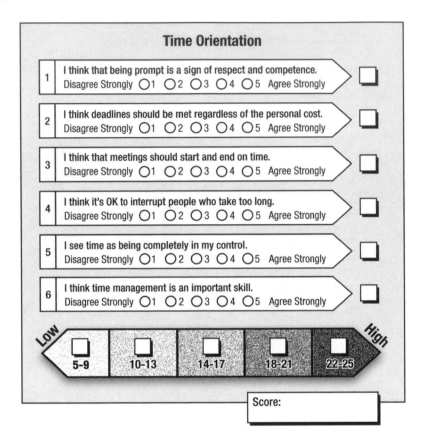

Figure 3-5f   Change tolerance questionnaire

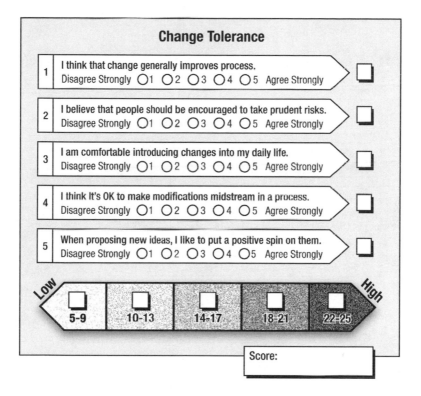

Figure 3-5g   Motivation/work-life balance questionnaire

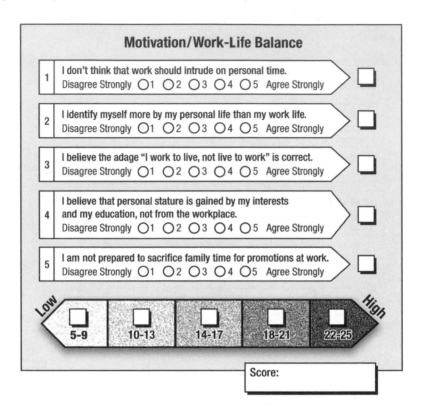

Motivation/Work-Life Balance

1   I don't think that work should intrude on personal time.
Disagree Strongly ○1 ○2 ○3 ○4 ○5 Agree Strongly

2   I identify myself more by my personal life than my work life.
Disagree Strongly ○1 ○2 ○3 ○4 ○5 Agree Strongly

3   I believe the adage "I work to live, not live to work" is correct.
Disagree Strongly ○1 ○2 ○3 ○4 ○5 Agree Strongly

4   I believe that personal stature is gained by my interests and my education, not from the workplace.
Disagree Strongly ○1 ○2 ○3 ○4 ○5 Agree Strongly

5   I am not prepared to sacrifice family time for promotions at work.
Disagree Strongly ○1 ○2 ○3 ○4 ○5 Agree Strongly

Low ☐ 5-9   ☐ 10-13   ☐ 14-17   ☐ 18-21   ☐ 22-25 **High**

Score:

DEFINITIONS FOR THIS CHAPTER

Visible culture: The outer layer of culture: what people say and do, how they dress and speak, their architecture, offices, and behavioral customs.

Hidden culture: The middle layer of culture: the values, beliefs, and philosophy that define a culture, such as attitudes toward time, communication, and religion and notions about good and evil.

(continued)

Core culture: The invisible layer, the principles people take for granted. Core or invisible culture harkens back to the essence of people's innermost beliefs about universal, nonnegotiable truths that were learned in childhood and retold generation after generation.

Stereotyping: The *American Heritage Dictionary* defines a stereotype as: "a conventional, formulaic, and oversimplified conception, opinion, or image."

Our definition continues as follows: When teaching culture, it is necessary to create generalizations because they provide a handy way to define a nationally based behavioral pattern. These descriptions should be treated as generalizations but remember that all people are different.

The seven keys, or dimensions: Hierarchy versus egalitarianism, group focus, relationships, communication styles, time orientation, change tolerance, and motivation/work-life balance.

Personal cultural style: Even though national cultures create behavioral standards, individuals are unique, and their behavior varies from the national norm. Understanding what your personal cultural preferences are helps you realize the differences between you and others.

Personal Cultural Profile: A profile of your specific preferences.

Diversity: Generally refers to different personal styles, behaviors, values, and subcultures.

Lessons Learned to Develop Your Cultural Skills

- The layers of culture

- The risk of generalization and stereotyping

- The seven key dimensions of the CW Model$^{©}$

- The concept of personal cultural style and the impact of diversity

Questions to Ponder

1. Think about the three or four cultural dimensions that you believe are the most crucial to understand. Why?
Directions: Go to http://book.culturewizard.com and join the discussion.

2. Why do you think it's important to position yourself on the CW Model© scale?
Directions: Go to http://book.culturewizard.com and join the discussion.

What Do You Think?

You have had your own experiences. Share them. Go to http://book .culturewizard.com and join the discussion.

Notes

1 Geert Hofstede, *Culture's Consequences: Comparing Values, Behaviors, Institutions, and Organizations across Nations*, Sage Publications, 2001.

2 Fons Trompenaars, *Riding the Waves of Culture: Understanding Diversity in Global Business*, Irwin Professional Publishing, 1993 and 1994.

3 *Culture, Leadership, and Organizations: The GLOBE Study of 62 Societies*, eds. Robert J. House, Paul J. Hanges, Mansour Javidan, Peter W. Dorfman, and Vipin Gupta, Sage Publications, Inc. 2004; Hofstede, *Culture's Consequences*; Trompenaars, *Riding the Waves of Culture*; and Geert Hofstede, *Cultures and Organizations: Software of the Mind*, McGraw-Hill, 1992.

4 Edward T. Hall, *Anthropology of Everyday Life*, Doubleday, 1993; *Dance of Life*, Doubleday, 1984; *The Hidden Dimension*, Doubleday, 1966; *The Silent Language*, Doubleday, 1959; E. H. and Mildred Reed Hall, *Understanding Cultural Differences*, Intercultural Press, 1990; Hofstede, *Cultures and Organizations: Software of the Mind*, McGraw-Hill, 2004.

PART

III

THE SEVEN KEYS TO MANAGING ACROSS CULTURES

Background to the Seven Key Dimensions

For years, researchers have been theorizing about what makes cultures different in terms of beliefs, attitudes, and behaviors and have come to a consensus (see Chapters 2 and 3). We believe that when you work across cultures, the best way to begin to understand values and attitudes is to watch for easily recognizable behaviors that give you clues to the deeper belief system that drives a society.

We have created the CW Model©, an easy-to-understand cultural template that focuses on seven distinct characteristics commonly referred to as cultural dimensions. These are the seven keys. The CW Model© is a tool for businesspeople who need to understand their own behaviors as well as those of the people with whom they're working.

Part III gives you insight into the seven dimensions of the CW Model©: hierarchy and egalitarianism, group focus, relationships, communication styles, time orientation, change tolerance, and motivation—work-life balance.

**THE SEVEN DIMENSIONS OF
THE CW MODEL©**

Hierarchy/Egalitarianism

The way people view authority and power, how much they defer to people in authority, whether they feel entitled to express themselves, and how empowered they feel to make independent decisions and take the initiative.

Group Focus

Whether people see accomplishment and responsibility as achieved through individual effort or collective effort and whether they identify themselves as individuals or as members of a group.

(continued)

Relationships

The importance and time devoted to building relationships and developing trust and whether trust and relationships are viewed as a prerequisite for working with someone.

Communication Styles

The way societies communicate, including the use of verbal and nonverbal expression, the amount of background information people need for understanding, and how directly (bluntly) or indirectly people speak. It also refers to whether brevity or detail is valued in a communication.

Time Orientation

The degree to which people believe they can control time and adhere to schedules or whether schedules are seen as deadlines or estimates. It also includes whether schedules or people are more important.

Change Tolerance

The perception of how much control people think they have over their lives and destiny and their comfort with change, risk taking, and innovation.

Motivation/Work-Life Balance

Whether people work to live or live to work, whether they can achieve status in a society by trading personal time for the opportunity to advance.

Hierarchy and Egalitarianism

What you'll learn in this chapter:

- How the Smart Guys at Wal-Mart Missed the Signals

- How Can You See Hierarchy?

- Hierarchical/Egalitarian Behaviors in Action

THE PHRASE *HIERARCHY AND EGALITARIANISM* REFERS TO
• How people view their relationship to people in power
• How casually or formally people relate to one another
• Whether a culture believes all people are created equal
• How much social mobility exists
• Who is responsible for decision making
• The degree of autonomy and personal initiative people feel they have

How the Smart Guys at Wal-Mart Missed the Signals

In 1997, Wal-Mart Stores, Inc., decided to take its successful business model to Germany. At that time, Wal-Mart was a $100 billion corporation with 750,000 employees in eight countries, including the United States. It had developed a business and customer service model that seemed to defy geography and appeared to be accepted internationally.

Germany was a good choice, Wal-Mart executives thought. After all, everyone knows that Germans love good bargains and are meticulous, careful shoppers. In addition, Germany was one of the world's largest economies, had a good-sized and relatively affluent population, and already had embraced two major comparable discount competitors that management felt had paved the way for the business to enter the market.

Thus, the German expansion was bound to succeed.

Of course, the Wal-Mart management, marketing, and customer service philosophy would be decidedly American in style. In other words, it would be extremely informal, friendly, and egalitarian. This was the formula that had made Wal-Mart the world's largest retailer, and there was no reason to doubt it. Senior managers strongly believed that its rah-rah, cheerleader management style was a winner.

In addition, Wal-Mart executives believed that since most Germans had a good grasp of English, the company could transport its corporate culture efficiently. They would send a man who successfully had managed 200 stores from the company's small-town-America headquarters in Bentonville, Arkansas, to run the new German operations. Never mind that he couldn't speak German. Never mind that that he required his store managers to work using English. The strategy couldn't fail. As it turned out, he would become the first of four CEOs in four years.[1]

The mighty Wal-Mart organization went to work and purchased retail operations from Wertkauf and Interspar, cobbling together 85 stores throughout the country. The company considered itself fortunate to acquire a full workforce with complete operating facilities. To make them Wal-Mart stores, they just needed to have the employees switch uniforms by donning blue Wal-Mart aprons and get some training in their friendly, helpful customer service style. To the American mind, they had a full, ready-to-go workforce, and with some additional training in the Wal-Mart service philosophy, the new team would be ready to go.

With their bright new aprons and some preparation, the former Wertkauf and Interspar German employees—now being addressed mostly in English—came to the morning preopening ceremony at which their managers would lead them in the Wal-Mart cheer. Each morning, as was the custom at Wal-Mart stores around the world, the employees would gather to chant "W-A-L-M-A-R-T." When the doors opened, smiling greeters would welcome German customers as they entered the store. Enthusiastic staff would help shoppers find what they wanted from the dizzying variety of products ranging from produce to televisions.

Fast-forward to July 28, 2006. Wal-Mart announced it was closing its German operations and absorbing $1 billion in losses. (It was the second such failure in two months, coming on the heels of the company's exit from South Korea.) Analysts said that beyond the huge monetary loss, it was an enormous strategic disappointment because Wal-Mart would have been able to use success in Germany to pave the way for entry into other parts of Europe and gained a greater ability to negotiate with local suppliers for its United Kingdom stores. It was a big blunder.[2]

What happened in that nine-year period to bring down the behemoth Wal-Mart in Germany? Could it be that ethnocentrism and cultural ignorance played a role along with the structural business elements, such as severely restrictive zoning, pricing, and operational codes?[3]

Absolutely. Wal-Mart's naïveté about doing business in Germany was exacerbated by its failure to plan for cultural differences. It wasn't just one cultural misadventure, either, but constant culture clashes that turned the Wal-Mart smiley face that had been so successful in North America into a grimace.

Remember those smiling greeters? Well, look at them from the German point of view. Everyone knows that Germany is a very formal, hierarchical society in which individuals reserve smiles for people they know. The Wal-Mart smiles that are effective in an egalitarian, informal culture were viewed by German customers as intrusive and presumptuous. In fact, many young women walking into the Wal-Mart stores thought the greeters were flirting with them. Others complained that strangers in the store were harassing them while they were shopping, although those people were staffers trying to help customers locate what they needed.[4]

The rah-rah cheers that start the Wal-Mart workday in Cincinnati and Charlotte were so foreign and uncomfortable to the German employees that they became an early-morning embarrassment rather than an early-morning inspiration. Having their leaders, whom Germans regard with some deference, orchestrating the embarrassing cheers made it worse. German workers see their bosses as having a more dignified role. In that hierarchical society, leaders are expected to demonstrate leadership by an upward connection, not a downward one. They are expected to dress in a somewhat more upscale way and show the trappings of power and authority. Thus, not only were the cheers out of place for the German workplace, but they put leaders into a role that Germans couldn't respect.

There were other cultural human resources bloopers as well. For example, Wal-Mart's prohibition of romantic encounters between employees and supervisors was particularly offensive to the Germans, who brought a lawsuit against the retailer to lift that dating prohibition.[5] Perhaps one of the most stunning cultural confrontations occurred when Wal-Mart's nonunion attitude ran full force against the immovable German works councils. Those works councils are formally independent of unions but work closely with them. They are the vehicle by which German workers participate with management in a spirit of mutual trust to ensure maximum workplace efficiency, and everyone knows that efficiency is a value that the German society holds dear. Wal-Mart's lack of appreciation of the role of the works councils eventually led the local union to organize a walkout in 30 stores that created bad publicity.[6]

Wal-Mart had other cultural problems as well. It discovered that Germans will go from store to store to take advantage of the lowest prices as opposed to the American preference for one-stop shopping. Other Wal-Mart practices, such as having clerks bag purchases, were unexpected and unwanted by German customers.

Franck Andreutti, a human resources manager in an American multinational corporation, working in Frankfurt, Germany, described the smiling German phenomenon: "While Americans pride themselves on being overtly friendly to everyone, that friendliness is misperceived in cultures that reserve warm greetings for friends." For example, when shopping in the United States, a clerk will ask, "How are you doing today?"

Franck explained that this is seen as intrusive: "If you're sincere and honest and give a complete answer like, 'I am feeling ill today,' the American shop clerk is surprised and can't handle the situation. It's not what they expect." Although Americans are extremely friendly and polite, Europeans view this behavior as intrusive and superficial. "Asking the question, 'How are you doing?' is a personal one," Franck said, "and you're asking it in a public place, not in private life. They should have more respect for position rather than assume they can ask such an impertinent question."

Franck also pointed out that these were the same German employees who had represented the companies that Wal-Mart had taken over. Trading the Wertkauf or Interspar jackets for the Wal-Mart apron didn't mean that their cultural values had changed as well. What's more, when Franck shopped in Wal-Mart, he was keenly aware that the product line had changed and he could no longer find the same local produce and products he'd previously found in that store. This change in product line also underscored "foreign" and "unfamiliar."

Clearly, there were many cultural challenges that Wal-Mart faced in Germany, but differences in attitudes toward hierarchy and egalitarianism were perhaps the most problematic. Let's look at the cultural dimension called hierarchy/egalitarianism and how it affects business behaviors.

WHAT IS HIERARCHY/ EGALITARIANISM?

Hierarchy/egalitarianism is the way individuals view authority and power, how much deference one gives to people in authority, whether people are entitled to express themselves, and how empowered they feel to make independent decisions and take the initiative. It is also one's relationship to power and authority. Are people in authority better or have they earned that status by merit, and is it open to others with the same degree of effort?

Figure 4-1 shows a general distribution of 50 countries on the hierarchy/egalitarianism scale. Keep in mind that even subtle differences can manifest themselves in profound ways. Using Figure 4-2, transfer your score on this dimension from the survey in Chapter 3 (Figure 3-5). Compare your personal preferences to the Country Rankings in Figure 4-1 to see where you are on this scale. You'll be using these scores to compile your complete Personal Cultural Profile in Chapter 11.

Figure 4-1   Country rankings for hierarchy/egalitarianism

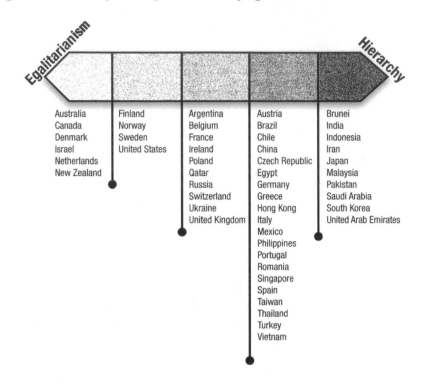

Australia	Finland	Argentina	Austria	Brunei
Canada	Norway	Belgium	Brazil	India
Denmark	Sweden	France	Chile	Indonesia
Israel	United States	Ireland	China	Iran
Netherlands		Poland	Czech Republic	Japan
New Zealand		Qatar	Egypt	Malaysia
		Russia	Germany	Pakistan
		Switzerland	Greece	Saudi Arabia
		Ukraine	Hong Kong	South Korea
		United Kingdom	Italy	United Arab Emirates
			Mexico	
			Philippines	
			Portugal	
			Romania	
			Singapore	
			Spain	
			Taiwan	
			Thailand	
			Turkey	
			Vietnam	

Figure 4-2

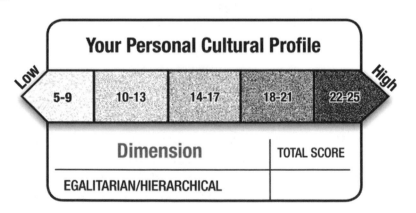

How Can You See Hierarchy?

In hierarchical societies, social and organizational structures are stratified, with fairly defined ways for people to interact with one another. People in positions of authority are treated with formality, respect, and deference. Titles are often important, and a chain of command is adhered to. In hierarchical cultures, the role of the leader may be authoritative, even paternalistic, and people look for direction from their leaders.

At the other end of the continuum, egalitarian societies have few stated barriers to opportunity and personal achievement. Authority is earned. Egalitarian societies tend to be more casual, open, and fluid, believing that individuals should have equal access to opportunities and all people should be treated with the same amount of respect.

In egalitarian societies, the business manager is viewed as a coach who provides the resources and motivation to realize individual potential. Managers empower employees to make decisions, and the employees are expected to take the initiative. In these societies, such as Canada, Australia, and the United States (See Figure 4-1), anyone can aspire to be the head of a multimillion-dollar business or attain preeminence in a career of his or her choice. Children are raised with rags-to-riches stories, and the culture encourages achievement regardless of one's economic origins. Americans, for example, can recount tales of individuals who overcame meager or modest beginnings to attain great status or power: Abraham Lincoln, Jack Welch, and Barack Obama, to name a few. These figures become the heroes of society and serve as proof that success isn't reserved for those in a specific social class.

However, in hierarchical cultures such as India, social ranking is somewhat fixed by birth, and family status plays a role in how much one can accomplish in the future. These societies have a different set of heroes and stories. They believe that people not only should make the best of their station but should dignify their position by accepting their rank. In hierarchical societies, individuals demonstrate their status by the way they dress, their accoutrements, and the trappings that surround them. They limit social interaction to people of similar status and show deference to power and authority.

Egalitarian societies often intentionally blur status distinctions. For example, in the Netherlands, individuals are viewed as equals regardless of the work they do. It's not unusual for a plumber who is repairing a faucet in a Dutch household to be invited to have a cup of tea with the owner of the house before embarking on any work. Contrast that to household helpers in Indonesia, who are confined to the "wet kitchen" and would never dream of entering the home itself.

These behaviors are based on long-standing beliefs, and even with globalization, the Internet, and mass communication, they change slowly. Ask any businessperson who works frequently with Japanese people, and he or she will tell you that rank can be a factor even in seating positions at a conference table.

Consider a business meeting in Japan at which Americans and Japanese were having their first gathering. The meeting was about to start when Jack, the midlevel operations guy in a small U.S. import-export firm, realized that being left-handed, he would be more comfortable sitting at the end of the table. He changed seats with another person on the team. To the Americans' surprise, the Japanese team rearranged themselves so that the person originally sitting opposite Jack moved to the end of the table as well. It didn't take the Americans long to realize that they were sitting across from a person of similar stature on the Japanese team.

Of course, in today's world of business, globalization has modified many cultural values and continues to do so. It appears that attitudes toward hierarchy are one of the ones that are in flux. Egalitarian bias has become a standard of the global corporation, and successful businesses think of themselves as being meritocracies, promoting and rewarding the best and brightest rather than favoring seniority or the historically privileged.

An experience at the author's firm, RW³ LLC, illustrates this point. RW³ is an online cross-cultural training firm that provides cultural resources, assessments, and virtual global team training. One of the cultural surveys asks global team members to answer questions to gauge hierarchical and egalitarian preferences so that team members can learn how to interact with others who may be different from themselves. One team had members from Saudi Arabia, Australia, the Netherlands, and the United States. As you can see in Figure 4-3, the team would face significant challenges in this area. However, in this company the Saudis knew that the corporate culture favored egalitarian principles, and they ranked themselves as being as egalitarian as the others on the team.

Figure 4-3 Comparing hierarchical scores for the United States, Saudi Arabia, the Netherlands, and Australia

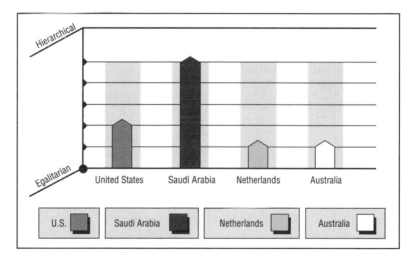

Although cultural values are deeply ingrained and don't change easily, globalization has brought with it certain behavioral standards, one of which is promoting on merit, which is obviously a corporate culture value that everyone on the team realized it would be important to ascribe to. However, the team members quickly realized that even though the Saudis and the Dutch both considered themselves to be individually egalitarian, they had very different approaches. For example, it was clear that the Saudis were more deferential to authority figures, were more likely to wait for clarification before assuming responsibilities, and were generally more formal in their attire and their interactions with others.

If you're doing business in the global marketplace, this is a dimension you need to understand because it is so fundamental to the success of a business endeavor.

Hierarchical/Egalitarian Behaviors in Action

Attitudes toward hierarchy and egalitarian principles exert a profound influence in business today even though many people are reluctant to admit it. Those attitudes affect the sense of empowerment and autonomy, leadership, decision making, and teamwork.

Empowerment and Autonomy

The hierarchical or egalitarian thinking of a society is woven throughout its business environment. You can see status in office design, in closed versus open doors, and in titles and dress. Hierarchical organizations have distinct layers, and everyone expects to see visible trappings of power and authority. Written and verbal communication is also more formal. For example, in extremely hierarchical societies (see Table 4-1), you'll find managers called by title, such as Herr Doktor or Herr Direktor. Don't make the mistake that Wal-Mart made. These are not superficial niceties. They are cues to others about how they should behave. Similarly, organizations have distinct lines of command, and it is poor form to go outside those lines of authority since it would be considered disrespectful and undermining.

TABLE 4-1   HIERARCHY/EGALITARIANISM: BELIEFS AND BEHAVIORS

Egalitarian	Hierarchical
• People believe in egalitarian principles.	• People assume that levels exist.
• People are mobile. They are able to rise in status.	• Individuals believe that one's position cannot change easily.
• Individuals should be treated with the same rights, privileges, and entitlements.	• People at different levels of the hierarchy do—and should—have different rights.
• People believe in empowerment, and everyone has a right to be heard.	• There are class distinctions and a belief that behavior, dress, and speech reflect hierarchical differences. Leaders dress expensively and should be addressed only with honorifics.
• Obvious symbols such as a fancy car, a big office, and elegant clothes are optional and sometimes are viewed as pretentious and an insensitive flaunting of power and wealth.	• Status symbols such as cars, fancy clothes, and jewelry are important cues to a person's rank in society.
• People typically call one another by their first names.	• Everyone is addressed according to his or her status, often by title. Even neighbors refer to each other with a title and never assume that they may call someone by a first name no matter how long they know that person.
• People dress for comfort, not to demonstrate their position or status. Dress may be informal both in the office and at home. Organizations may have "dress-down days" for the comfort of employees.	• Dress is typically more formal. People also dress to show respect for others.
• Language is typically direct and informal.	• Languages have several words for *you*, indicating different levels of familiarity.

Source: Adapted from Michael S. Schell and Charlene Marmer Solomon, *Capitalizing on the Global Workforce: A Strategic Guide for Expatriate Managers*, McGraw-Hill, 1996.

One of the most profound implications of this dimension is the amount of freedom employees have to express themselves, assume authority, and make independent decisions. How much ownership do people feel for the overall success of a business endeavor? In other words, do they feel responsible for completing a task or are they ready to take the initiative for the successful execution of the entire project?

When people from egalitarian cultures work with those from hierarchical ones (who may not feel empowered), they encounter some of the most significant stumbling blocks to working together successfully. What is empowerment?

Empowerment is a sense that employees in egalitarian cultures have (intuitively) that their roles are to ensure the successful accomplishment of a business activity rather than dutifully following task-based instructions. When you feel empowered, you feel entitled to express an opinion to almost anybody regardless of that person's rank in the organization. You participate in the outcome as well as in the process of the work. The senior member of an egalitarian business team looks for candid input and relies on empowered employees to make decisions and take action.

There's a good example about mechanics at American Airlines. For years, those mechanics had been authorized (empowered) to inspect planes, and if they saw something suspicious that might indicate damage to a plane, they were empowered to take the aircraft offline on their own volition and order a detailed inspection. Each mechanic was authorized to do this on the basis of his or her judgment. They didn't have to ask a supervisor if it was all right; they could go ahead and just do it.

This is a natural way for employees in an egalitarian society to behave. But when American Airlines, in an effort to improve efficiency, tried to institute a structure that would curb the individual mechanic's ability to exercise this kind of initiative, it had to do so with a host of guidelines and instructions that clearly specified the circumstances under which a mechanic could take a plane offline. In an empowered society, it is easier to allow people to take the initiative than to curb them with guidelines, whereas the reverse is true in a hierarchical environment.[7]

A skilled, empowerment-based manager approaches a business team in an egalitarian society with the question, "How do we best manage this situation?" A hierarchical manager, however, approaches the team with a specific set of directions. The potential for difficulties is clear. Understanding this particular aspect of hierarchy is especially important because so much of current business activity involves emerging cultures that have deep hierarchical traditions.

In today's world, many of the more merit-based egalitarian ideas are popular. Organizations around the world are tending to reward, promote, and recognize their employees on the basis of achievement and accomplishment because they are beginning to recognize that a collegial manner is an extremely effective way to ensure the intellectual contribution of an employee. However, it's more complicated than that.

Take, for example, Depak, the senior manager who was in charge of a night shift at a call center in Hyderabad, India. He was commended by his fellow employees and had complimentary letters from clients for being an outstanding performer.

The company decided to promote him to the day shift, where he was the number two guy in a much larger organization with many more employees and more people reporting to him. Unexpectedly, Depak's performance started to suffer. Instead of being able to give clear directions to his direct reports, he sought additional approvals before completing tasks.

Why would an exemplary performer who had taken the initiative in one setting expect to be told what to do in another when the jobs were almost identical?

When Depak was the senior person, he knew exactly what his responsibilities were and was authorized to make whatever decisions were necessary to keep the process flowing. He was at the top of the night shift ladder. As number two, he no longer felt the same sense of authority because he had a direct supervisor. He felt reluctant to take the initiative in many instances even though he knew what to do and instead waited to ask his boss for answers as a sign of respect. In this case, it wasn't the company or the direct supervisor who had the problem; Depak's own internal value system inhibited his performance.

As you can imagine, his customers began to suffer, his performance rating was lower, and the previously exemplary performer was in danger of being demoted because he was no longer competent. The fact is that his competence level didn't change. What changed was the way he interpreted his role and range of responsibilities. No one prohibited him from acting as he always had acted.

What was his manager to do? The important thing is to recognize that people who come from hierarchical cultures prefer to have a situation in which there is a clearly defined scope of responsibility and are uncomfortable when their supervisors give them more authority than they are culturally prepared for. Depak's manager could have told him at the time of his promotion the specific range of responsibilities his new job would entail. He should have made that clear to him. The second step would have been to have a regular review process designed to reinforce the scope of responsibility and confirm that it was being put into practice. In other words, people don't automatically feel empowered just because you tell them they are. When working with people from hierarchical cultures, you want to give them careful guidance.

Role of Hierarchy in Leadership

What makes a good leader? It all depends on the culture with which you're dealing. Just as we've learned to expect different behaviors from employees in hierarchical versus egalitarian societies, we find that leadership is significantly differently. In egalitarian cultures such as Canada and Scandinavia, a leader often is seen as a peer with additional responsibilities. Supervisors are those who have demonstrated leadership and manifest it in a collegial way. Leaders often are seen as coaches who ask colleagues how they would do something rather than telling them how to do it. Empowerment not only defines employee behavior, but it defines effective leadership. An effective leader in an egalitarian environment fosters a symbiotic relationship: The leader solicits input to make wise decisions, and the employees feel that their perspective is valued because they participate in the dialogue. The absence of either one leaves an unbalanced business equation.

In egalitarian societies, leadership is something that goes to those who demonstrate unique behaviors that are most beneficial to accomplishing the job rather than to the oldest person in the group or the one with the longest tenure. An egalitarian leader who is coaching an empowered workforce sees that role as trying to help those employees make the most of their skills and resources. Employees expect to be able to challenge, question, and debate their leaders, and a good leader is seen as one who is open to that kind of discussion, who reaches out for input from direct reports and considers what employees are saying.

The role of a manager with a hierarchical team is different. A hierarchical employee needs greater input from the leader, more frequent supervision, and a clear, detailed statement of role expectation. An egalitarian manager crossing this cultural barrier also needs to check frequently for understanding because employees will be less likely to raise questions. Egalitarian managers may think of this as micromanaging and inefficient, but it is necessary and is what employees expect.

Decision Making

Cultural values affect the way people make decisions. In hierarchical societies, decisions typically are made by strong leaders who may—or may not—confer with colleagues or direct reports. However, whether or not direct reports are consulted on decisions, only the leader feels empowered to make them, and people of lesser stature will defer to the most senior person even if they feel empowered to participate in the debate.

By contrast, in egalitarian cultures everyone feels empowered to participate in the debate and at least vote in the final decision. Good leaders will elicit those opinions and hold the entire team responsible for the decision and its successful execution. They expect that when someone makes a decision, he or she will take responsibility for it. People feel the right to postpone implementing a plan until they have bought into it and can see how it will be implemented.

Team and Meeting Behavior

Participation in teams and meetings also follows hierarchical levels. Typically, in hierarchical societies, meetings are conducted for the purpose of discussing decisions that already have been made or will be made by the leaders. It is considered embarrassing and inappropriate to ask subordinates for their opinion in the presence of senior managers. Time and again we hear stories about Chinese, Indian, and Japanese workers who won't speak during a meeting because someone of higher status is present.

By contrast, in egalitarian cultures, meetings often are conducted to make decisions and determine implementation tactics. Similarly, when working on teams, people in hierarchical societies look for direction from the team leader and are less likely to initiate independent action than are those from egalitarian societies. (For a fuller discussion of teams, see Chapter 12.)

Table 4-2 shows the challenges you'll face when crossing cultures. Use it to help tailor your expectations and business behavior.

TABLE 4-2   CROSSING CULTURES: HIERARCHICAL TO EGALITARIAN, EGALITARIAN TO HIERARCHICAL

From Hierarchical to Egalitarian	From Egalitarian to Hierarchical
• Don't expect to make decisions alone. Employees expect to be treated as equals and to have a say in important decisions. They feel comfortable giving unsolicited opinions, providing ideas, and speaking up in meetings.	• Although subordinates may contribute to the decision-making process, the responsibility for making the decision rests largely with the boss. Asking too much in regard to the opinions or ideas of subordinates may make a supervisor appear ineffective.
• Even on important issues, your subordinates will expect to participate with you. Thus, it is important to delegate responsibility to subordinates.	• Subordinates will not expect you to involve them in all decision making. Soliciting opinions of lower-level employees will diminish your credibility.
• Don't be surprised when everyone—colleagues and subordinates as well as supervisors—uses your first name to address you. They all expect you to do the same thing.	• Don't be surprised when colleagues, subordinates, or supervisors call you by your surname or even your title. This is considered good business and social behavior.
• Obvious signs of power and position are considered inappropriate. Therefore, status symbols are less important and may be seen as pretentious.	• Proper use of office space, business cards, cars, and clothing is important to communicate your position clearly.
• Managers try to empower their employees to make their own decisions. Managers may go to a subordinate's office for meetings to highlight the equality in their relationship.	• Attempts to empower employees can be disruptive. You will be making the informal rules of the organization, such as when how, where, and to whom you should communicate.
• Meetings often combine levels and disciplines to encourage a free flow of communication and ideas. You will be expected to speak up regardless of who else is present.	• Meetings will be held with individuals of similar rank and position. When subordinates join the meeting, they aren't expected to participate.

DEFINITIONS FOR
THIS CHAPTER

Empowerment: The expectation of managers in egalitarian societies that employees will take the initiative without prior authorization.

The team apron culture: The risk of misinterpreting familiar, visible, but superficial signs such as uniforms, jackets, and aprons as indicative of deeper attitudes and beliefs.

Lessons Learned to Develop Your Cultural Skills

- The powerful role of hierarchy and egalitarianism in leadership
- What to expect from employees in hierarchical and egalitarian cultures
- The role of hierarchy and egalitarianism in empowerment, leadership, decision making, and teamwork

Questions to Ponder

1. You're working with an outsource team in India that consists of very smart people, some of whom have been educated outside India. You're surprised that when an aspect of the project is finished, the team waits for you before proceeding to the next logical step. Why do you think this is happening? Directions: Go to http://book.culturewizard.com and join the discussion.

2. You're attending a meeting in the Netherlands with Dutch, Swiss, and Norwegian colleagues. You're finding it difficult for

the group to come to a decision because everyone is expressing opinions—both agreeing and disagreeing—and being extremely blunt. Is there any way to curtail the dialogue and force a quick decision?

Directions: Go to http://book.culturewizard.com and join the discussion.

What Do You Think?

You have had your own experiences. Share them. Go to http://book .culturewizard.com and join the discussion.

Notes

1 Andreas Knorr and Andreas Arndt, "Why Did Wal-Mart Fail in Germany?" Universität Bremen, Institute for World Economics and International Management, June 2003, p. 20.

2 Ann Zimmerman and Emily Nelson, "With Profit Elusive, Wal-Mart to Exit Germany," *The Wall Street Journal*, July 29, 2006.

3 Knorr and Arndt, p. 17.

4 Ibid., pp. 22–23.

5 Zimmerman and Nelson.

6 Knorr and Arndt, page 21.

5

Group Focus

What you'll learn in this chapter:

- Do I Have to Listen to *Everyone's* Opinion?

- How Do You Recognize Group Focus?

- Where Does This Come From?

- Group Focus in Action

GROUP FOCUS
REFERS TO

- The importance of the group in relation to the individual

- Whether people want to be distinguished from the group—seen as individuals—or considered part of a particular group

- The idea that group harmony is necessary to achieve business goals

- The importance of living and working together in harmony

Do I Have to Listen to *Everyone's* Opinion?

On a spring afternoon Jeri Hawthorne, an American human resources professional who specializes in intercultural awareness and training, gathered a group of eight people in a small conference room at Novo Nordisk in Copenhagen. Jeri's team was in the final stages of creating a three-day intensive intercultural training program for HR professionals. She had a lot of credibility riding on the success of that very visible program.

Ordinarily, at her company such a content-intensive meeting would include only those who were steeped in intercultural theory and program design. But this time Jeri included the team's administrative support staff because they were responsible for helping with travel plans for the event. There was likely to be some discussion about logistics, including hotels and lodging, and she figured it was more efficient to include those issues now and enhance the cohesiveness of the team.

Familiar with the Danish sense of group identity and strong egalitarian values, Jeri was aware that everyone in the meeting would be expected to contribute. Everyone would expect to have his or her opinion taken into serious consideration—from her most experienced and academically degreed peer to the newest clerk who had just joined the organization. All considered themselves equals in the group.

Jeri had worked very hard preparing for the meeting because the training was for high-level professionals and this session was the only chance all of her team members had to get together for the final preparation. She had a packed agenda in which every moment counted.

Jeri moved to the front of the room and began showing the content-laden slides that would make up the bulk of the training program. Unexpectedly, a young woman chimed in, "I don't think you should say it that way. Someone might be offended. You should say it this way," and she offered another choice of words.

Jeri tried to move past that statement and continue, but other colleagues began to come in with additional opinions that Jeri felt were of minor value. Suddenly, Jeri felt her carefully crafted agenda falling apart. She had planned for a densely scheduled day, and this preliminary subject was not one she expected to have to discuss. Precious time was being taken out of the day to address a concern raised by someone who by most standards wasn't qualified to pose such a roadblock. Yet the whole group felt it was important to engage in the discussion.

Much to her chagrin, Jeri knew she had to stifle her personal cultural preference to put quick closure to the discussion. She was aware that in the group-focused, egalitarian Danish culture, every opinion needed to be explored, and in many cases consensus was necessary.

She couldn't help but imagine how she would have handled this at home, in Washington, D.C. There, in the individualist American culture, as discussion leader, she could have put an end to the dialogue and imposed her individual will, especially since it had majority support. She was accustomed to soliciting input from knowledgeable colleagues and then making a decision. She prided herself on how quickly and effectively she could make good decisions and how tolerant she was to acceptable business risks. Others acknowledged her capabilities in that area.

Now Jeri could hear her own cultural lessons playing in her mind. "You have to listen and at least acknowledge this point of view," she said to herself. "If you don't agree, you have to explain why and give the theoretical explanation. Otherwise, you might find other people jumping in to say, 'We never thought of it that way, and even though the academic definition is correct, this novice has a good point and we might want to change the phrasing.'"

By the time the discussion ended, Jeri had to figure out a way to recover the hour that she'd lost from the dialogue. She was frustrated but knew it would have been unproductive to try to push the interaction in any other way.

"When it works, this type of group dynamic means you get the best thinking of several people," she said. "When it doesn't, you can end up having to rephrase thoughts to take into account everyone's opinion. You risk ending up with something so watered down that it doesn't resemble the original idea."

You have to be prepared for that. Fortunately, Jeri understood the importance of allowing and seeking full group participation and endorsement. All too often people from individualist societies do not allow for that kind of consensus process. They quickly lose patience with the consensus process, and although they may succeed in driving their point across, they are unlikely to get the group support needed to bring the project to a successful outcome.

Group focus, however, is not always intertwined with egalitarianism, as it is in the Scandinavian countries. Anyone who has worked with Asian group-focused cultures such as Japan and Thailand probably has experienced equally frustrating situations in which there is apparent agreement around a concept (or schedule) from the senior members of an organization who are attending a meeting, only to hear them say that they need to take the idea back to their reports to get approval and buy-in. Even though this is from a hierarchical rather than egalitarian perspective, people from group-focused societies nevertheless feel the need to come to a collective decision.

WHAT IS GROUP FOCUS?

Group focus describes whether people identify themselves as part of a group or by their individual responsibility and whether work should be a collective output or a series of individual contributions.

Figure 5-1 shows the degree of group focus in 50 countries. Transfer your scores on this dimension from the survey in Chapter 3 (Figure 3-5) to Figure 5-2. Compare your personal preferences to the country rankings in Figure 5-1 to see where you are on this scale. You'll be using these scores to compile your complete Personal Cultural Profile in Chapter 11.

Figure 5-1   Country rankings: group focus

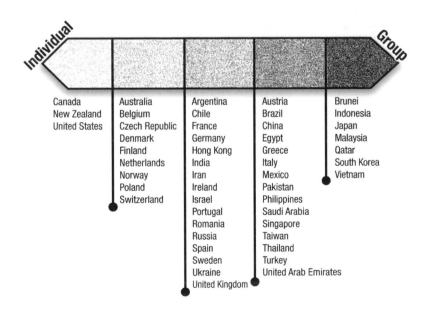

Canada	Australia	Argentina	Austria	Brunei
New Zealand	Belgium	Chile	Brazil	Indonesia
United States	Czech Republic	France	China	Japan
	Denmark	Germany	Egypt	Malaysia
	Finland	Hong Kong	Greece	Qatar
	Netherlands	India	Italy	South Korea
	Norway	Iran	Mexico	Vietnam
	Poland	Ireland	Pakistan	
	Switzerland	Israel	Philippines	
		Portugal	Saudi Arabia	
		Romania	Singapore	
		Russia	Taiwan	
		Spain	Thailand	
		Sweden	Turkey	
		Ukraine	United Arab Emirates	
		United Kingdom		

Figure 5-2

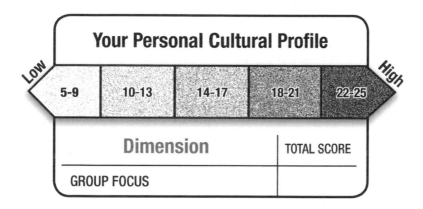

How Do you Recognize Group Focus?

You will find that in group cultures people define themselves by their affiliation with a group: its identity, values, and achievements. People look for consensus in decisions and rarely impose new procedures and program modifications without dialogue and group buy-in. Often these societies believe that maintaining a harmonious work environment is both important and beneficial to all the members of the group.

On the other end of the continuum, individualistic societies recognize and reward unique personal contributions. These societies encourage people to express their distinctiveness and uniqueness. Cultures low on the group focus scale focus on individuality, have laws protecting the rights of the individual, focus on individual achievement, and encourage individuals to distinguish themselves from the masses. People in these cultures may prefer to work and spend time alone; when they are part of a team, they focus on their individual roles.

The concern for individual rights is pervasive in cultures that rank low in group focus, such as the United States (see Figure 5-1). In some cases, the individual is more fully protected than the society is.

Group-focused societies have strong admonitions and punishments for people accused of committing crimes. Loyalty to the larger group is paramount for the individual in a group-focused society and is considered appropriate because the individual is cared for and protected by the family and group. People believe that the group is always greater than the sum of the individuals who constitute it.

Jeri Hawthorne discovered that Denmark's group orientation manifests itself in every aspect of personal and business life and is introduced at the earliest stages of life. For example, children are enrolled in full-time day care from the age of nine months. Parents who don't conform are seen as doing their children a disservice because they aren't socializing their kids to be part of the group. You'll often see this playing out in collective spaces where people clean up after themselves on picnic grounds and outwardly demonstrate their concern for the common good. Even teenagers and children may conscientiously show their concern.

You can see how pervasive the differences in attitude is when you look at the United States, where children in nursery school and kindergarten are taught to stand in front of the class for "show and tell," which provides an opportunity for the little ones to talk about something important to them. It's not unusual for a tot to bring in a special toy or picture and talk about a unique experience. This begins to establish the idea not only that children should be comfortable calling attention to themselves but also that their unique experiences are of interest to everyone else. Contrast this with Japanese kindergartners, who will consult with one another and draw similar pictures when asked to draw their families.

Where Does This Come From?

If you really want to see how people think, examine their heroes, folktales, and children's stories. The archetypal American superhero is Superman.

He acts independently, disregards the accepted way of doing things, and saves people with his superhuman strength. What does he do when he's low on energy or overly stressed? He goes off to his icy retreat, where he's isolated. He gets strength by sequestering himself.

American children are raised on the story *The Little Engine That Could.*[1] This tale is about a small train engine that dreams of pulling a long train of freight cars over a high mountain. The little engine wishes and wishes he could be big and strong, but even if he's not, he believes that if he tries hard enough—regardless of insurmountable odds—he can achieve his dreams. One day his chance comes. None of the other locomotives is available do the job. The Little Engine must pull all the cars that are laden with children's toys and deliver them over the mountain.

"I-think-I-can, I-think-I-can, I-think-I-can" is the Little Engine's mantra. Sure enough, he delivers the toys in time, and the children are happy. The story illustrates the American tenet that if you believe enough in yourself and work exceptionally hard, you will succeed single-handedly. It teaches individuality, optimism, and self-reliance.

People display their individuality in the way they dress, the things they do, and the way they speak. They're encouraged to "make it on their own" or do it their own way. The French children's stories featuring the little girl Madeleine show that her individuality and tenaciousness sometimes get her into trouble, but her cleverness saves her.

Collectivist cultures such as Japan teach that one can succeed best through communal efforts. The frequently told Japanese tale about Momotaro, the Peach Boy, is an excellent example. Once upon a time, the story goes, an old man and woman were very lonely because they had no children. One day the old woman found a peach floating down the river. She took it home, and the peach split open. Out came a baby boy who told them that he had been sent from heaven to make them happy. The boy grew to be a teenager and one day told his parents that since they had always been so good to him, he was going to help all the people in his country by going to Ogre Island, killing the ogres, and bringing back the treasure.

In an individualist country, Momotaro would have trained and done it himself, much like Jack in *Jack and the Beanstalk*. But in this tale Momotaro meets a dog, a monkey, and a pheasant who befriend him. They become a little "community." When they get to Ogre Island, they discover that they need the talents of each of them: The pheasant can fly and start pecking at the eyes of the ogres while the monkey climbs the walls of the fort and opens the gate for Momotaro and the dog. The animals help Momotaro defeat the ogres, who bow down to him and promise never to do wicked things again. The little band finds a wonderful treasure that they bring back to the old man and woman, and everyone lives together.

In this society, the boy can succeed only with the help of the group. It's not only a matter of his initiative or his ingenuity; it's his ability to enlist the community in a cooperative endeavor that results in his success and the community's well-being.[2]

Look at the difference in proverbs from one culture to another. In the West people say, "The squeaky wheel gets the grease." This means that if you stand out of the crowd, your needs are more likely to be met. By contrast, in Asia the saying is "The nail that stands out gets pounded down," or, "The pig that squeals goes to slaughter." This is an obvious reference to the dangers of being different. It carries a strong admonition to remain part of the group.

Group Focus in Action

The significant issues related to group focus have to do with the way people work together and how they can be motivated and rewarded. This affects the way managers make assignments and people solve problems. Group focus determines whether teams or individuals are given assignments and whether problems are solved individually or as a group process. Is decision making and production a group process? Do people like to work in close proximity to one another and share developments as the process continues, or would they prefer to go off and work alone?

Hiring

Group focus plays an important role in the way employees and candidates present themselves in interviews and interactions with management. Obviously, it would be inappropriate for someone in a group-focused society to talk about his or her individual achievements, either academic or in previous work-related situations.

In contrast, qualified candidates in an individualist culture are clear and even outspoken about their accomplishments and perhaps never acknowledge the contributing roles that others have played in those achievements. Managers with a global mindset quickly recognize this culturally based preference and find ways to get to the necessary understanding to determine the candidate's or employee's readiness to take on the tasks in question. To evaluate a high-group-focus candidate, you have to think in a high-group-focus context. Since they won't tell you what they have done, you might explore a little more deeply how work was accomplished and how successes were achieved by the previous team. That is not always easy for people from individualistic societies. Of course, if a recruiting manager does not understand this cultural dimension, he or she is likely to make some profound errors that have an adverse effect on both the candidate and the business mission. (See Chapter 13 for specific guidance on how to approach hiring and selection.)

Recognizing Talent

In individualistic countries, employees are singled out for praise and recognition. Companies in these cultures have employee-of-the-month programs, recognize individual achievement with preferred parking spaces, provide individual incentive compensation, and in general celebrate individual performance. Employees who receive this recognition are applauded and serve as role models for the rest of the organization. They are proud to be singled out for acknowledgment. Individuals like to work on their own and work out problems by themselves. An individual may be singled out for praise and criticism. The shared belief is that individuals are responsible for their actions. Motivation in individualistic cultures is related to power and achievement. People are hired, fired, or promoted because of their skills, past achievements, and technical know-how. They are selected for international assignments because they are viewed as individuals who can get the job done.

The opposite holds true in cultures with a high group focus. There, singling out an individual at best would be embarrassing and at worst would confuse and even demoralize the individual and the group. Since success is dependent on a cooperative effort, it would be completely inappropriate to single out one individual for praise or recognition.

A foreign manager arrived in Japan and was impressed by the young woman who introduced him to others in the plant. He thanked her publicly, complimented her, and held her up as an example to the rest of the staff. He could not understand why she never came back to work afterward.

In high-group-dependent cultures, people are motivated by the assurance of greater security and the opportunity for affiliation, which means that they expect their organizations to take care of them, develop their talents, and fairly compensate them. High-group-dependent cultures can still be meritocracies, but managers need a different skill to recognize and promote talent than they need in a more individualist culture. Employees thrive on the basis of their ability to fit into the group and accomplish tasks by building consensus and working toward organizational goals.

They focus on organizational policies, harmony, and the needs of the group. Because loyalty and seniority are important, promotions often are generated from within the organization. Achievement originates from the creative talents of the group, not the capabilities of one outstanding member.

Decision Making

To a large extent, business is based on the ability to manage risk and make effective decisions. Individualistic societies read and value individualistic decision makers: people who have the ability to evaluate risk and data and make quick decisions. Even when a decision cannot be made individually, these cultures are happy to go along with a majority decision, even if the minority doesn't agree.

Businesspeople in group-focused societies also need to make decisions, but the process is entirely different. As illustrated in Jeri's situation in Copenhagen, people involved in decisions expect to be consulted. No responsible businessperson would make a far-reaching decision without involving others and gaining agreement from all the parties involved. It's easy to see how this process could create frustration for people working in intercultural situations.

A common concern among Western business leaders in dealing with some Asian counterparts is the ongoing need for meetings to reach a decision. Part of the reason is that high-group-dependent cultures never allow a single person to make decisions. Rather, a delegation is brought to business meetings. Members confer before they make a decision and also need to discuss certain business issues with the home office. Anyone affected by a business decision is expected to be consulted, and decisions are made only after consensus has been reached.

Collaboration, Harmony, and Team Behavior

The need for harmony is also a culturally determined behavior and is often part of the group-focused environment. People in these cultures often like to come together for meetings, and this reinforces the sense of affiliation that comes from being together. The forces of the need for affiliation and harmony make the purpose of meetings different from the purpose in individualistic societies. The sense of being part of a harmonious group is a positive experience. The purpose and objective of the meeting may not be as clearly defined as it is in individualist cultures.

People from individualistic cultures prefer to work alone, and when they are part of a team, they want to do their individual best to help the team succeed. When given a task, the individual works on it until satisfied that it's complete regardless of whether another team member is struggling. The best performer is the team leader, and everyone acknowledges the status of that position. Individual contribution to the team is what's important, what's going to propel the team forward.

Table 5-1 illustrates the overt behaviors you can expect.

Table 5-2 shows the challenges you'll face when crossing cultures. Use this table to help tailor your expectations and business behavior.

TABLE 5-1   GROUP FOCUS BELIEFS AND BEHAVIORS

Individual Focus

- Individualism reigns supreme. People are encouraged to be self-sufficient, to "make it" on their own, to "think for themselves."
- Individual accomplishment is recognized and rewarded.

- Individual freedom is very important. There is an "I" consciousness and an orientation to one's self.

Group Focus

- Values the team and the community. The individual's identity is important as he or she relates to the whole group.
- Harmony is important. Every person in a group must be comfortable for the group to work together.
- Taking into consideration how the group "feels" about an issue is more important than how an individual reacts.

(continued)

TABLE 5-1   GROUP FOCUS BELIEFS AND BEHAVIORS (CONT'D)

Individual Focus	Group Focus
• Decision making often is achieved by majority decision. People are encouraged to speak up, but if they don't take responsibility for their own actions, no one in the group feels it is necessary to make his or her wishes known.	• In group activities, everyone must be heard; consequently, decision making takes much longer.
• Meetings are scheduled to maximize time. Decisions are expected.	• Meetings may take considerably more time, and people resent being forced to adhere to a schedule rather than being allowed to voice their concerns or perspectives.
• Meetings are devoted to collaboration and the exchange of information.	• The point of many meetings is simply to gather the group so that everyone can voice his or her opinion. Meetings aren't simply for feedback and approval of ideas.
• Individual taste and style is reflected in home decoration, offices, dress, and even choice of cars.	• People may not value the need to "express themselves."
• The focus is on the nuclear family with fewer children.	• The emphasis is on the extended family and the community.

Source: Adapted from Michael S. Schell and Charlene Solomon, *Capitalizing on the Global Workforce: A Strategic Guide for Expatriate Management*, McGraw-Hill, 1996.

TABLE 5-2   CROSSING CULTURES: GROUP FOCUS

Group Focus to Individualistic	Individualistic to Group Focus
• Don't expect to rely on the group to provide answers. An individual's importance and self-worth are determined by that person's ability to think and work independently.	• Expect people to rely on the group to provide ideas and answers. People value and identify themselves first as part of a group, then as individuals.

(continued)

TABLE 5-2   CROSSING CULTURES: GROUP FOCUS (CONT'D)

Group Focus to Individualistic	Individualistic to Group Focus
• Don't praise a group if one member did an outstanding job. Individuals claim credit for work done alone and expect managers to acknowledge their achievement. Credit, promotions, and raises are given to individuals, not groups.	• Remember that individuals do not take sole credit for accomplishments even when credit is due primarily to one individual. Instead, employees are rewarded in groups. Do not single people out to answer questions, provide ideas, or complete a project.
• Promotions routinely are based on performance and achievement. High performers are more likely to gain positions of authority and leadership.	• Promotions are based on seniority and experience, not solely on performance and achievement.
• Decision making is usually rapid because decisions are made by an individual or by majority vote. Implementation can be delayed by subsequent challenges and questions brought up by colleagues.	• Once a decision is reached, implementation is usually quite rapid. Many meetings may be necessary to gain group consensus and reach a decision.
• Employees look for opportunities to demonstrate their abilities. In meetings and presentations, individuals strive to distinguish themselves. Presentations are dynamic and interactive.	• Presentations tend not to integrate the group. Spontaneous questions and problem-solving exercises may embarrass the group or disrupt the way the group functions.
• Provide employees with opportunities for independent problem solving.	• Provide employees with opportunities to work in a group since they believe that groups maximize ideas, helping them reach an optimal solution.

**DEFINITION FOR THIS
CHAPTER**

Harmony: The need to have a comfortable, noncontentious working environment.

Lessons Learned to Develop Your Cultural Skills

- The impact of group focus on business meetings and working on a team

- The role of harmony in a society

- How people in group-oriented cultures view individual accomplishment

- How to recognize individual skills in a group-oriented society

Questions to Ponder

1. You have a limited amount of time on your visit to introduce a new quality control procedure to your company's Naples, Italy, office. You can't seem to get agreement on an implementation plan. It seems that the group won't accept majority rule. This is preventing a decision. What do you think this is happening?
   Directions: Go to http://book.culturewizard.com and join the discussion.

2. You've been asked to create an employee-of-the-month recognition program in your Jakarta, Indonesia, office. You're on a conference call with a group of local managers who can't

seem to come up with a single employee's name for the first month's award. What do you think is happening?
Directions: Go to http://book.culturewizard.com and join the discussion.

What Do You Think?

You have had your own experiences. Share them. Go to http://book.culturewizard.com and join the discussion.

Notes

[1] Watty Piper, with illustrations by Lois Lenski, *The Little Engine That Could*, A Platt & Munk Classic, originally published in 1930.

[2] Momotaro, the Peach Boy, ancient Japanese folk tale.

Relationships

THE TERM *RELATIONSHIPS* REFERS TO
• The importance of developing a personal relationship before conducting business
• The implied expectations and obligations of a relationship
• Whether trust is assumed or earned
• Whether rules are interpreted equally or there are special conditions for friends
• The value of connections

The Dutch and Chinese Cultural Exchange

Anke Puscher was a Dutch national who worked for a leading multinational postal and direct marketing company headquartered in Holland. Anke had been with the company for eight years in various international commercial management roles. During her tenure, she had driven business development initiatives in European countries, and when a position in Shanghai was offered to her in early 2006, she enthusiastically accepted it. The company believed she'd had enough international experience to take on the new challenge even though she knew little about China.

Three years before Anke's assignment, the company recognized the potential of direct mail marketing in China. Until that time, Chinese marketing had focused predominantly on broadcasts and billboards. The company saw its growth in China as a natural expansion of its global ambitions and was pleased that it had developed a unique product focused on the Chinese market.

As it turned out, Anke was the right person to take on the challenge. As the sales and consultancy director, she needed to identify the market for the newly developed services among Chinese and global companies and develop a Chinese sales force to reach that market. In the process she would need to learn who the decision makers were and how to reach them with a compelling sales pitch. Coincidentally, the company was not the only global direct marketing firm launching a Chinese initiative. Among Anke's challenges was the need to win business away from competitors.

It was quite a task for a China novice, as Anke was to discover. In the Netherlands, the business development approach was to research and study the marketplace carefully, identify the needs, and develop focused products uniquely suited to industries and service lines. Once the plan was developed, the sales force would build on the credibility of previous successes within that industry. For example, if a direct marketing campaign for one major food market chain worked, they would take the story of that success to other food markets.

In China, Anke realized to her dismay that no market segmentation study was being conducted, and there was no uniformly applied sales strategy. Instead, her sales team pursued opportunities without rhyme, reason, or direction. Instead of the focus on industry and market segmentation that worked so well in Europe, the Chinese sales team appeared to approach the market in a haphazard way. Consequently, market penetration was slower than what management had anticipated.

Anke carefully developed a sales strategy that was based on the business segmentation approach, supported it with analysis, and presented it to the Chinese sales team. The strategy was heavily dependent on defining a unique need in an industry and contacting (cold calling) potential buyers in companies within that industry.

Although her Chinese colleagues greeted the strategy and its logic with nods and apparent agreement, Anke was astounded to find that no one followed it: "They said, 'Very nice idea. We are going to develop our sales plan accordingly.' And they just continued contacting the same people they knew—as they'd always done."

She soon discovered a key lesson of working in China. Even though her team was highly educated and many of them had lived abroad, they were unable to implement a strategy focused on anything other than using their existing relationships. Asking her team in China to make cold calls was like asking a weight lifter to run a marathon. "They pretended that they were following my strategic direction, but they believed I was wrong. I could tell they were working in exactly the same way, but they put a little shell around it."

Anke continued: "They thought, 'Here comes a Westerner who thinks she knows what's right, but she doesn't understand.' Initially they were polite and wouldn't tell me to my face because they thought I was making a mistake. It's not polite to tell your boss she's making a mistake."

Anke realized she had to prove that her direct marketing approach could work in China, that her team could earn more money, get performance bonuses, and win recognition if it followed the strategy. Anke was up to the challenge and decided to pursue a client directly to show that the plan could succeed. But where would she find the right contacts after being in China only one month?

Through a European connection with a retail chain in China, she learned that a French leisure clothing retail chain was seeking professional support to advertise new store openings. Its challenge was to target households that actively pursued sports and outdoor activities to minimize the use of leaflets. Using the company's consulting capability, consumer data, and distribution network, she helped the client solve that problem and delivered one of the biggest successes that year in the company.

Now, with a successful experience to build on, she used the retail chain relationship to win another significant piece of business and used that to demonstrate how the industry segmentation strategy could work. Encouraged by the outcome of this different way to approach the market, her Chinese sales force became more interested in trying it.

It was her chance to make the strategy work. She purchased cold-call lists and gave them to the team, but when she asked how the calls were going, team members told her that no one was reachable and the lists were no good. She knew they hadn't tried the names she'd given them and was becoming increasingly concerned about how to implement the strategy. However, Anke gave them a little time to see what they would do. That was a good idea because once they saw that market segmentation was effective, the team members adapted Anke's approach to fit into their relationship-oriented way of doing business. They all contacted people within their own networks and asked for referrals to new contacts in the market they were approaching. In other words, they asked their networks to help them build relationships in the new area of opportunity. After several months, the joint effort resulted in significant sales growth for the company in Shanghai.

In the final analysis, Anke and her Chinese colleagues learned from each other. Anke's plan of industry and product segmentation worked, but her Chinese colleagues had to change it from a pure market approach to a relationship-based approach. They called on people they knew and asked for referrals to individuals within the market segment on which they were focusing. They relied on recommendations and introductions but focused them within an industry. "In the end," she said, "we were aiming for the same target, but everybody did it in their own way."

Anke succeeded in creating an environment where new techniques could be introduced and work in a cultural context different from the one in which they had been created. Although her Dutch background prepared her well for a logical, methodical direct approach, her Chinese colleagues were able to show her that a culturally appropriate adaptation could be developed, retaining the high relationship context of their culture. Anke also learned from them to reach out to her

WHAT ARE
RELATIONSHIPS?

The relationships dimension describes the importance a society ascribes to building extensive connections and developing trust and how central relationships are as a prerequisite to working with someone.

contacts: "I adapted the contextual approach from my Chinese colleagues. In the end, without the European network contact, I wouldn't have had the initial success."

Figure 6-1 shows the ranking of relationships for 50 countries. Transfer your scores on this dimension from the survey in Chapter 3 (Figure 3-5) into Figure 6-2. Compare your personal preferences to the country rankings in Figure 6-1 to see where you are on this scale. You'll be using these scores to compile your complete Personal Cultural Profile in Chapter 11.

How Do You Recognize the Relationships Dimension?

Cultures around the world have different perspectives on the importance of relationships in business. However, in most societies, the relationship dimension is an important element of business, if not the foundation of all interpersonal interactions, both business and social. As Anke discovered, her team members couldn't conceive of doing work in a way that circumvented their contacts and connections. (In Figure 6-1 you'll note that there are many more relationship-oriented countries than transactional countries.)

Some cultures require a level of trust before embarking on any work, whereas at the other extreme, some are so transactional they are able to get down to work without having to know you at all beforehand.

Figure 6-1   Country rankings: relationships

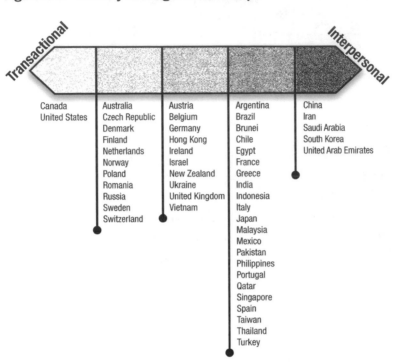

Figure 6-2

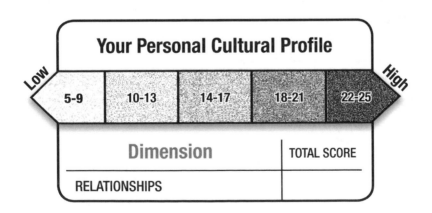

In cultures such as China and India, for example, if you don't under-stand the depth of obligation associated with relationships, you'll be confounded by some of your colleagues' actions and expectations. Rela-tionships take center stage and direct many of the activities in the work-place as well as outside it. Often individuals will not enter into a business relationship until you establish trust. Since relationships are crucial to the entire interpersonal interaction, it's not surprising that entertaining and other social activities are part of business dealings. Furthermore, in China it's almost impossible to conduct business without having a solid relationship or getting an introduction from someone who has one.

Figure 6-3 shows that relationship-oriented societies require time before individuals allow you to become friends and penetrate barriers. In cultures in which you don't make friends with everyone quickly, the friends you make are close and the relationships are abiding. Once you've gotten through the initial barriers, you become trusted and will reap the benefits of those powerful associations. Contrast that with transactional cultures. You'll see that transactional individuals are easy to get to know quickly, but only on a surface level. Friends are made easily, and relationships are taken more lightly. Barriers arise and are just as difficult to break through. The risk is that people from relation-ship-oriented cultures may misinterpret the initial ease of getting to know transactional individuals and experience it as superficiality. They may even mistrust you as a result.

In relationship-oriented societies, relationships develop slowly, are stable, and sometimes pass from generation to generation. Although they are slow to develop, they're built atop a framework that transcends time and place and probably will endure even if one person moves to another city or country (see Figure 6-3).

Since knowing the "right" people and being networked with them is an important part of life, individuals devote a lot of time, considera-tion, and effort to building relationships. In fact, friendships are often

Figure 6-3   Graphic comparison of how some cultures have a hard outer shell and are slow to form relationships while others form superficial relationships easily.

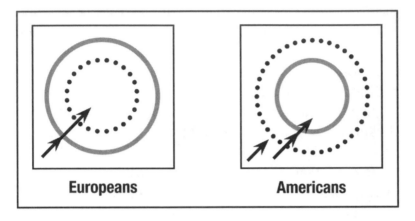

multidimensional because people believe that an enduring friendship is a strong criterion for a business relationship since you know you can trust the person. Indeed, having a relationship is not an impediment to making an objective decision; it is often an important factor in the decision. Trust and long-standing connections often are viewed as being as important as contract and price, and maintaining a deep and extensive network of trusted contacts takes precedence over deadlines, cost, and efficiency. People surround themselves both professionally and socially with those they've known for many years.

At the other end of the spectrum are cultures that are more transactional, such as the Netherlands, Canada, the United States, and Sweden. People don't need to know others well before they do business or have significant social interaction, and associations develop quickly, but may last for only a short period. Even neighbors who see each other socially every day may not stay in touch if one of them moves to another city, for example. Social relationships may be superficial, with people sharing few of their private feelings. Americans, for instance, are easy to get to know on a surface level and then become private.

In transactional societies people are eager to get down to business even without having a prior personal connection. When you see this behavior, you can assume that although there is openness to meeting new people, relationships can be short term, and there are few implied obligations in a relationship. The important point to remember is that you want to avoid unintentional ill feelings. Others often view people from transactional cultures as being superficial and their generous spirit as insincere.

Mark Burchell, business development director at Interdean International Relocations, tells a story about when he moved to the United States from England. He wrote home about how much he liked it here and how quickly he made friends. On his first day he had been invited to people's homes. Later he was shocked when he realized that those invitations, though generously proffered, were not intended to be taken up.

These ideas about the importance of relationships fundamentally affect the way individuals approach business. Transactional cultures tend to rely on legal systems to protect the rights of businesses and individuals, whereas relationship societies believe that trust compels people to act honestly and fairly with each other.

Relationships and Trust

In relationship cultures, trust is critical for successful business transactions, but make no mistake: Trust is a necessary component in *all* cultures. However, in some cultures trust is assumed (with the legal system as a backup), and in others it has to be earned. Whether articulated or not, trust is one of the biggest potential stumbling blocks to working across cultures and is made all the more important by the fact that much of today's work is done virtually without the benefit of getting to know one another face to face.

Research in the field points out that trust is an important component of teamwork and is critical to effective business interactions.[1]

Even if this is unspoken, in a monocultural environment, people make certain assumptions about trust, and certain behaviors reinforce or challenge those assumptions. This represents the intercultural challenge of trust. Not only do different cultures have varying needs for trust and relationships as an underlying component of doing business, but they also have different ways of manifesting trust and commitment. One of the early pitfalls in intercultural interactions is failure to recognize the importance of establishing trust and being able to recognize behavior associated with building it.

In American society, when one individual says to another, "Trust me, I know," or, "Trust me, I will do it," the presumption is that there is no need to question or doubt that statement. This can be a cross-cultural land mine, however, because it is one of those hidden aspects of culture that you need to examine when you work beyond your own borders.

What is trust? Is it a feeling? Is it an act of faith? Or can trust be measured by actions? Trust can be demonstrated, according to Roy J. Lewicki, a Distinguished Teaching Professor and Professor of Management and Human Resources at the Max M. Fisher College of Business at Ohio State University.

Lewicki and his coauthors, who work in the field of conflict resolution, offer a system for examining trustworthy behavior. In this model, the aspects of trust are ability, integrity, and benevolence. "Our trust in another individual can be grounded in our evaluation of his/her ability, integrity, and benevolence," they state. "That is, the more we observe these characteristics in another person, our level of trust in that person is likely to grow."[2]

Why is this important? If you're going from a more transactional culture to one in which you need to take time to build a relationship by establishing trust, you need to know *how* to go about doing that. In other words, Anke couldn't simply say to her Chinese colleagues, "Trust me, I know." She had to build their confidence in her and also exhibit her respect for them.

Lewicki offers this guidance:

Ability refers to an assessment of the other's knowledge, skill, or competency. This dimension recognizes that trust requires some sense that the other is able to perform in a manner that meets our expectations.

Integrity is the degree to which the trustee adheres to principles that are acceptable to the trustor. This dimension leads to trust based on consistency of past actions, credibility of communication, commitment to standards of fairness, and the congruence of the other's word and deed.

Benevolence is our assessment that the trusted individual is concerned enough about our welfare to either advance our interests or at least not impede them. The other's perceived intentions or motives of the trustee are most central. Honest and open communication, delegating decisions, and sharing control indicate evidence of one's benevolence.[3]

Lewicki and colleagues go on to say: "Although . . . linked to each other, they each contribute separately to influence the level of trust in another within a relationship. However, ability and integrity are likely to be most influential early in a relationship. . . ."[4]

What are they suggesting? In societies that require trust building before embarking on a business relationship, these experts suggest that you need to demonstrate skill and integrity. As a result, you may need to spend more time in activities you don't ordinarily perceive as being valuable. In other words, although you may think that chatting about personal issues before a business meeting or spending time outside of work socializing with colleagues is a simple nicety or a waste of time, think again. They are actually the building blocks of trust, opportunities for you to demonstrate your talents and heighten your credibility.

Figure 6-4 shows where each type of culture begins the business interaction. High-relationship societies start with the personal and

Figure 6-4   High relationship cultures build trust and confidence before starting a business activity while transactional cultures go straight to the business activity that may evolve into a more personal relationship after the business deal is made.

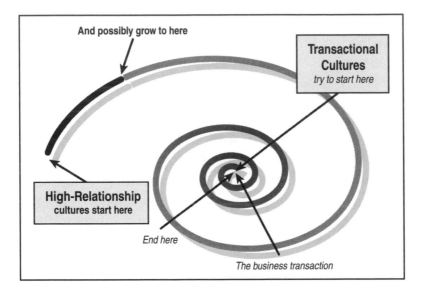

build trust. As they get to know you, people become more comfortable doing business with you. Transactional societies can begin with the business dealings and slowly get more personal and build trust, depending on their inclination.

There is no uniform way or easy formula for establishing trust. Trust takes time and needs to be built at whatever pace the individuals require. Effective global business leaders need to understand the importance of creating trust with colleagues and team members and recognize that its absence will undermine the effective functioning of a group.

Expectations of Relationships

If you're from a transactional culture, you expect that those with whom you interact will be honest and feel compelled to do the best job possible simply because they're motivated by an internal drive to do well. There are no further obligations beyond the transaction. In other words, you're not obligated to socialize, offer out-of-work time for favors, or take a personal interest in the people with whom you work. Also, you'd think twice before hiring your friend's child for a job in your company.

By contrast, in relationship-based cultures, friends are expected to put friendship above business transactions and in some cases even above the law. Fons Trompenaars[5] describes a phenomenon that he refers to as "particularism versus universalism," which defines cultures as having behavioral standards that are different for "particular people" (namely, friends and family) or believing that behavioral standards are the same for everybody.

He cites the following scenario: An individual is the cause of an automobile accident. Should his friend testify in his favor regardless of his degree of responsibility, or is the friend supposed to tell the truth? In this example, people in particularist (high-relationship) societies are expected to put the relationship above all else, whereas universalist (transactional) societies would find it very bad form to expect a friend to be less than honest.

You may never be called on to lie for a friend, but if you're hiring for a position in your company, do you wonder whether you'd give your friend an advantage over someone you don't know? Whom would the job go to? Your friend (who you know is trustworthy) or someone more qualified whom you don't know?

A Word about *Guanxi*

China, along with many societies heavily influenced by the Chinese, has a particular type of relationship called *guanxi*. Although relationships are fundamental in Chinese society, *guanxi* means more than just close and trusted relationships. It also refers to a complex network of connections that is at the core of Chinese life. *Guanxi* (pronounced "gwan-SHE") is one of the most powerful forces in Chinese culture, encompassing the idea of a complex series of connections to individuals and families with whom a person is networked. *Guanxi* is built and deepened over time and carries with it a profound sense of responsibility. The term also includes a sense of commitment and obligation built over time by the reciprocation of social exchanges and favors.

People who have *guanxi* are quick to act on each other's behalf, do favors for each other, and, depending on the depth of the relationship, support each other's families as the need arises. Think of *guanxi* as a type of currency that can be saved and spent between individuals and families (and organizations). Like money, it can be exhausted if it is not replenished with reciprocity, and so people must be sensitive not to overextend the *guanxi* that has been established. Failure to repay favors is equivalent to not repaying a financial obligation.

The reciprocal nature of *guanxi* and its implied obligations are one of the main reasons the Chinese are reluctant to engage in deeper relationships with people they do not know. Beginning such a relationship can put them in a compromising position from which it is difficult to withdraw. Additionally, they are concerned that establishing *guanxi* with someone who later proves unworthy will tarnish their reputation. Thus, if you want to begin a relationship with a Chinese individual or company, it's best if you can be introduced by a mutual friend or associate who can vouch for you. However, the intermediary is expending *guanxi* to make the introduction, and so you will need to repay the favor.

Understanding the role of *guanxi* in business is essential for building fruitful relationships in China. However, the specific questions of how, when, where, and with whom to build *guanxi* can vary greatly from location to location and industry to industry. Government employees require different treatment than do businesspeople, and there are variations based on age, personality, and education. In short, there are no formulas and no guarantees.

Michael Bruck, currently Managing Director of Tripod Capital in China, was the general manager of Intel China. During his tenure, he realized how important it was to express a strong interest in the well-being of his Chinese employees. He invested time, energy, and resources in their training. He helped develop their strengths so that they could grow their careers. This not only resulted in significant success for Intel in China but also built deep friendships between Michael and his employees. Those friendships and relationships still exist, many years later, to everyone's advantage.

Hospitality and Extended Family Ties

Hospitality is one way people strengthen important relationships. In India, hospitality is a central value that not only includes individuals but extends to the larger family and even to a professional extended family. Observe how misunderstandings can occur.

An American director decided he had to have a firsthand look at his company's operations in Mumbai and told his peers in the Mumbai office that he was coming soon. His colleague in India told his assistant to make all the travel arrangements, including plans for hotels and any other needs the director might have, and cleared his own calendar for the entire week and weekend of the director's trip. He told his family that they would be entertaining his American colleague during the weekend, taking him sightseeing, and generally making sure he had a good time. The family was delighted to be able to invite him to a distant cousin's wedding that was taking place that weekend.

The American found the visit fruitful and enjoyed the hospitality of his Indian associate but was a bit surprised by the level of generosity shown by the man's family members. It was an interesting visit for him, but it seemed somewhat strange that he'd been invited to join so many family activities. When the Indian colleague had occasion to visit the United States, the American made sure to take him out to a lovely lunch and even took him and some of the guys in the office out for drinks at the end of the day. The Indian was very surprised at what he read as a lack of interest, feeling that his generosity was not being reciprocated.

"They embrace you into the culture, into their family beyond the business bottom line," explains Aaron Arun Baharani, president of Manage the Globe, headquartered in New York City. "It's how they define the relationship. Indians spend a lot of time being hospitable as part of the way they build trust.

"In the business context, it's all part of the extended family. Professional colleagues are constantly being entertained by the family, and in fact the personal extended family and the business extended family overlap." When an Indian visits the United Sates and his hospitality is not reciprocated in the same way, the Indian leader wonders if he's not being valued as a partner.

It's hard to miss the business implications of this cross-cultural misunderstanding, but many people do miss it. Sometimes it is very difficult to anticipate the depth and extent of family ties and their impact on the workplace.

Take, for example, the young Indian engineer in Detroit who came to his manager and told him that he had to leave the United States right away and would not be able to return for three weeks. The manager was perplexed because the young man had been extremely diligent in his work and was aware of an important impending deadline.

After a significant amount of probing, the manager discovered that the engineer's mother had insisted that he come back to Bangalore to meet a prospective bride whom the mother had selected. He felt he had no choice but to follow his mother's directions.

It seemed incongruous that this highly trained engineer, working with the most sophisticated technology, would adhere to ideas of arranged marriage and hold values so closely aligned to his traditional culture that he would follow his mother's wishes even if they conflicted with work demands. Fascinated by this seeming paradox, the manager began to realize that many individuals from relationship-based cultures need to integrate the relationship element into their lives, regardless of how traditional their lives are and regardless of their educational level or seeming degree of acculturation.

How Relationships Win Business

In the early 1980s, an American and a European power-generating supplier were competing for a $600 million contract in Malaysia to upgrade that country's power-generating system. Malaysia's economy was growing, and the country was modernizing at a breakneck pace. Malaysia's Kuala Lumpur was in a race with Singapore, Hong Kong, and Indonesia's Jakarta to attract foreign capital and build its economy.

It needed to attract local attention to capture the imagination of the world's investment communities. Who would have the best educated workforce? Who would have the tallest buildings? Who could develop the best and most stable municipal infrastructures? It quickly became apparent to the government of Malaysia that the electrical grid needed upgrading: everything from its power generation system to its electrical distribution network.

Whoever won the contract, it would be a monster contract. All the companies bidding for the job arrayed their best sales teams for the competition. Each planned to come up with a winning strategy. After the preliminary vetting, the competition came down to two companies. Convinced that they could demonstrate the greater efficiency of their manufacturing and construction, as well as the cost benefit over their competitor's product, the executives at the American company were feeling very confident. The American company's competitive advantages were well known to the executives of the European competitor, and they had good reason to be concerned because both companies had stellar reputations and excellent histories with the Malaysians.

However, the Europeans had invested heavily in Malaysia, the city of Kuala Lumpur, and the long-term strategic direction of the government. They had sponsored local events and had a significant team on the ground that met frequently with government officials and other decision makers to be sure they understood the decision-making process.

The negotiations that followed were intense, as one would expect for a contract of this size. The American technological advantage seemed insurmountable. However, the Europeans felt that their long-standing relationship and long history of support of the government and its people, together with a better than adequate product, gave them cause for optimism. How right they were! Although the decision was a tough one, the relationship-oriented Malays decided that their sense of trust and confidence in a long-standing partner was more important than a small product advantage.

The Malays knew the European organization better; they had built up a personal relationship with that company's executives, and if anything went wrong, that relationship would be extremely valuable in making sure things were set right. They felt that the European management was more invested in the well-being and future of Kuala Lumpur, and those values were more important to them than a small gain in efficiency.

This high-stakes example shows that people from transactional societies can misread the potency of longer-term relationships and trust. Are price and quality the key determinants, or are trust and likability more important? Are sales made on the basis of relationships and connections? Certain cultures mistakenly believe that quality, price, and value are the only factors that have to be taken into account in making business decisions.

This goes beyond sales. For example, in many Western cultures it is assumed that nepotism is a negative. But it is possible that because someone is your friend, giving that person the job is a good decision. That person will be more reliable because of the friendship and never would do anything injurious.

Team Behavior

The relationship dimension manifests itself in several ways on teams. Whom do you invite to be part of your team? Is it the people who can do the best job or the people you most like to work with? If you're from a transactional culture, you assume that others have been chosen for your team on the basis of their relevant experience and technical competence. If you're from a relationship-based culture, it's likely that your team will consist of people with whom you like to work. Don't be surprised that certain people are selected for the team on the basis of who they know and the influence they have in the larger organization.

You can see the potential for problems in dealing across cultures. If you're from a transactional culture and are working in a relationship-based team, you may wonder why specific people were chosen for the team. The answer may not be obvious.

Beyond that, people from transactional cultures expect meetings to proceed on schedule with little deviation from the agenda and to focus on strategy and action. When making decisions, you try to be objective and dispassionate, focusing on business rather than personal issues. Those on the team who are relationship-oriented invest a lot of time and effort in developing relationships with team members, believing that the time invested in personal conversations will build trusting relationships that can facilitate a smooth, productive team experience. (This issue is examined in detail in Chapter 12.)

Table 6-1 lists some of the behaviors you can expect.

Table 6-2 illustrates the challenges you'll face when crossing cultures. Use it to help tailor your expectations and business behavior.

TABLE 6-1 RELATIONSHIPS: BELIEFS AND BEHAVIORS

Low-Relationship Culture
- Relationships and business agreements may continue for only a short period.
- Individuals are willing to engage in many activities immediately with the assumption that if the activities don't work out, they can end them. Personal trust isn't a prerequisite to business dealings.

High-Relationship Culture
- Relationships and friendships are extremely stable over long periods.
- Trust is a prerequisite to business dealings and must be established and nurtured over time; it is essential for initial and further business dealings.

(continued)

TABLE 6-1   RELATIONSHIPS: BELIEFS AND BEHAVIORS (CONT'D)

Low-Relationship Culture	High-Relationship Culture
• Business agreements must be protected by contracts and lawyers.	• People won't do business with someone until they've built a relationship and know they can trust that person. Recourse to the law is secondary to honoring any commitments to a "partner."
• Fax and phone suffice for most business interactions. Only high-level decisions and information exchange have to be conducted in person.	• Face-to-face meetings are always preferred.
• Conversations on both business and social occasions tend to focus on business issues. Getting to know the other individual is considered irrelevant to business.	• It's important to show an interest in the individual as well as in the business issues. It is helpful to gather information about the individual and the business before meetings so that it is apparent that you care about the person, not just the success of the joint business endeavors.
• People begin relationships easily. There is more transience in friendships.	• It takes time to build relationships, but they are impermeable to distance and the passing of time.
• Relationships are seen as transactional and a necessity of working together. Even on a social level, neighbors who consider themselves to be fairly close may have little to do with one another if either neighbor moves to a new location.	• Relationships tend to remain stable even if great distances separate the people.

Source: Adapted from Michael S. Schell and Charlene Marmer Solomon, *Capitalizing on the Global Workforce: A Strategic Guide for Expatriate Managers,* McGraw-Hill, 1996.

TABLE 6-2 CROSSING CULTURES: RELATIONSHIPS

Relationship to Transactional

- Relationships are highly transactional, so they can be built quickly and dissolved easily if they are no longer expedient.

- Established personal relationships are not necessary to completing a business deal. Don't expect these agreements to be long-lasting.
- Financial issues and concrete business factors are of great significance to potential business partners in deciding whether to work with you.
- Being able to focus on business concerns and reach closure is highly valued. Engaging in discussions of issues not related to the current business is considered distracting. Once business agreements have been completed, the various parties may discuss non-business-related topics.

- When arriving in a new location, your ability to fit into the business environment and your willingness to work hard are important. Your commitment to your work will be what encourages your colleagues to build relations with you.

Transactional to Relationship

- Business partners will be receptive to getting to know you only after time has passed. You can jump-start the process by having common acquaintances and having individuals with credibility introduce you.
- Trying to do business with someone you have just met may be very difficult. Build strong relationships as the key to successful business dealings.
- Give potential partners an opportunity to get to know you. Share meals, after-dinner activities, or golf.

- When doing business with external clients, focusing only on business concerns may seem narrow to your counterparts. Instead, be open to discussing history and cultural issues, family concerns, or other nonbusiness topics. Demonstrating that your completing a business transaction is very important.
- When arriving in a new location, building relationships with colleagues and subordinates is appropriate. Discussions at work, over lunch, and during after-work activities ensure that business will progress smoothly.

Source: Adapted from Michael S. Schell and Charlene Marmer Solomon, *Capitalizing on the Global Workforce: A Strategic Guide for Expatriate Managers,* McGraw-Hill, 1996.

DEFINITIONS FOR THIS CHAPTER

Guanxi: The complex nature of personalized networks of influence and social relationships that is a central concept in Chinese society.[6]

Connections: Interrelated contacts.

Hospitality: The elaborate ways individuals treat each other outside the workplace; may include extended family.

Lessons Learned to Develop Your Cultural Skills

- The impact of relationships in a business setting

- Expectations of relationships

- The importance of building trust

- *Guanxi* and other extended family connections

- The role of relationships in winning business, keeping talent, and working on teams

Questions to Ponder

1. You're going to India and know that as soon as you land, your Indian peers are going to meet you at the plane, take you out for dinner, and keep you entertained for the duration of the visit. Last time, you were exhausted because you weren't able to have any private time. You would like to have more time to rest and recuperate. How can you create some private time for yourself? Directions: Go to http://book.culturewizard.com and join the discussion.

2. There is a Swahili proverb, "A man alone cannot push a boat into the sea."[7] What do you think it means?
   Directions: Go to http://book.culturewizard.com and join the discussion.

What Do You Think?

You have had your own experiences. Share them. Go to http://book .culturewizard.com and join the discussion.

Notes

[1] Roy J. Lewicki and Edward C. Tomlinson, "Trust and Trust Building." In *Beyond Intractability*, Guy Burgess and Heidi Burgess, eds. Conflict Research Consortium, University of Colorado, Boulder. Posted December 2003, http://www.beyondintractability.org/essay/trust_ building; The Beyond Intractability Knowledge Base Project, Guy Burgess and Heidi Burgess, codirectors and editors, Conflict Information Consortium (formerly Conflict Research Consortium), University of Colorado, Boulder, CO.

[2] R. J. Lewicki, D. J. McAllister, and R. J. Bies, "Trust and Distrust: New Relationships and Realities," *Academy of Management Review* 23, 1998, pp. 438–458.

[3] Ibid.

[4] Ibid.

[5] Fons Trompenaars, *Riding the Waves of Culture: Understanding Diversity in Global Business.* Irwin, 1993 and 1994, pp. 35–38.

[6] Definition from Wikipedia.

[7] Axel Schelffler, *Let Sleeping Dogs Lie and Other Proverbs from Around the World*, Barrons Educational Series, 1997, p. 89.

Communication Styles

What you'll learn in this chapter:

- How Genentech Continues Its Quest for Best Practices

- What Is Communication Style?

- The Elements of Effective Cross-Cultural Communication

- Recognizing Different Communication Styles

- How to "Read" Nonverbal Cues

- Using Silence and "Yes" to Avoid Conflict

- The Impact of Language

COMMUNICATION STYLES REFERS TO

- The ways societies use language, both verbal and nonverbal.

- The amount of information people need to receive or share in order to understand a message. Is it brief and task-relevant, or does it include background information as well?

- The directness or subtleness of the language people use.

- The way people use words or gestures to express feelings or moods.

- The importance of harmony and saving face.

How Genentech Continues Its Quest for Best Practices

Genentech is one of the most highly regarded companies in the world. Since its founding in 1976, it has been a leader in creating biotechnology products. With U.S. product sales of $8,540 million for 2007 (a 19 percent increase over sales in 2006), it was on *Fortune*'s 2008 list of the fastest growing companies in the United States, was ranked number one in pharmaceuticals on *Fortune*'s 2008 list of America's most admired companies, ranked forty-first among *Barron's* 500 best American companies in 2008, and was on *BusinessWeek*'s list of the 100 most innovative companies in 2007.[1] It has been voted one of *Fortune*'s 100 best companies to work for for 10 consecutive years.

As in other pharmaceutical companies, product development requires a significant amount of testing and clinical trials that must be conducted on patients who haven't been treated under other protocols. (Clinical trials are the testing grounds where researchers discover whether new drugs are safe, what doses are the most effective, and whether already approved pharmaceuticals have other uses.)

However, it's not easy to find patients. In the United States, for example, the patient population is being used up because there are so many trials being conducted by so many companies. Therefore, Genentech, like others, needs to look around the world to find patients. However, that's not at all simple. Beyond the logistical issues of labeling, writing directions, and transporting medications in new ways that comply with foreign laws, there is the thorny cultural issue of explaining to patients what a clinical trial is and what is expected in terms of their participation.

Cross-cultural communication is always a challenge, and one can see this especially vividly in health care. In the best circumstances, communication between doctor and patient is a very sensitive area, and when cultural differences come into play, it becomes even more complex. The very notion of questioning one's doctor and being involved in the selection of one's treatment is foreign to many societies. What's more, in many places physicians are not accustomed to explaining why treatment decisions were made, and patients don't ask. In clinical trials, however, it's crucial to communicate with patients in a way they understand so that their *informed consent* is obtained. Researchers and clinicians need to document carefully that patients understand the risks and benefits of an experimental treatment.

What does a best-practices company such as Genentech do when faced with the challenges of communicating drug-testing objectives and protocols in a way that ensures the cooperation it needs for effective clinical trials? Keep in mind that the trials are being conducted on patients who have been selected carefully to ensure that they are not involved in other testing protocols. Almost by definition, that means that the patients probably will be coming from non-Western countries and that they need to be communicated with uniquely.

For starters, Genentech tasked Nazma Muhammad-Rosado, director of clinical operations, to convey to the Genentech workforce the importance of cultural awareness in its global expansion. It recognized that introducing cultural competency was a full-on business requirement with a person who has a business title and business group responsibilities. Nazma saw that adapting the communication aspect of clinical trials in a foreign environment was critical for success. More than simply the packaging of the drugs, treatments needed to have cultural redefinition in the area of communication.

Nazma recognized that as a part of the globalization implementation, there was a need to develop communications that would address two audiences: the patient and the physician. Of course, Nazma was aware that physician-patient communications are unique and that the nonverbal aspects are always important. In other words, it's not only the words the doctor use, it's the tone of voice, facial expression, and gestures.

Doctor-patient communication is also unique by culture and reflective of the general cultural values of a society. For example, in an egalitarian society, it's not unusual for patients to feel somewhat responsible for their own treatment and question a doctor, whereas that level of involvement would be unusual in a hierarchical society. Obviously, the communication directives and documents that Nazma's team needed to prepare would have to be culturally appropriate, especially in areas where informed consent and careful compliance by the patient were critical.

Doctors had to be communicated with differently and had to be given a different message to convey to their patients. For example, patients in some countries in Latin America would tend to do whatever the physician told them to do without question. Thus, the doctors had to be taught to communicate differently during the explanation of the experiment to secure informed consent. The doctor also needed to be clear in empowering the patients to be sure they knew they were volunteering for an experiment and knew the risks as well as the potential benefits.

Nazma and her team now not only needed to translate instructions and labels but also had to create communications scripts for physicians and health-care providers that were culturally appropriate, and wherever possible, provide communication training. Nazma knew from her previous cultural training that people have different expectations regarding communication, and so her team would have to tailor communications for each region of the world. People receive and send messages differently depending on their culture's perception. She knew that communicating across cultures involves careful attention to more than language: Some cultures need more background and context than others, some cultures demand direct messages, and all cultures have different reactions to tone of voice and nonverbal language. All this is complicated further by being part of a relationship in which the patient looks to the physician as a lifeline.

Nazma's colleagues addressed this challenge on three levels: (1) They translated the messages into the local language, (2) hired an intercultural firm so that the entire organization could learn about cultural differences, and (3) developed relationships with local service providers for advertising and patient recruitment who could make sure that communication was delivered effectively.

What Is Communication Style?

Communication style is the confluence of several cultural values. It reflects the following elements:

- Hierarchical beliefs of a society through body language and level of politeness

- Importance of relationships in word choice and tactful language

- Attitudes toward saving face and avoiding conflict by the emotion (or lack of emotion) of the message

In the Genentech story, the deference of the Latin Americans could create a situation in which they might accept what the doctor would say without question, which would be counterproductive to the company's goals. The life-and-death messages that Genentech had to convey illustrate in the most graphic way the spectrum of what goes into effective communication. Communication involves what you say, how much you say, and how you say it. It illuminates the cultural programming of both the listener and the speaker.

Figure 7-1 shows rankings for communication styles for 50 countries. Transfer your scores on this dimension from the survey in Chapter 3 (Figure 3-5) into Figure 7-2. Compare your personal preferences to the country rankings in Figure 7-1 to see where you are on this scale. You'll be using these scores to compile your complete Personal Cultural Profile in Chapter 11.

The Elements of Effective Cross-Cultural Communication

The way a society communicates provides remarkable insights into the way it thinks and the way it conducts business. In fact, communication style transcends the actual words. It encompasses the way people

Figure 7-1   Country rankings: communication styles

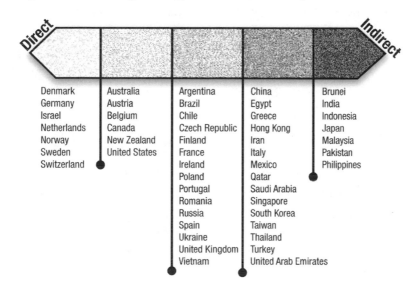

Direct				Indirect
Denmark	Australia	Argentina	China	Brunei
Germany	Austria	Brazil	Egypt	India
Israel	Belgium	Chile	Greece	Indonesia
Netherlands	Canada	Czech Republic	Hong Kong	Japan
Norway	New Zealand	Finland	Iran	Malaysia
Sweden	United States	France	Italy	Pakistan
Switzerland		Ireland	Mexico	Philippines
		Poland	Qatar	
		Portugal	Saudi Arabia	
		Romania	Singapore	
		Russia	South Korea	
		Spain	Taiwan	
		Ukraine	Thailand	
		United Kingdom	Turkey	
		Vietnam	United Arab Emirates	

Figure 7-2

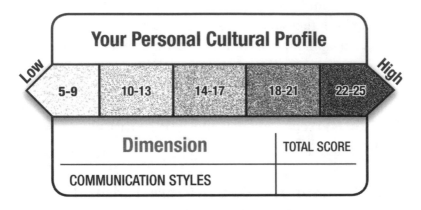

transfer verbal and nonverbal messages through voice, body language, and actions. Of course, much of this behavior becomes unconsciously embedded into the collective psyche and isn't acknowledged. However, the differences become glaringly apparent when cultures interact, and of course, the more sensitive the message, the greater the potential for miscommunication. A question that's phrased in an inappropriate manner or a gesture that's not expected can send the wrong message. If you provide too much information, the recipient may not be able to distinguish what's important, whereas too little information could leave the receiver unable to complete the task.

Recognizing Different Communication Styles

Watch people talk with each other. Watch their body language. Watch their hand gestures. Do people speak frankly, in a straightforward manner, or is that considered rude? Is it a good thing to be brief, to get to the point, or are elaborate explanations with impressive vocabulary more common?

We divide communication style into four categories to help you recognize and understand behavior: direct–indirect, high context–low context, nonverbal communication (including body language), and avoiding conflict or saving face.

Direct–Indirect

Cultures that favor direct communication value succinct messages that are to the point. In cultures with a direct communication style, people say what they mean as clearly and briefly as possible without adding a lot of background information. There are few nonverbal nuances or explanatory gestures, and though body language is used, it isn't confused with the real message, which is contained in the words. Direct communicators like to be taken at their word. They make eye contact and may express disagreement openly without being considered disrespectful. If you are going to a society that uses direct communication, you can feel comfortable that if you understand the verbal message, you probably have received all or at least most of the important parts of the communication.

In contrast, indirect communicators value the way the message is relayed and the elegance of the language. There is less reliance on the explicit verbal message to convey meaning. Instead, tone of voice, facial expressions, body language, and nonverbal gestures are important contributing parts of the message in addition to the context in which the conversation is taking place. Your eloquence and ability to elaborate are extremely significant and will be part of the way your friends, colleagues, and subordinates judge your message. Communication in these cultures is far more subtle, and that means you must work to interpret the meaning of the gestures, tones, and context that come from below the surface. Many languages, for example, have hierarchy built into them. Special endings to words and certain pronouns express deference or superiority.

Cultures that favor indirect communication use business meetings to demonstrate understanding and knowledge of the topic. Imparting new information is secondary and much less important. Deep, meaningful discussions of the topic almost always occur before the meeting. Cultures that place a premium on communication, such as France, reward eloquent speeches, which become the cornerstone of a successful meeting.

Contrast that with direct cultures, such as Australia, in which meetings are called to deliver information. Discussions are limited to general information that is needed to get the job done. You ask questions if you need additional information, and everyone expects to reach decisions at the conclusion of the meeting. In these cultures presenting and adhering to an agenda are essential because that is what moves the meeting along and ensures that all information is covered.

High Context–Low Context

Are you someone who wants a lot of background to be able to understand what someone is saying? Or do you want people to get to the point? In low-context cultures, individuals expect only as much information as they need to accomplish a specific task. When they are given more data, they may end up confused and annoyed at the wasted time. By contrast, people from high-context cultures want a comprehensive picture of the entire project, their role in it, and the role everyone else is playing.

Imagine the frustration of a pressured American executive trying to convey succinctly a straightforward task to a Spanish colleague. Kept on the phone for 30 minutes being asked questions that appear to be irrelevant to the task, he inadvertently can appear to be rude because he doesn't understand the need for context. The Spaniard, in contrast, turns to her colleagues at the conclusion of the phone call and complains that it's difficult to understand Americans who call requesting help without describing the project.

Of course, even in low-context cultures there are high-context individuals. These are the people who go into a lot of detail in their stories and often need more information about projects. Although others consider this a waste of time, high-context individuals know more about the entire process of a project. Not surprisingly, low-context individuals often need frequent meetings to review progress on projects during which participants share new information, whereas high-context cultures will have fewer meetings with relatively little new information being shared.

Nonverbal Communication

Nonverbal communication conveyed through body language, eye contact, tone of voice, and hand and body gestures is as important as the words people use in many societies. In fact, research shows that from 60 to 70 percent of communication is nonverbal. Only 7 percent comes from the actual words a person uses.[2] Cultures that favor indirect communication tend to use a lot of body language, facial expressions, and tone of voice as part of the message.

Even if you don't speak the language, it's a good idea to become versed in a culture's nonverbal expressions, such as touching or bowing, personal gestures, and the display of emotions. The section below on nonverbal communication goes into detail.

Avoiding Conflict or Saving Face

Not surprisingly, avoiding conflict and saving face are of great importance in many cultures. Avoiding conflict is a major way to confer honor and respect to another person. In most Asian cultures, in which the concept of face has been raised to a fine art, it's possible to act in a way that helps one save face or in a way that causes someone to lose face. In addition to overt conflict, directing a public reprimand at a subordinate or singling out one person from a group can cause that person to lose face.

Jan Jung-Min Sunoo is the project director for the ILO/Vietnam Industrial Relations Project attached to the International Labour Organization in Hanoi. He works with many private and foreign-owned enterprises to help improve labor relations. In some years, as many as 60 percent of the strikes occurred in Korean- and Taiwanese-owned factories, a number disproportionate to their presence in Vietnam.[3]

Although there are numerous reasons for strikes in Vietnam, one of the reasons related to culture is that the Korean management style is tougher and more direct than the Vietnamese style. If someone makes a mistake, that person may be reprimanded in front of peers in a Korean or Taiwanese factory. This may be accepted behavior in Korea or in Taiwan but causes great loss of face and is considered excessive in Vietnam. Any open display of temper or impatience by a superior is viewed as immaturity and poor breeding and would cause a Vietnamese superior, as well as the person being shouted at, to lose face.

"Public reprimands absolutely don't go over at all in Vietnamese culture," says Jan, "because they are really into saving face with each other and do not practice public humiliation." Vietnamese never shout; if they have to discipline someone, they do it in private because you have to save face. You never want to make someone lose his or her dignity.

"Abusive behavior is absolutely unacceptable," Jan said. In fact, in the recent past, many labor strikes resulted from such basic cultural misunderstandings. The workers simply walked out of the factory because they wouldn't abide the behavior and didn't know how to handle this type of loss of face among their peers.

How to "Read" Nonverbal Clues

A person conveys nonverbal communication through body language, eye contact, hand and body gestures, and seating positions at business meetings and even by how much time he or she spends with others. In many societies, the way people look when they are saying something as well as the way they look at another person can be more important than the words they use.

"You shouldn't underestimate the importance of being aware of nonverbal communication, especially in a multicultural context," Jan explained.

Body Language, Gestures, and Smiles

The way people use their bodies to deliver a message mirrors underlying values in their society. Bowing, for example, illustrates deference in hierarchical cultures; sitting up straight or standing tall may indicate respect in egalitarian societies.

Facial expressions are also important. Does a weak smile mean, "Yes, I agree," or, "I have listened to you and don't want to disagree openly"? People smile for different reasons. Western managers who say what they mean and mean only what they say often are confused about how to interpret critical subtle messages, especially when trying to understand Asian colleagues.

"A smile can be just a general human-to-human harmonizing lubricant and is meant to show a pleasant countenance between people," Jan Jung-Min Sunoo explained. "The key is not to assume that what a smile or a nod or any other familiar gesture means in your own culture can automatically be interpreted in another. Often it does, but often it doesn't."

In Japan, frowning while someone is speaking is interpreted as a sign of disagreement. Consequently, because the Japanese value harmony, they try to maintain an impassive expression when listening. Expressions to watch out for include inhaling through clenched teeth, tilting the head, and scratching the eyebrow or the back of the head. It is also important not to misinterpret a smile, which can mean anything from "I agree" to "I understand and do not agree" or can mask the discomfort of someone conveying bad news.

Then there are gestures that can be simply baffling. Joyce Thorne, director of training and professional development for Integreon, a firm that does knowledge process outsourcing (see Chapter 11 for Integreon's complete story), recalls the first time she encountered head bobbing in India. Joyce is no novice to India. An American who lived in India for four years and has worked directly with Indians for six years, she was responsible for helping to orient new staff members to the Western style of doing business. The company employs individuals who run the gamut from those with advanced degrees to those who do data processing.

Joyce said, "We were a very small company at that time, and I was leading a group of people who were going to be doing document processing. They were globally aware individuals with a good deal of education, but they were not used to interacting with people from other countries.

"I went into the class and explained a particular concept. Then I said, 'Does everybody understand that?' Everybody gave me an up-and-down head shake, but it was a little bit sideways, too. I thought, That looks like a yes to me. That's great. Then later I said, 'Okay, do you understand that concept?' and everybody shook their heads from side to side, like no. So I explained it again, and I said, 'Did you understand that part?' And everybody did the same head back-and-forth movement."

She didn't know what was going on. Did they understand or didn't they? Fortunately for Joyce, there was a person helping her who had previous experience with questions and answers in that group.

"What am I doing wrong?" she asked. "Why don't these people understand me?" He explained that in this situation, when you turn your head from side to side, it means, "I get it. I'm hearing you, and I understand you." When you put your head up and down, it may mean "I'm trying to get what you mean, but I'm not really sure."

This use of body language is often confusing to those unfamiliar with Indian communication. It sometimes gives the impression that people are saying yes and sometimes makes it seem that they're saying no. In fact, they're just trying to figure out what the person is trying to say.

In many Middle Eastern societies, common ways to denote negative responses include raising the eyebrows with the head tilted back, clicking the tongue to make a *tsk* sound, and repeatedly moving the forefinger from right to left. Shaking the head from side to side often indicates a lack of understanding rather than disagreement.

Eye Contact

As with body and facial gestures, eye contact is culturally determined. In many Latin American cultures, eye contact with those in superior positions is generally indirect to demonstrate proper respect. A person may misinterpret direct, intense eye contact as aggression. The Chinese also may consider it disrespectful to stare into another individual's eyes, particularly if that person is senior in rank because of age or status. A Chinese person may take prolonged eye contact as a challenge, whereas brief eye contact can communicate interest in the other person. In China and Japan, avoiding eye contact also indicates a sense of privacy. Many Japanese will close their eyes during meetings or while riding in an elevator, but do not mistake this for falling asleep.

At the other end of the spectrum, in many Middle Eastern countries eye contact is critical while conversing. If you glance away, it may be taken as lack of interest in the discussion or even lack of respect toward the speaker. In many Western cultures with a direct communication style, eye contact is crucial and represents sincerity, strong intent, and even intelligence.

Personal Space and Touching

The use of touch, the distance from each other at which people stand when they speak, and where people are positioned around a conference table are indicators you should observe carefully. In some cultures touching is appropriate in almost any kind of communication; in others it can be offensive and is reserved for close friends and family. In some cultures putting one's feet up on a desk is a contemplative posture; in others it is the most offensive of gestures. In some cultures the gesture in which you create a circle with the thumb and forefinger shows that everything is okay; in other cultures it is an obscene gesture. In other words, if you're going somewhere or working with people from other cultures, you need to learn how to be sure that your body language and gestures are consistent with the message you're trying to deliver. When some of these gestures surprise you, be patient.

Paul Grogan, an Australian human resources manager living and working in London, was part of a due-diligence team that was meeting with a new acquisition's management team in Al Khobar, Saudi Arabia. His team was finding it difficult to obtain information from the Saudis.

The Saudis were unfailingly courteous and wonderful hosts, but they wouldn't provide the information that Paul's group was seeking. Paul's colleague, a native of Philadelphia in the United States, age 63, was extremely frustrated with not getting anywhere. In desperation, he and Paul approached the young son of one of the key managers who happened to work there. Paul's colleague explained his background in the industry and the experience and knowledge he had gained over 40 years and asked for this young fellow's help.

He agreed, and as Paul and his colleague left his office, the young Saudi walked out with them. Paul walked in front. When he looked back, the young Saudi had taken the hand of Paul's colleague and they were walking hand in hand.

"My colleague looked at me with panic in his eyes but went with it," Paul said. "He had his hand held for the next hour by another man, but at the same time, we were given the information he had access to." Later they discovered that this was a sign of respect by the Saudi for the 63-year-old's years of experience and "elderly/knowledgeable" status.

"The memory of this still brings tears to my eyes when I remember the look on the face of my friend who liked to describe himself as a 'hardass from Philly,'" Paul said.

Surprised or not, he did the right thing. Many Middle Easterners stand extremely close when speaking to someone of the same gender; however, they increase the space considerably when speaking to someone of the opposite sex. Although they often touch others while conversing to enhance communication, they do not use sweeping hand gestures and feel more comfortable when others restrain their hand movements.

In Latin America, however, it is not uncommon to use big gestures and touch the shoulders or hold the arm of the other person while conversing to emphasize a point or show involvement and camaraderie. A person may perceive withdrawing from these gestures as an insult. In some cultures looking someone in the eye is a sign of character; in others it is a sign of aggression.

Delivering Bad News

An important aspect of nonverbal communication is the way cultures deal with delivering bad news. Some cultures, such as that in the United States, respect the idea of giving direct, hard-hitting information. The idea is to "tell it to me straight because I can handle it; I'm a grown-up."

There are a variety of ways to do this. Even in cultures that respect direct communication, people often tend to say, "Let me tell you to get it over with." The rush to get past the unpleasant experience of conveying bad news may cause the speaker to omit important details that a high-context person may need. This is a matter of personal style. The fact is that some cultures cannot convey information in a way that low-context, direct-communication cultures want to receive it.

For example, we often hear about Western managers complaining that their Indian direct reports and colleagues won't give them the "straight story." In a similar way, certain Germanic cultures will be confused by the subtle way their English colleagues give them negative feedback and may miss the core of the message. The English colleague is likely to cushion the bad news and sandwich it between positive messages.

For example, upon completing a performance review with his British manager, the American walked out saying, "Ah, that wasn't too bad."

He never understood what the manager was telling him. Just a few months later, he couldn't comprehend why his salary wasn't raised.

Using Silence and "Yes" to Avoid Conflict

The use of silence may be difficult to interpret by those from direct-communication societies, but it is as much a part of the message as are the words. As with other aspects of nonverbal language, the prevalence of this behavior largely depends on the individual's background. Perhaps one of the most misinterpreted aspects of communication, silence is often a way of showing contemplation and respect for the speaker. Many societies consider it rude not to show that you are giving adequate thought to what has been verbalized to you.

John, an American sales representative for a women's clothing manufacturer, recently called on one of the company's customers in Japan. It was his second trip and meeting with Sato-san, and John felt they had a nice relationship. Consequently, John felt it was a good time to push the sale and ask for the order. To his surprise, as soon as he quoted the fee, Sato-san fell silent. In his discomfort with the silence, John assumed that he must have surprised Sato-san with the amount and, because he had some negotiating room, quickly lowered the price. To his chagrin, Sato-san remained silent.

Uncomfortable but wanting the deal, John adjusted the price again, realizing that he now had no more margin for negotiating and could do no more. Sato-san said he would let John know the next day because he had to speak with his team. Eventually, Sato-san indicated that he was willing to go ahead and place the order. Of course, by the time the deal closed, it was much less lucrative for John and his company, and he wondered how he'd gotten it so wrong. Sometime later, John and Sato-san's British assistant were having drinks at a bar, and John commented on what a powerful negotiator Sato-san was. The assistant looked at him and asked why he kept lowering his price. He then commented, "All Sato-san was doing was contemplating the deal." The moral of the story: Nonverbal communication affects business outcomes.

Hesitancy is another form of silence. Indian communication, which values harmony and subtle communication, historically has relied heavily on nonverbal language. When someone hesitates and then says no after being asked to perform a certain task, that person may be expressing willingness but may be concerned about his or her ability to complete the task. Indian society has a group culture that attempts to avoid giving an overt negative response, which could offend or disappoint the person with whom one is speaking. This consideration also may be seen in silence and reluctance to offer a dissenting position. It is a good idea to be alert for long pauses or other nonverbal cues, such as avoiding the eyes or evasive responses, as they may indicate a negative response.

As one would expect in cultures that prize harmony, such as many Asian societies, people have difficulty giving an overtly negative response. Communication is meant to allow both parties to retain face, which means that they avoid showing anger or other negative emotions. At times people may respond with long silent pauses or the word *yes* even though they mean the opposite. In general, one should consider responses such as "maybe," "probably," and "I'm thinking about it" as "perhaps," whereas the response "I'll consider it" is frequently negative. It is often a good idea to ask the same question several different ways to ensure that you have understood what the response you received actually meant.

The Impact of Language

It was George Bernard Shaw who said that the British and Americans are divided by a common language. Shaw's quip cuts to the core: The fact that we use the same words doesn't mean we use the same language. This is especially true in global business; the international language may be English, but that doesn't mean it's understood universally. In fact, people who make that assumption do so at considerable peril. If common expressions differ between the United States and the United Kingdom and proper ways to ask questions also differ, how different must they be for individuals who are not native speakers of English.

When operating in a multicultural environment, you want to be sensitive to different levels of language fluency and comprehension. Even though people may speak well, their comprehension of English may lag far behind their speech. It is more difficult to understand native speakers of a language than to construct and speak that language oneself. No matter what language is being used, in international business we're often dealing with people whose native language is different from the one being spoken. The result? Often at least one person in the communication is struggling with both comprehension and word selection.

At the same time, this individual is having to work harder to understand the communication. Then there's the added challenge of trying to decipher an accent and idiosyncratic word usage. For example, when a Vietnamese agrees with fellow Vietnamese, he or she usually says, "*Roi, roi, roi*" (meaning "okay"). But when Vietnamese people use the word *okay* in English, they inadvertently retain the same tone they use in Vietnamese, which in English sounds rude: "Okay! Okay! Okay!" Not knowing this, an American might feel insulted by the Vietnamese and overreact to what is actually affirmation.

Moreover, what must a non-American think when we talk about a bootstrap operation, grassroots support, or movers and shakers? What does an American think when a British person uses the word *puncture* or *flat*? Add to all this the nonverbal communication that's taking place, and the potential for problems expands exponentially.

When people speak with their team in a language other than their native one, it often affects their ability to interact with the group. It potentially affects spontaneity, clarity of expression (vocabulary and pronunciation), and willingness to express ideas. This is more challenging if your culture is indirect or your personal style is more introverted.

HELPFUL HINTS FOR READING NONVERBAL COMMUNICATION

This sidebar gives a few pointers that will enhance your comfort with nonverbal communication. Whatever society you find yourself in or whatever nationalities you deal with, it is always a good idea to watch carefully how locals interact and adjust your nonverbal communication accordingly:

- Limit hand gestures and maintain a moderate body posture.

- When conducting a conference call, follow up meetings with written communication and be sure that all the members understand the discussion and outcome.

- Silence can mean agreement, disagreement, or contemplation. Be careful not to make assumptions and express the overt message whenever possible.

- Do not interpret the absence of disagreement as agreement.

- Nonverbal communication is powerful. Learn about the ways in which members express negative concepts. Silence is often one way to do this, but it also may show respect and allow contemplation of another person's comment.

- Provide additional opportunities for all team members to contribute more easily. Give people a chance to write notes to each other, provide follow-up materials to phone calls in which input is requested, and offer a detailed agenda before the call or meeting so that individuals can prepare for it.

Table 7-1 lists some of the overt behaviors you can expect.

Table 7-2 describes the challenges you'll face when crossing cultures. Use the table to tailor your expectations and business behavior.

TABLE 7-1 COMMUNICATION STYLES: BELIEFS AND BEHAVIORS

Direct, Brief	Indirect, Background Needed
• People look for content, not what surrounds the content. They expect that all the information they need to communicate is contained within the words they use. What is spoken matters, not how or where it is spoken. Even the expressions used are not that important.	• The context of the communication is very important. It isn't only what people talk about that is important; it's the tone of voice and where the conversation takes place. What is being said may not be as important as how it is said.
• Information is held very closely and shared on a need-to-know basis. People in positions of power have more information.	• People share information and expect to have a constant flow of input.
• People are direct and expect to be taken at their word.	• People tend to be indirect. Listeners are expected to interpret statements and questions to infer what the speaker is saying.
• Body language usually won't be acknowledged as having a major impact on the content of the message. Verbalized information is key.	• Nonverbal nuances, including gestures and voice quality, are important. The same verbal message may mean something totally different to different people because of the nonverbals that accompany the words at the time they are stated.
• Clarity of communication in words is paramount, and open dialogue with probing/challenging questions is acceptable. Simplicity is admired, and language may be punctuated with vulgarity for effect.	• Speaking eloquently but indirectly is a prized art.
• Saving face is not important. Sometimes openly challenging someone you disagree with is admired.	• In some societies, the idea of saving face is an essential part of information exchange.

Source: Adapted from Michael S. Schell and Charlene Marmer Solomon, *Capitalizing on the Global Workforce: A Strategic Guide for Expatriate Managers*, McGraw-Hill, 1996.

TABLE 7-2 CROSSING CULTURES: COMMUNICATION STYLES

From Indirect to Direct

- Being indirect and eloquent is not valued as much as being simple and direct. Intelligence is judged by the ability to communicate one's meaning clearly and concisely.
- Indirect communication may be perceived as evasive and untruthful.

- It is expected that if someone has something to say, he or she will say it, whether it involves criticism or praise.
- Good questions are highly valued. Don't be reluctant to ask questions that may confound a speaker.

- Don't expect to obtain a lot of business-related information informally. Colleagues typically share business-related information at business meetings.

- Indirect statements may be misunderstood. Focus on saying or requesting precisely what you need.
- Subordinates will not expect to share all information with you. They will involve you only when you have requested it or they have issues that they feel are relevant to you. A constant flow of information interferes with the ability to work effectively.

From Direct to Indirect

- Being direct and concise may not communicate information most effectively. Remember that form is as important as content.
- All aspects of communication have meaning. Much is communicated implicitly through nonverbals.
- Direct communication of criticism is seen as coarse and unsophisticated.

- Eloquent answers are highly valued. Questions may not be raised publicly if they confound a speaker.

- Don't expect to obtain all business-related information at meetings. Get involved in the informal information exchange network over lunch, coffee breaks, or golf.

- Direct statements may be seen as rude. Focus on saying things more indirectly.
- Don't insulate yourself from your subordinates. They will expect to share a constant flow of information with you.

DEFINITIONS OF TERMS IN THIS CHAPTER

Direct versus indirect communication: Brief, concise messages versus those that use subtlety and body language.

Contextual versus brief communication: The amount of background information an individual needs to understand, appreciate, and feel satisfied with the message.

Nonverbal language: Messages conveyed through body position, eye contact, tone of voice, and hand and body gestures.

The concept of face: Face is an intangible quality that reflects a person's reputation, dignity, and prestige. You may lose face, save face, or give face to another person. Companies, as well as individuals, have face, and this often provides the rationale behind business and personal interactions.

Lessons Learned to Develop Your Cultural Skills

- How communication styles affect every element of managing across cultures
- How to understand nonverbal language and gestures
- The impact of language

Questions to Ponder

1. You are introducing a new performance review process and have designed a form that makes it quick and easy to give feedback. It worked well in your home country, and everyone appreciated how it delivered both performance evaluations

and 360-degree feedback. To your surprise, your local managers don't want you to introduce the form. Why?
Directions: Go to http://book.culturewizard.com and join the discussion.

2. You're an innovative manager of a global team of software developers. You lead many conference calls and believe many of them are a waste of time. What can you do to improve the use of time?
Directions: Go to http://book.culturewizard.com and join the discussion.

What Do You Think?

You have had your own experiences. Share them. Go to http://book .culturewizard.com and join the discussion.

Notes

1 http://www.gene.com/gene/about/corporate/awards/index.html.

2 A. Mehrabian, *Silent Messages: Implicit Communication of Emotions and Attitudes,* Wadsworth, 1981; Barbara and Allan Pease, *Understanding the Basics: The Definitive Book of Body Language,* Bantam, 2008.

3 2008 interview with Jan Jung-Min Sunoo, project director of ILO/Vietnam Industrial Relations Project in the International Labour Organization.

Time Orientation

> ## *TIME ORIENTATION*
> ## REFERS TO
>
> - The amount of control people feel they have over time. Do you control time, or is it out of your control?
>
> - The importance society places on relationships versus keeping schedules.
>
> - Attitudes toward timekeeping and punctuality.
>
> - Comfort level with short-range versus longer-term planning.
>
> - The appropriateness of assigning set times for social functions or business meetings to start and finish.

Understanding Time Orientation Can Save Your Business

Paul Burger, the newly appointed American manager in an aeronautics engineering company, was assigned to grow a Spanish engineering subsidiary. Paul loved Spain and could speak Spanish fairly well, and his family had built a vacation home in Palma de Majorca. As a result, he was very familiar with the way things got done and how much time it took to accomplish things in Spain. His family home had been completed nearly two years behind schedule, and so he was prepared for the types of delays he was likely to encounter.

One of the early tasks Paul was given was to identify a new engineering manager who would be responsible for designing and implementing the new production processes for which a specific facility would be built. It was a highly demanding position. Paul had made a commitment to his management team to get the facility expanded and running within a reasonable but ambitious time frame.

Paul met the Spanish staff and was impressed by a young engineer who had joined the company recently. Raul had every characteristic Paul was looking for: He was smart and well respected by his colleagues, had had a good education, and had an excellent track record at the company. Paul proposed him for the position of the new engineering manager for the expanded facility.

Raul was sent to the Kansas City headquarters for an interview. To Paul's disappointment, the management in Kansas City rejected Raul for the position.

They called Paul to tell him to keep looking. The reason? Raul didn't have the sense of urgency they were looking for. Although he had all the other credentials, they said he never stressed adherence to production schedules. Even though he acknowledged that schedules were important, he insisted that other elements of the project were equally critical. In addition, he had shown up a little late to two of the meetings.

Paul felt it was partially his fault that this had occurred because he should have told Raul that Americans expect punctuality and that commitment to deadlines and schedules is considered a critical management skill. He understood that Raul lacked a cultural under-standing of the U.S. firm. Raul didn't realize that he should have emphasized that schedules are critical and maintaining on-time performance from subordinates is a management skill that U.S. man-agement would demand. Paul's assessment of Raul as a good candidate was correct because Raul was an excellent manager for a Spanish work-force, but he failed to help Raul recognize that in a global environment a manager needs to manage "up" as well as "down." Managing up required understanding the criticality of on-time performance, whereas managing down required awareness of relationships and the strong hierarchical perspective on him that his employees would have because of his stature. Unfortunately, they both lost out.

The culture clash around time orientation is common and frustrating and plagues Western managers perhaps more than any other of the seven dimensions. In spite of the simplicity of the definition, this dimension is often complicated and compounded by other cultural values, such as relationships and hierarchy.

TIME ORIENTATION

Time orientation is the degree to which people believe they can control time and whether schedules or people are more important. It affects time management, long- and short-term planning, schedules, and adherence to agendas and deadlines.

Figure 8-1 shows the rankings for time orientation for 50 countries. Transfer your scores on this dimension from the survey in Chapter 3 (Figure 3-5) into Figure 8-2. Compare your personal preferences to the country rankings in Figure 8-1 to see where you are on this scale. You'll be using these scores to compile your complete Personal Cultural Profile in Chapter 11.

Figure 8-1

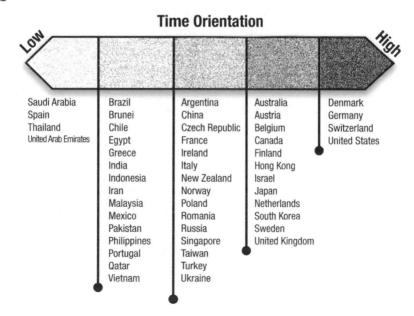

Time Orientation

Low — High

Saudi Arabia	Brazil	Argentina	Australia	Denmark
Spain	Brunei	China	Austria	Germany
Thailand	Chile	Czech Republic	Belgium	Switzerland
United Arab Emirates	Egypt	France	Canada	United States
	Greece	Ireland	Finland	
	India	Italy	Hong Kong	
	Indonesia	New Zealand	Israel	
	Iran	Norway	Japan	
	Malaysia	Poland	Netherlands	
	Mexico	Romania	South Korea	
	Pakistan	Russia	Sweden	
	Philippines	Singapore	United Kingdom	
	Portugal	Taiwan		
	Qatar	Turkey		
	Vietnam	Ukraine		

Figure 8-2

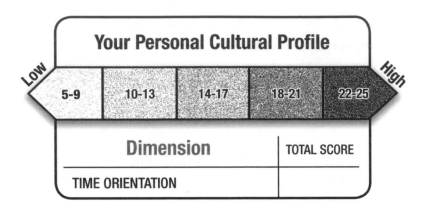

Recognizing Time Orientation

Your orientation to time is so all-encompassing that it is one of the pivotal factors influencing meetings and agendas, adherence to deadlines and production timelines, and social and business dealings. Anyone functioning in the international arena—whether in business or in social situations—will recognize the relative emphasis that each culture places on time. As the definition indicates, cultural perception of time is both complex and multifaceted. Since this is also a readily recognizable behavior, it can provide early clues for understanding and adjusting to other societies.

Time orientation is both simple and complex. It is simple to recognize. You can see it in the promptness of meeting start times, the speed with which people move, and how important it is to get something done on schedule. At the same time it is complex. It is often compounded by other cultural dimensions, such as the need for harmony in the workplace and the importance of investing in relationships.

Moreover, it is often disguised. In today's business world, no one will argue with the need for a schedule, and there is agreement about and investment in a carefully crafted sequence of events. However, because of a variety of conflicting needs, those timelines may not be adhered to. For example, you may arrive at a meeting and receive a comprehensive two-day program agenda containing items such as 15-minute summaries by business units, only to find that speaker after speaker goes on for twice that long. Thus, although it is simple to set up the agenda, getting different cultures to adhere to it can be very complex. Or you may find at the conclusion of the meeting (during which time much discussion took place) that the members of the group put together a comprehensive, detailed schedule and task document, only to find three months later that some of the individuals seem to be working from a completely different schedule. Therefore, although the behavior is simple to identify and there is seeming agreement about the schedule and tasks, the meaning of that agreement can vary dramatically among colleagues from different cultures. Whereas some see time as absolute, for others it is a more fluid measure.

To examine the time orientation dimension, we begin with the fundamental issues: (1) whether you believe time is a commodity that can be saved and spent like money, (2) whether you believe staying on schedule and following tasks is important even if it imposes on personal relationships, and (3) whether your credentials as a manager are dependent on your ability to deliver quality work on schedule.

Do You Believe You Control Time?

It is extraordinarily difficult for people in cultures that believe they can control time to appreciate that some cultures believe that time is not controllable but is like predicting the weather. People who are from cultures that don't believe they control time often are bemused by those who get anxious about "managing time." What's more, they wonder what lasting value this activity brings.

We refer to cultures that believe they control time as high-time cultures and those that don't as low-time cultures. High-time cultures such as northern Europe and the United States and Canada view time as something that is finite, an entity that can—and must—be controlled lest it be wasted and used up. Activities are scheduled carefully to fit within a limited number of hours, and individuals continually select and prioritize those activities. These cultures value time so highly that they take time management courses and plan their days with precision.

As with other cultural phenomena, people develop their attitudes towards time as children. Think of the proverbs that American youngsters learn that relate to time: "A stitch in time saves nine," "Make haste, not waste," and, "The early bird gets the worm."

By contrast, in the world's many low-time cultures, including southern Europe, Latin America, the Middle East, and Africa, people believe that time is a variable. Time is not their taskmaster, and they pay greater attention to relationships than to deadlines and schedules. Moreover, scheduling time is viewed as a very limiting activity. In terms of action, this means that plans change frequently. Consequently, when someone is late, it doesn't reflect negatively on that person's character or ability to organize life. (Asia is variable, depending on the individual country.)

Of course, no matter what type of time orientation you have, today's multicultural business world demands that most business activities begin relatively promptly. However, don't interpret the fact that most meetings begin on time as a sign that everyone believes time is controllable. Global standards of timeliness mean that most business-people today respect the idea of arriving at a meeting when it is scheduled to start. This tends to mask some of the other characteristics of low-time cultures that are still present.

If you work with people from low-time cultures, don't expect time and deadline commitments to mean the same thing they mean in a high-time culture. For example, these individuals wonder how you can be effective if you create an arbitrary ending time for a meeting. Perhaps not all the participants will have been able to speak; perhaps some event may have delayed the beginning of the meeting. In these cultures, people believe time is fluid, and though it is somewhat controllable, rigidity comes at the expense of relationships and a thorough understanding of another person's perspective. Be prepared to manage schedules more actively than you would at home.

People in low-time cultures also find constructive ways to use their waiting time. Paul Bailey of RW[3] recently attended a meeting in Qatar. He arrived on schedule and took a seat at the table. About half the participants already had arrived and were engaged in active dialogue about a variety of issues; they continued to talk while Paul sat with his BlackBerry, somewhat perturbed about the late starting time, and busily sent e-mails. It wasn't until just before the meeting actually came to order (about 20 minutes later) that he became aware that some of the "chatting" was about issues that were going to be discussed at the meeting. It didn't take Paul long to realize that he was the one who hadn't been using the time to the best advantage and how important that time was.

In low-time cultures people may agree to a time schedule, but the way they accomplish work may be different. They often place greater emphasis on relationships and are more flexible about the way work is accomplished. Levels of punctuality vary tremendously, and being late for a social event isn't considered rude; it actually can mean arriving at the "right" time. In low-time cultures, people believe that many things are more important than adhering to schedules and so there's no need to make time an absolute value; it's better to be flexible.

The potential conflict between people operating in high-time versus low-time societies is obvious. In high-time cultures, your effectiveness is judged by your on-time performance. The corporate financial structure is designed to perform and report achievement at quarterly intervals. Inability to adhere to those related schedules has profound ramifications for corporatewide earnings, and therefore managers are evaluated on their ability to adhere to schedules and punished when they miss their targets.

Managers in a high-time culture believe that everyone understands and must accept these rules. However, when you're managing and working with people from low-time cultures, you should not be misled into believing that the acceptance of a deadline means that an individual is as committed as you are to adhering to it. The ways in which societies utilize strategic or tactical planning to achieve business solutions constitutes another enormous difference between societies. Although both may agree on a long-term strategic objective, cultures that are highly sensitive to time immediately set forth an elaborate, comprehensive tactical timeline and adhere to it. Low-time cultures take a more fluid approach, always focusing on the strategic end but feeling no compunction about modifying it as it progresses. You can see how stressful this would be for an intercultural team whose members are working together on a single strategic mission. Does the timeline govern, do the tactical steps govern, or does the most comfortable way to achieve the desired result govern? If you recognize that you're managing in a low-time culture, it's incumbent on you to manage the schedules and timelines very carefully. You'll need to micromanage the timelines because the participants may have the same dedication to the quality of the performance but probably don't have the same internal drive to achieve on-time performance. People in low-time cultures tend to appreciate rather than resent this kind of close management of schedules.

Time and the Impact of Relationships

In high-time cultures, making yourself available or "giving up time" is considered a great compliment to a friend or colleague. Since "time is money" and free time is "discretionary funds"—and carries an additional premium—it is the most valuable gift one high-time individual can give to another. However, a low-time recipient, who typically would be high on relationships, may view this as an expectation and not display the anticipated appreciation.

Here is another example: High-time cultures schedule a beginning and ending time for meetings and social gatherings. In contrast, planning the length of a meeting or party in a low-time culture is considered impossible or rude. How can people plan the amount of time necessary to discuss specific topics or determine in advance when the "good time" at a party will be over and people should leave?

Imagine how difficult it was for a certain Latin American executive we know. He traveled to a New York conference to make a presentation, and to his bewilderment and shock, people apologized and said they had to leave for another meeting after he exceeded the 25-minute time slot he had been allotted. He perceived them as being rude; they perceived him as being insensitive to their schedules. Neither was wrong, but all were offended.

Schedules are adhered to rigidly, and people who are "considerate" and "responsible" usually confirm times for meetings to begin and end far in advance. Think of the phone call confirming such a business appointment. To someone in a high-time culture, this simply ensures the efficient use of time: No one is confused about the beginning time for a meeting. This prevents one individual from waiting for another (and thus wasting time); in a low-time culture this confirmation would not be related to time but rather to deference for the meeting participants.

The Impact of Monochronic and Polychronic Time on Business

Edward T. Hall identified a cultural characteristic that he called monochronic and polychronic.[1] Hall's dimension provides even greater depth to time orientation. Monochronic refers to high-time cultures and polychronic to low-time cultures, but Hall's paradigm involves more than time. It relates to one's perspective on the nature of time as being linear or somewhat circular. Whereas in monochronic and polychronic societies people have different attitudes and comfort levels about setting agendas, meeting schedules, and fulfilling deadlines, this is also reflective of people's attitude toward relationships. Polychronic people tend to be more comfortable with multitasking and prefer to focus on doing several things at one time. They move between activities and subjects with ease.

Geremie Sawadogo, program manager for global mobility for human resources at the World Bank, has talked about his experiences working with the polychronic cultures of Africa. Geremie has worked for years in Africa, including: South Africa, Senegal, Niger, and Burkina Faso, and was the Peace Corps country director for Benin from 1997 to 2002. He explained some of the polychronic behaviors that can seem bewildering to monochronic observers.

"Walk into an African civil servant's office and you'll find that they organize differently. To a monochronic observer, things may seem out of control: Papers are stacked on desks, the office might also serve as a meeting place with friends, and several conversations are taking place at one time," he said. "Meetings are different as well. There is a lot of spontaneity, topics are likely to be introduced and discussed simultaneously, and agendas—while used—aren't carefully followed. There are several strands of conversation going on at one time, but those who are familiar with the culture are adept at keeping up with the essentials. Multitasking is elevated to a fine art.

"Staff meetings can be social events," he explained, "where side conversations take place because socializing is very important."

Monochronic managers coming into polychronic cultures in which relationships are important need to be tolerant of the behavioral preferences they're confronting.

Relationships and Time

Yang Zhang, Ph.D., was working in Shanghai with a French high-tech company. The organization recently had brought in a Belgian national, Christophe, to fill one of six senior vice president positions in China. The other senior vice presidents were Asian: Chinese, Korean, Taiwanese, and Indian. Before accepting the assignment, the Belgian vice president had been briefed thoroughly about the challenge the French office was having with the Shanghai employees. The French management encouraged Christophe to bring a greater focus to staying on schedule and meeting deadlines when he was in Shanghai. Soon after his arrival, he realized the severity of the problem. Although his Asian colleagues could see the problem of not meeting deadlines, they weren't able to solve it. They agreed to work with a Swiss management consultant whom Christophe had worked with successfully on his last assignment.

He was pleased that his colleagues were enthusiastic about the suggestion and scheduled a three-day program. The consultant arrived and laid out a six-step management improvement process, and the team began discussing it. It was clear at the outset that the Asian members were uncomfortable jumping immediately into the substance of the agenda. They hadn't gotten to know Christophe well and had no rapport with the consultant. Furthermore, they all doubted that the home office appreciated the complexity of achieving the targeted time frames. During the three days, the consultant continually stressed tasks and deadlines to members of the team and was disappointed at their reluctance to accept the "perfectly reasonable" schedule he was putting forward.

Although they were ready to take on the tasks, they were not willing to accept the imposed schedule. At the end of the program, Christophe, by default, had accepted the responsibility for completing the bulk of the tasks because none of his colleagues was willing to accept the deadlines.

When Yang debriefed the team members, they told her that they weren't sure that all the other related business units had been briefed adequately and had bought into the process. They wouldn't feel comfortable with the schedule the consultant had presented until they had visited and consulted with all the people involved with the other business units. Upon reflection, Yang realized that there was an absence of a sense of trust in Christophe and the consultant and a lack in the relationship the related business units had with Christophe for the deadlines to be maintained. Although the six-step solution covered all the tactics, it didn't recognize the preliminary need to establish relationships with all the people and business units involved in the process. Although the Asians were prepared to take on the tasks, they felt they couldn't commit to on-time performance because they first needed to be sure that others had bought in.

Some cultures need to start by creating a relationship; once it has been established, they can accomplish a task efficiently. Other cultures begin with the task, and the relationship may evolve afterward. (See Figure 6-3)

Joyce Thorne is Integreon's director of training and professional development (see Chapter 11 for details about Integreon). She spent several years living in India and knows the frustrations that await if you don't have the proper expectations about time. As you learned in Chapter 7, Indians strongly prefer to say yes and want to be helpful but may overcommit because they don't want to say no.

Joyce said, "In India, they'll sometimes say, 'I'll be right with you. Give me two minutes.' But this can be misinterpreted. What two minutes means is 'as soon as I'm finished with what I'm doing right now,' which might be an hour or two." In other words, because Indians don't want to say no, they say "I'll be right with you," which means something completely different.

Of course, you can see what can happen. This commonly accepted term in India will drive a Westerner crazy. If you say "two minutes" and then take an hour or more, you've got trouble.

Since Joyce's firm works with American and British lawyers and other professional services people, she provides programs on the science of how people manage time from a polychronic perspective. They build into the culture a set of agreements around timeliness and about doing what one says one is going to do within the deadlines. They're measurable items, both by quality and by timeliness, and so people are reminded constantly about whether they are meeting their objectives around time and timeliness. What Westerners may disparagingly call micromanaging is one way to be sure that the focus remains on the milestones related to promptness and to meeting the promised deadlines. Using check-in points regularly helps everyone stay on target and on time.

Table 8-1 lists some of the overt behaviors you can expect in regard to time orientation.

Taking Time Seriously

Paul Grogan, an Australian human resources manager living and working in London, recalled the frustration of a new finance manager who had started a rotational role in Algeria. He was working one month on and one month off.

His role was to move the company's operations from Houston to Algeria, and in that role he was seen as hardworking, conscientious, and destined to move up the ladder. He hit the ground hard and wanted to get everything done within his first four-week rotation since he knew that he would be off for four weeks and did not want his replacement, who would cover the next four weeks, to have to do any work that was left over from his stint. In Houston, he was appreciated and rewarded

TABLE 8-1   TIME: BELIEFS AND BEHAVIORS

Low	High
• Time is uncontrollable. If you are late, it cannot be helped.	• Time can be measured, saved, and controlled. If you're late, you're being disrespectful or disorganized.
• People who place less emphasis on the dictates of time focus on numerous things at once and are more concerned about people's feelings than about adhering to a schedule (polychronic).	• People who ascribe a great deal of importance to controlling time also generally prefer to do one thing at a time (monochronic).
• Maintaining a harmonious working environment is more important than adhering to arbitrary schedules.	• If you drive people to accomplish time-driven deadlines, you are considered a good manager. If you do not know how to use time effectively, especially in business, you're viewed negatively. One of the highest compliments is to say that someone is extremely efficient with time.
• People change plans often and easily.	• People tend to schedule events and plan as if they are fixed. Schedules are sacrosanct.
• Individuals don't expect to allot a certain length of time to business meetings because they consider it impossible to plan in advance how long it will take to discuss relevant business concerns.	• People set times for the beginning and ending of social and business engagements, viewing time as precious and not easily compromised.
• Scheduling business meetings ahead of time isn't expected, especially because people often will not arrange their schedules until the last minute.	• Providing significant lead time before an event or meeting is a sign of respect, reflecting the individual's status as well as the business goals.

Source: Adapted from Michael S. Schell and Charlene Marmer Solomon, *Capitalizing on the Global Workforce: A Strategic Guide for Expatriate Managers*, McGraw-Hill, 1996.

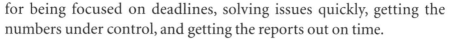

for being focused on deadlines, solving issues quickly, getting the numbers under control, and getting the reports out on time.

To his great dismay, at the end of the first four weeks, he hadn't gotten anything accomplished. The local staff simply had not worked with him. In fact, they had done what they always did, which didn't include doing what they were told to do.

He was very angry and did not understand how these staff people could refuse to follow reasonable instructions. At the start of his next four weeks, the project manager, who had been there for three years, told him, "Don't try to do any work for the first two weeks other than drink coffee with your team, go out with them when they have a cigarette, and have dinner with them in the evenings." He urged the finance manager to take an interest in the employees' lives outside the workplace: "Find out if they are married, if they have children, what their hobbies are."

This was not what he was used to!

In the final two weeks, the financial work he needed to get done was done. He came to appreciate that in Algeria the relationship you form with your staff is critical if you want to accomplish any task in a timely manner. As the boss, you are personally responsible for your employees' welfare not just at work but in their daily lives. Unless you accept that responsibility, you will face an uphill battle.

If you're dealing with a low-time culture, you need to be more careful about how to manage time or what your expectations are of your colleagues' commitment to time. You need to be aware that your colleagues don't approach time the way you do, and you need to manage a schedule more proactively if you want a project to stay on a timeline.

Table 8-2 lists some of the challenges you face when crossing cultures. Use the table to help tailor your expectations and business behavior.

TABLE 8-2 CROSSING CULTURES: TIME ORIENTATION

From High Time to Low Time

- Don't expect people to adhere strictly to schedules. Buffer your appointments with people. Leave time between when you anticipate one meeting ending and the next one starting.
- Do not judge an individual's competence, care, or concern by that person's adherence to schedules. Identify other cultural values that define competence and evaluate staff according to those criteria.
- Don't abruptly end meetings because you have "run out of time." Participants will feel comfortable extending the length of the meeting if there is still productive discussion.
- Don't expect to be able to plan all activities. Time and schedules are vulnerable to forces beyond an individual's control. Incorporate local "time" into performance and productivity projections for the organization.
- Don't be surprised if people come late to meetings or do not attend at all. Plan fewer meetings and explain why promptness is necessary if you feel it is important that meetings begin on time.

From Low Time to High Time

- People and events are scheduled. They will expect you to begin and finish on time. Coming late to a meeting is a sign of disrespect. Coming late to work is a sign of lack of concern or disorganization.
- Do not judge an individual's competence by his or her concern for people compared with his or her concern for time. Attitudes toward time are seen as defining features of individual attitudes toward work.
- Beginning and ending times for meetings often are agreed on. Don't allow meetings to continue beyond the time that has been allocated for the meeting even if the group is engaged in a productive discussion.
- It is assumed that all activities can be planned and scheduled. It is expected that timetables will be adhered to.
- All staff members are expected to attend all business meetings and arrive on time. Discussions with colleagues may not be acceptable excuses for tardiness.

> ## DEFINITIONS FOR THIS CHAPTER
>
> *High time–low time*: Refers to a culture's sense of an individual's ability to control time and perform on a schedule and the relative importance of promptness and keeping to a schedule.
>
> *Monochronic and polychronic*: Terms popularized by Edward Hall. A monochromic culture is one that believes time is linear. These cultures emphasize scheduling, promptness, and doing one thing at a time. Polychronic cultures believe that interaction with others and relationships are the most important things, certainly more important than meeting schedules. These cultures do several things at one time and expect interruptions to divert focus.[2]

Lessons Learned to Develop Your Cultural Skills

- How to recognize time orientation

- How your attitude toward relationships affects your attitude toward time

- The importance of monochronic and polychronic attitudes

Questions to Ponder

1. Your French colleagues insisted that you take an extended lunch at a restaurant even though you were getting close to your deadline and hadn't finished all the work you had planned. The Canadians on the team were dismayed. Why? What was going on?

Directions: Go to http://book.culturewizard.com and join the discussion.

2. You're running an international meeting and have a lengthy agenda that requires you to curtail debate and discussion. You feel good about how you've stayed on schedule by limiting people to two minutes of speaking time. When you break for lunch the first day, you're told that your Mexican delegates do not want to return to the meeting. What happened? Directions: Go to http://book.culturewizard.com and join the discussion.

What Do You Think?

You have had your own experiences. Share them. Go to http://book .culturewizard.com and join the discussion.

Notes

[1] Edward T. Hall, *The Dance of Life: The Other Dimension of Time*, Anchor Books, 1989.

[2] Ibid.

Change Tolerance

> **CHANGE TOLERANCE REFERS TO**
>
> - Openness to change and innovation
>
> - Willingness to take risks
>
> - If people feel they control their destiny or if their environment controls them
>
> - Preference for rules and structure
>
> - How the organization encourages and rewards initiative and deals with failure

Six Sigma, Italian Style

In 1993, John Kovach, who had been a human resources manager at General Electric Power Generation Systems in upstate New York, was tapped to go to Italy to support the transition of a new acquisition, Nuovo Pignone. That Italian company designed and manufactured industrial compressors as well as small to medium-sized steam and gas turbine systems. In making the acquisition, GE knew that Nuovo Pignone was the "class act" in the industrial compressor sector. Everyone knew that Nuovo Pignone had high standards for quality and prided itself on them.

In preparation for the assignment, John took time to study the Italian culture and focused on learning as much as he could about the work culture at Nuovo Pignone. Of course, no amount of preparation could prepare him fully for the challenge he was about to encounter.

Under Jack Welch, GE had developed a very strong corporate culture. Although each GE unit thought of itself as unique—with its own corporate culture—there was a strong "GE way," and a part of John's role was to make Nuovo Pignone a GE company. At that time GE was a highly disciplined organization that attacked new challenges with across-the-board commitment. That was very much in the Jack Welch tradition, in which the leadership would lay out a plan and the whole organization would buy into it and enthusiastically pursue the target.

John's charter was not only to make Novo Pignone fit GE but to do it fast and thoroughly. One of John's early challenges was to institute a Six Sigma[1] quality management process. Jack Welch had previously decided that Six Sigma would be GE's corporatewide quality control management process, and all its divisions and employees were being trained and evaluated in terms of the Six Sigma structure.

In the United States, Six Sigma was accepted (sometimes grudgingly) without exception because Jack wanted it. There was not much discussion about whether it fit a business style; the discussion was always about *how* to implement the plan as fast as possible.

However, John encountered a very different decision-making environment at Nuovo Pignone. Decisions weren't accepted merely because they were mandated, at least not if one wanted them to work. In this environment new ideas had to be discussed, sold, and bought into. People affected by a decision needed to express them- selves, challenge and question the new approach, and find a locally acceptable way before moving to institute a new process. That never happened fast.

This was very different from the rest of GE, where decisions were accepted because "Jack said so" and people made commitments quickly because speed of implementation was critical. John knew that he would have to find a culturally acceptable way to introduce Six Sigma to Nuovo Pignone if he wanted it to take hold. He was aware that it would take longer in Italy than it did in the United States. He also knew that he had to keep his American managers advised of the progress, although it would be slower than they would want it to be. He would have to buy time for the plan to work in Italy.

He worked diligently with his Italian colleagues to help them understand why they needed to adopt Six Sigma yet managed to give them enough time to find an acceptable way for it to work in the Nuovo

Pignone culture. Different levels would be given a plan and given time to meet to discuss it and involve all the necessary people in the new procedures.

"Little by little we got the senior leaders onboard. We got some things translated into Italian, and then we started with the key manufacturing and technical people too," John explained.

He also had to make sure that his American managers knew he was making progress and keep explaining to them why movement was so slow. To be credible, he had to demonstrate some progress to get the additional time. At the same time, he went from meeting to meeting showing the slow progress he was making and explaining as best as he could how the local culture made decisions differently.

As a good global manager should, John recognized that decisions in Italy and the introduction of a new system in Nuovo Pignone couldn't be done with the speed that his management group in the United States was accustomed to. The trick was to keep the process moving forward at Nuovo Pignone as quickly as it could while buying time with GE management. John explained that Italians generally embrace change a little more slowly than Americans do.

By having preliminary discussions and getting buy-in throughout the organization once decisions were made, he believed they would be implemented more quickly and with fewer errors or adjustments downstream.

"There is an element, particularly in Italian culture, where they spend the time with their decision-making process up front. They make what they believe to be good decisions and ones that the group can agree to. They shorten the cycle on implementation and rework because they don't have to go back and fix things afterward," he explained.

It took a long time.

John realized that the Nuovo Pignone culture and the Italian culture had a level of change tolerance different from that in the United States. In the Italian culture, new systems change has to be discussed, tested, probed, and examined. Unlike the United States, where change is assumed to be an improvement, Italians make no such assumption.

New systems are not agreed to until they are thoroughly understood. In Italy's less change-tolerant environment, changes can be made, but for them to work, they have to respect the local culture, and local management needs the space and time to absorb and integrate the changes.

Interestingly, two years after completing his assignment, John was delighted to see Nuovo Pignone getting the Six Sigma award in Global GE.

WHAT IS CHANGE TOLERANCE?

Change tolerance refers to the perception of how much control we believe we have over our lives and destinies (is our life determined by us or by external forces?) and our comfort level with change, innovation, and risk taking. Do we see change as bringing opportunities or as threats to be avoided?

Figure 9-1 on page 189 shows the rankings for change tolerance for 50 countries. Transfer your scores on this dimension from the survey in Chapter 3 (Figure 3-5) into Figure 9-2 (page 190). Compare your personal preferences to the country rankings in Figure 9-1 to see where you are on this scale. You'll be using these scores to compile your complete Personal Cultural Profile in Chapter 11.

How Open Are People to Change and Innovation?

The dimension of change tolerance is extremely important in a rapidly evolving world where technology is propelling social change at an ever-increasing pace. Most organizations have embraced the idea that change is vital for success, but that doesn't mean that societies and individuals are comfortable with it. Why? Not all cultures view change as a positive force, and this creates an important distinction for organizations to reckon with.

Think of the American proverb, "Nothing ventured, nothing gained," as opposed to the British proverb, "Let sleeping dogs lie,"[2] or the Saudi Arabian proverb, "The chameleon does not leave one tree until he is sure of another."[3]

Figure 9-1 Country rankings: change tolerance

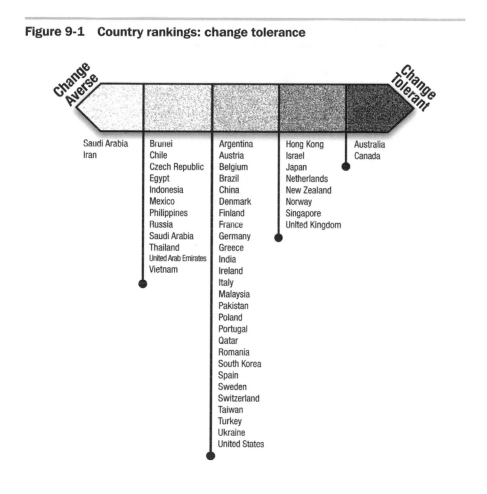

Change Averse				Change Tolerant
Saudi Arabia	Brunei	Argentina	Hong Kong	Australia
Iran	Chile	Austria	Israel	Canada
	Czech Republic	Belgium	Japan	
	Egypt	Brazil	Netherlands	
	Indonesia	China	New Zealand	
	Mexico	Denmark	Norway	
	Philippines	Finland	Singapore	
	Russia	France	United Kingdom	
	Saudi Arabia	Germany		
	Thailand	Greece		
	United Arab Emirates	India		
	Vietnam	Ireland		
		Italy		
		Malaysia		
		Pakistan		
		Poland		
		Portugal		
		Qatar		
		Romania		
		South Korea		
		Spain		
		Sweden		
		Switzerland		
		Taiwan		
		Turkey		
		Ukraine		
		United States		

Figure 9-2

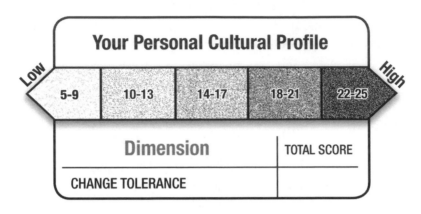

Societies that feel comfortable with change believe they are in charge of our own futures and expect transitions to take place constantly, viewing them as part of the natural order. They see change as necessary and accept it as such—the way many people view evolution. Organizations have greater flexibility in their structure, and employees are often comfortable expressing their feelings about company policy to colleagues and supervisors. In those societies, leaders are expected to be change agents; they're looked to as the visionaries who direct the course. Think about the American political realm, in which even conservatives running for office talk about the need for change.

In contrast, societies that have a low threshold for change view it as a threat to their fundamental values. Cultures that believe they are controlled by external events strive to maintain the status quo and see new opportunities as creating problems.

Leaders are expected to be champions of tradition. This dimension defines the need for rules, the ability to take risks, and the ideas we all hold about how much control we have over our own destiny. At the most fundamental levels of society, it affects the freedom we allow our children for self-expression, with change-averse cultures being restrictive whereas change-tolerant cultures encourage children's freedom to explore.

In change-averse cultures organizations demonstrate their concern about risk taking by building structures with clearly defined approval systems. Young employees do not present bold new concepts and tend leave the decision making to older and more senior managers. People in change-averse cultures take much more time making decisions and undertaking new ventures. To them, failure is something to be ashamed of even when it brings with it valuable lessons. In contrast, in the change-tolerant, risk-taking culture of the high-tech industry in the United States, if you have learned from an experience, you can put that information to good use. You may have preferred to succeed, but it's not shameful if you don't.

Risk versus Caution

In today's petroleum-hungry world, it's hard to imagine how a major petroleum exploration organization could pass up excellent opportunities. However, that's what was happening to the British division of a major oil and gas company.

How could this happen? The British division of the company was identifying excellent exploration locations in the Persian Gulf regularly and conducting the appropriate preliminary tests. It discovered that many of the fields were worthy of further exploration, yet invariably its proposals were rejected by its Houston counterparts (who were in charge of the decisions) in favor of far less promising ventures.

The decisions about which fields to explore were being made in the petroleum capital of the United States by Texas oilmen. The proposals were being written by the best European-trained exploration engineers, and the manager of the team was befuddled about why his team's proposals were being rejected routinely. He and the other senior members of his team became convinced that there was some kind of cultural communication breakdown.

The reason for the situation was the culture clash between the cautious Brits and the "go-get-'em" American culture of the Texans. It seems that when the teams got together, the Americans perceived their English colleagues as unnecessarily negative, focusing on why things wouldn't get done and ultimately stifling the creativity and productivity of the team in the United States.

The situation got severe enough that the Americans at one point adjourned a three-day meeting prematurely, saying that the environment had become so negatively charged that they were unable to continue. They returned to Houston and reported this to their management team, and as a result the senior team considered closing the European office.

As a last resort, both the Houston and the United Kingdom leadership decided to examine what kind of communication breakdown could be at the root of the problem. What could bring otherwise mature and sensible business managers and engineers to this level of negativity and frustration?

By all external visible signs, there were no cultural barriers. They liked getting together for beers after hours and talking about the great exploration adventures they had, and they laughed at one another's jokes. No cultural differences? Of course there were.

The cultural culprit was the degree of risk aversion that the respective cultures had. Whereas the Americans were extremely risk-tolerant, the British were less so. In the U.S. culture, failure is considered a learning experience, but in the European culture, it is not.

Ultimately, it came down to how each culture observed and communicated risk. The British started their proposals with a list of the risks of the project, followed by a history of the region. It was not until all the risks were discussed that they would move on to the opportunities. Their proposals closed with the potential rewards, couched in more understated language than would be used in the United States. Although the Americans recognized the risk, they focused on the potential for success. They optimistically projected the value of an exploration project as the leading component of their proposals.

The British believed that the Americans refused to examine risks seriously, that they were inappropriately optimistic and casual and were prepared to fund high-risk projects carelessly. The Americans felt that the Brits were being negative and looking for excuses for failure on every project. They were convinced that the British would not work hard for success since they were poised to accept failure and thus would not be adequately dedicated to a successful outcome. The net result was that there was never a uniform approval of a project and the American management refused to fund the British team's proposals.

As a solution, management decided to create a uniform proposal format in which risks and rewards would be identified, and the same empirical measures would be used by the British and American teams. They also were encouraged to discuss their cultural perceptions of risk to gain a better understanding of each other.

Table 9-1 lists some of the behaviors you can expect to see regarding change tolerance.

How You See Change Tolerance in Business

Examine organizations in change-tolerant cultures and it is obvious that one of the most important aspects of a corporate culture is rapid change. Those cultures view something new as synonymous with something good. They value individuals whose creative genius leads to fresh organizational plans and strategies. Compare countries that have high change tolerance with ones that have low change tolerance and it's clear that they have profoundly different ideas about lifetime employment, receptivity to new ideas, and attitudes toward moving or beginning new ventures. Today few Americans would consider holding the same job for life. In fact, changing jobs generally is viewed as highly desirable because it can broaden one's knowledge and skills.

TABLE 9-1   CHANGE TOLERANCE: BELIEFS AND BEHAVIORS

Change-Averse

- People's ideas generally can be described as, "We have always done it this way; why change now?"

- Change represents a threat to traditional ways. It must be controlled and limited.
- Child rearing tends to be strict. Children are given fewer freedoms.

- People believe that nature cannot be controlled easily. Instead, people must learn how to respond to the fluid, ever-changing character of nature.
- Employees like clear outlines of requirements, rules, and instructions and believe that rules cannot be broken easily.
- There is less willingness to compromise, and employees view competition as inappropriate.

Change-Tolerant

- People tend to be receptive to new ideas. They like innovation and tend to accept alternative ways of doing things.
- Societal changes are more common, and creativity and experimentation are highly valued.
- Child rearing may be more permissive. Children are encouraged to be innovative and creative.
- People believe in their abilities to control the environment and harness the forces of nature.

- Employees prefer broad plans and guidelines and feel that rules can be changed for pragmatic reasons.

- There is greater readiness to compromise with opponents, and employees perceive competition as acceptable.

Source: Adapted from Michael S. Schell and Charlene Marmer Solomon, *Capitalizing on the Global Workforce: A Strategic Guide for Expatriate Managers,* McGraw-Hill, 1996.

Japan, by contrast, is a country with a low tolerance for change, as witnessed by the lifetime employment assumption (which is being eroded slowly by economic realities) and centuries-old traditions in dress and art and music. Interestingly, new economic realities have caused the Japanese to embrace change in technology and business while cherishing and retaining tradition and the status quo in social structure and personal life.

In cultures that are wary of change, companies demonstrate their aversion to risk by building structured organizations with clearly defined approval systems. Organizations from cultures that embrace change view it as a means of self-improvement both for the business and for the individual. They tend to have greater fluidity and flexibility in their organizational structure. Employees are often comfortable expressing their feelings about company policy to colleagues and supervisors.

Companies that view change favorably have higher employee turnover because employees see change as a positive step in their own careers. Industries tend to be more innovative and creative. These societies are usually the ones that develop new products, register a disproportionately high number of new patents, and promote technological advances.

Whereas risk taking is rewarded in these cultures even if doesn't always lead to a breakthrough or bottom-line success, that isn't the case in risk-averse societies. Obviously, cultures with lower change tolerance can and do introduce innovations, and one need look no farther than Japan to see that the security created by this work environment can and does lead to innovation and consistent progress. In addition, this system of conformity and lifelong loyalty allows the Japanese to succeed at manufacturing and to turn out high-quality manufactured items such as televisions, VCRs, and cars at price points others can't match.

Predictably, companies in change-averse cultures experience stress when organizational issues are not clear. As a result, they detail job and task responsibilities at a level that might seem excessive to others. What's more, managers ensure that subordinates clearly understand all aspects of a project before a company sinks money into research and development or manufacturing. Finally, loyalty is a legitimate basis for promotion. Structure is perceived as empowering employees. By contrast, change-tolerant cultures develop broad project guidelines that focus on achieving the goal but don't define how to get there. Individual innovation and creativity supply the fuel, and it's believed that multiple paths are possible. Loyalty to the organization is not highly valued, and that translates into short-term planning and the need for built-in redundancies.

"Try, Try Again"

Peter Bregman of Bregman Partners, a change management and leadership development consulting firm headquartered in the United States, recently was helping a client in Mexico select a new chief technology officer to help define its Web and Internet strategy. He was asked by his Mexican client to sit in on an interview that was being con-ducter with a candidate for that position who was from the United States.

After the general discussion, the candidate began talking about his background in the technology arena. It was impressive. He had been on the staff of many well-known successes and failures. He spoke at length about a couple of the Web-based strategies he had worked on for other organizations and went into detail about how and why some of them had failed. He even talked about the amount of money that was lost in those failures. He positioned each story in terms of what had been done right and what had been done wrong.

To Peter, the candidate clearly was well qualified and appeared to have an adequate grasp of the challenges faced by his client. At the conclusion of the meeting with the candidate, Peter asked the client what he thought of the candidate. He was amazed to see the generally negative reaction. When Peter asked why, the client said, "How could we hire someone who failed so often?"

Peter explained to his client the role of failure from the candidate's point of view. Clearly, he saw success and failure in the same light: They were both part of the learning experience. The candidate had cataloged the errors as things not to repeat, using them as a learning experience; that was why he talked about them during the interview. His perception was that as long as he learned from a mistake, it was a valuable experience and worthy of being cited on a résumé.

Peter's client looked at him in astonishment. He couldn't fathom being proud of failures. His risk-averse culture saw failure as a disgrace with no redeeming value. It was something to hide because one never could recover from it. Peter explained the American adage, "If at first you don't succeed, try, try again."

People in change-averse cultures take much more time making decisions and undertaking new ventures. To them, failure is something to be ashamed of even when it brings with it valuable lessons. In contrast, in the change-tolerant, risk-taking culture of the high-tech industry in the United States, if you have learned from an experience, you can put the information to good use. You may have preferred to succeed, but failure is not considered shameful.

The net result is that the process of change management is dramatically different between change-tolerant and change-averse cultures. Change-tolerant cultures tend to view change and even risk as a manner of moving forward and building. When they look at opportunity, they predominantly see the lavish rewards of success. In contrast, change-averse cultures see change as risky, to be undertaken only after all the potential pitfalls have been accounted for. When people in those cultures look at an opportunity with risk, they see the embarrassing potential of failure.

Table 9-2 lists some of the challenges you'll face when crossing cultures. Use the table to tailor your expectations and business behavior.

TABLE 9-2   CROSSING CULTURES: CHANGE TOLERANCE

Change-Tolerant to Change-Averse

- Don't expect people to change production methods rapidly. They will find it difficult to innovate and prefer to remain with the status quo.
- Don't expect people to accept innovation easily. Try to build support for new methods or procedures so that there will be less resistance to implementation.
- Employees expect to remain in the same company for much of their careers. Don't threaten poor performers with job action. This may be difficult legally or unacceptable culturally.
- Employees typically are promoted by seniority. Don't carelessly discuss promoting a young high performer over a more senior employee.
- Don't provide broad descriptions of your expectations for employees. They want your expectations to be described and specified clearly.

Change-Averse to Change-Tolerant

- People view new methods of production with enthusiastic support. Try to become more flexible in your approach to doing things.
- You often will be judged on your ability to innovate and adapt to change. Suggesting new ideas and developing new methods or procedures will be appreciated.
- Employees do not expect to remain with the company for their entire work history. Unsatisfied employees may begin looking elsewhere for employment. Valuable employees may need special perks and privileges to ensure loyalty to the company.
- Employees are promoted on the basis of performance. Employees resent individuals who are promoted because of seniority or connections rather than because of ability.
- Don't be too detailed in describing the expectations you have for your employees. They prefer to have a general outline and have your expectations evolve as you understand their capabilities.

Lessons Learned to Develop Your Cultural Skills

- The way in which people handle changes in the environment
- The business problems associated with risk aversion
- How change affects business dealings

Questions to Ponder

1. You're in a meeting in Brazil and need to talk about a business venture that did not succeed. How would you position it and your role in it?
   Directions: Go to http://book.culturewizard.com and join the discussion.

2. You've been sent to India to critique and modify a local accounting system. How will you introduce your role to the Indian management team? What should you be prepared for? Directions: Go to http://book.culturewizard.com and join the discussion.

What Do You Think?

You have had your own experiences. Share them. Go to http://book .culturewizard.com and join the discussion.

Notes

[1] Six Sigma is a business management strategy originally developed by Motorola that today has widespread application in many sectors of industry. Six Sigma seeks to identify and remove the causes of defects and errors in manufacturing and business processes. It uses a set of quality management methods, including statistical methods, and creates a special infrastructure of people within the organization ("Black Belts," etc.) who are experts in those methods. Each Six Sigma project carried out within an organization follows a defined sequence of steps and has quantified financial targets (cost reduction or profit increase). Definition from Wikipedia: http://en.wikipedia.org/wiki/Six_Sigma.

[2] Axel Scheffler, Let *Sleeping Dogs Lie and Other Proverbs from around the World*, Barron's Educational Series, 1997, p. 77.

[3] Ibid, p. 79.

Motivation/Work-Life Balance

What you'll learn in this chapter:

- Espresso Culture at Work

- How Motivation/Work-Life Balance Is Reflected in Society

- The Impact of Motivation/Work-Life Balance in Business

MOTIVATION/WORK-LIFE BALANCE REFERS TO
• How people identify the ways they gain status, whether through achievement or personal life; how people define their status in society, whether from personal life or work achievements.
• How one's work influences one's self-image and self-perception.
• Motivation for success: why people work and what it means.
• How much work-life balance is valued.
• Which is more motivating: time off or a promotion.
• The presence or absence of laws and policies promoting family benefits.
• What constitutes status.

Espresso Culture at Work

Joshua Sturtevant, director of technology for RW³ LLC, tells a story about when he was at the university in Genoa, Italy. He was completing a master's degree in music technology for New York University. The program divided students into three groups on the basis of their primary interests: dancers, musicians, and technicians. The first two groups were made up of students from various countries, but the tech team consisted of only Italians except Joshua. The team members communicated well because they all spoke "technology," whether in English or in Italian.

From the outset, there had been differences in the way the three teams approached their assignments. The dancers worked all the time. The musicians loved music, sat and played together, and built a strong camaraderie in an attempt to support one another and make one another sound great. The Italian technical team was extremely competent but felt that work was only one part of life and should be integrated with one's social life, not dominate it. They took long lunches and many coffee breaks, and since all of them except Josh were Italian, they couldn't understand why he was always focused on his work and trying to exceed the director's expectations at the expense of having a good time.

At the end of the semester, the class was preparing for its culmination performance, which was to be held at a prestigious venue for a student performance, and the entire class was excited and nervous in anticipation. The agreement was that tech team would set up the equipment two hours before the dress rehearsal to be sure that everything was there and worked flawlessly. At the time the dress rehearsal was scheduled to begin, all the equipment was set up, but none of the members of the tech team except Joshua was there. The achievement-oriented dancers were in costume, and musicians were at their instruments. The Italians on the tech team, who were much more focused on being with their friends, were nowhere to be found.

"The director, who was a teacher at New York University and a perfectionist who was focused on getting work done before anything else, was livid," Joshua said.

Joshua was beside himself. Thinking that perhaps his fellow team members had been held up at the university, he took off at a run across the town and up a huge hill to the university. About halfway up the steep cobblestone hill, Joshua paused to catch his breath and caught sight of his tech team classmates having espressos after a long lunch in a sidewalk café!

Breathless and drenched in sweat, he approached them, astounded that they were still there, only to discover that he was unable to speed them up. He was surprised that they couldn't understand why he was so stressed.

In spite of his cajoling, they finished their espressos. It was painfully clear to Joshua, an American from the Midwest, that to the Italians work-life balance meant that a social lunch followed by a coffee was as important as promptness in arriving at the dress rehearsal. To Joshua, commitment and accomplishment were primary motivators, whereas to his Italian colleagues, who wouldn't have wanted to disappoint their fellow students and also had high standards, the primary purpose of life was to balance enjoyment of everyday pleasures with their work.

The performance went well, and at its conclusion Joshua's Italian teammates pointed out to that everything had gone well. They made a point of emphasizing how unnecessary his anxiety was. So what if they were a bit late?

It's obvious that culture determines people's priorities. Clearly, Joshua's top priority was to succeed and excel at work, and he couldn't have enjoyed leisure time when he knew that the tasks needed for a successful performance were outstanding.

Figure 10-1 shows the dimension of motivation/work-life balance in 50 countries. Transfer your scores on this dimension from the survey in Chapter 3 (Figure 3-5) into Figure 10-2. Compare your personal preferences to the country rankings in Figure 10-1 to see where you are on this scale. You'll be using these scores to compile your complete Personal Cultural Profile in Chapter 11.

WHAT IS MOTIVATION/WORK-LIFE BALANCE?

Motivation/work-life balance describes the emphasis that people in a society place on achievement and status by hard work versus the focus on personal time and activities.

Figure 10-1 Country rankings: motivation/work-life balance

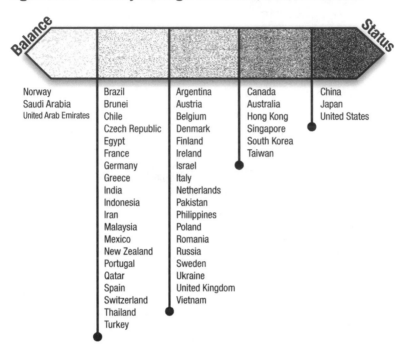

Figure 10-2

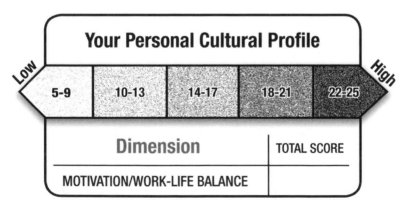

How Motivation/Work-Life Balance Is Reflected in Society

Motivation/work-life balance refers to how much work-life balance is valued in a society. Which is more motivating: personal time or a promotion at work? What do you consider personal sacrifices, and what do you consider reasonable requests for work? It is reasonable to be asked to work on a weekend or to reschedule a vacation? What's the separation between your work and personal life? Do you live to work or work to live?

Although we'd all like to think we strive for balance in our professional and personal lives, cultures differ in the values they hold regarding the importance of work versus personal time. Those differing values are reinforced by organizational and government policies regarding vacation time, flexible work arrangements, child care provisions, and other family benefits. The dimension of motivation/work-life balance covers this tug-of-war.

Generally speaking, more individualistic societies tend to produce people who are driven by the ideals of personal achievement, self-fulfillment, and possibly economic gain and material rewards. To achieve their goals, those individuals are willing to sacrifice personal time, work into the night and on weekends, take their laptops with them on vacation, and hop onto a plane at a moment's notice. Although the outward signs are obvious, under the surface what motivates people may not be financial security as much as status and personal satisfaction. This isn't just a matter of individual choice. Countries with a work-oriented culture tend not to have state-mandated vacations or welfare benefits for those who are out of work.

In cultures at the other end of the continuum—strong motivation/work-life countries—there's a feeling that one's personal life always takes precedence over work. People work to live, not live to work. People are not likely to socialize with colleagues outside of work and rarely, if ever, discuss business at a social function. Personal achievement and economic gain take second place to the quality of one's life. When you're asked, "What do you do?" it is just as likely to be a question about your hobbies as about your career.

In France, for example, it's against the law for employees to work more than 35 hours in a week. Dimitra Manis of AXA Corporation is an Australian who transferred to France in 2005. Dimitra told several stories about her adjustment in terms of her work ethic and commitment to the job to being a manager in a French workplace in which the 35-hour workweek is mandatory and month-long vacations are common.

"During my first year, I would come to work on public holidays and almost every weekend," she said. "Of course, the office was a ghost town. When members of my team learned that I had been working on holidays and weekends, they assumed that I didn't have a happy home life."

"I didn't take much leave the first year while I mastered the job and accomplished the significant challenges I had taken on for myself, but I decided to take a month off during the summer after that first year.

"My colleagues said to me, 'It has taken you a long time, but now you are French!'"

Dimitra also talked about how her Australian work ethic had her carrying an extremely heavy workload—working from 8 a.m. to 10 p.m. almost daily—and how the local human relations department had to warn her that she was pushing her team too hard and might encounter problems with the French labor "secret police."

In many countries that are high in work-life balance, government or corporate policies enforce long vacations and limit work hours. There are programs, such as lengthy maternity leave, to help parents. Failure to take one's full quota of paid leave is considered foolish. The people who are always last to leave the office are considered not dedicated but inefficient—they can't complete their work within the allotted time.

Typically countries that are high in motivation/work-life balance are also cultures that are somewhat hierarchical; status may be bestowed at birth and derives from attendance at preferred schools and universities. In those cultures, family connections and school ties are important and valued. Many arrangements are made on the basis of whom you know rather than what you've accomplished. For example, do you speak about someone in terms of what he or she does or in terms of who his or her family is and how important that family is in the society?

Some societies view work as what needs to be done to survive and enjoy life. Since people in those societies don't gain power and status by dint of hard work, they typically limit their time at work and concentrate their energies on family, friends, and vacations. On the other end of the spectrum are cultures in which people work hard and sacrifice personal time and family because work-related achievements are a key means of gaining power and status.

Organizations in cultures that value achievement over work-life balance think nothing of asking employees to give up family time or sacrifice vacations for work responsibilities. Self-fulfillment comes from economic gain and recognition at work.

Another differentiator of societies is how much people identify themselves by their personal lives or their work titles and achievements. For example, is it appropriate to discuss business during social interactions?

The Impact of Motivation/Work-Life Balance in Business

Attitudes toward motivation affect the hours you work, your willingness to have organizations interfere during your personal time, and the relationship between how you think about yourself and what you do for a living. In high-status countries, people feel that you should accomplish many things and that what you achieve is determined by hard work. Work and accomplishment should be rewarded and recognized.

What you achieve defines your importance and status in the world, leading to a sense of well-being. People are valued for their measurable contributions, and these high-motivation cultures are goal-oriented, measuring people's values against their abilities to achieve those goals.

In those cultures, objectives are clearly defined and on-the-job performance is measured against those objectives for bonuses, promotions, retention, and recruitment for participation in special projects. People are always available on their BlackBerries and check their e-mails. They don't resent receiving phone calls during off-work hours. People in the other types of cultures think it is rude to interrupt their evening and think you'd be crazy to give up family time or postpone a vacation.

In cultures in which the primary motivation is for work-life balance, great value is placed on relationships and personal characteristics. For example, job satisfaction is often more important than setting and reaching arbitrary goals. Since status isn't determined by individual accomplishments, people more often seek harmony in the work environment.

In high-balance cultures, people work to live rather than live to work. The organization cannot interfere in the private lives of individuals easily. Since expectations directly affect motivation, status is tied closely to reward structures. People aren't as likely to be motivated by compensation because money isn't a source of status. As a result, finding common ground for rewarding and motivating workers is a significant challenge in dealing with employees.

Although people in these societies are reluctant to talk about their personal accomplishments, that doesn't mean they don't have such accomplishments. This is a big error high-status-attainment individuals make when interviewing potential job candidates from low-status-attainment societies. In high-status-attainment cultures, people are more comfortable talking about what they've accomplished. When going on job interviews, they are coached to emphasize the amount of money they've earned for the company and the number of people they've managed. The objective is to show that they were an integral component in the company's success. In low-status-attainment cultures, individuals may consider it inappropriate to flaunt personal achievement. Instead, résumés are expected to be more comprehensive and outline the jobs and skills individuals have mastered. Recommendations from prominent individuals have great value. Additionally, information related to age, schools attended, and other affiliations may be more significant to an interviewer in a low-status-attainment culture.

In high-status cultures in which achievement is coveted, people are willing to work on weekends when necessary to get the job done. In most of the low-status-attainment countries in Europe people will never surrender their six-week vacations and are unlikely to work on weekends to earn more money. Contrast that to the United States where executives rarely take their allotted vacations and regularly take work home on weekends after putting in a 60-hour week.

The motivation/work-life balance dimension is very subtle and sometimes difficult to recognize. For example, the fact that an English person may find it intrusive to work on a holiday doesn't mean that she or he is unmotivated. It means that achievement—and working hard—is not part of that person's way to achieve status. Living to work is not part of the culture, and long hours at the office do not constitute status attainment to an English person. Contrast the English afternoon high tea break with an American coffee break that consists of standing and gulping coffee from a Styrofoam cup. The British society makes sure that it allocates time to pursue other interests on Saturday and Sunday.

In high-status-attainment cultures, families readily allow work demands to interfere with a person's private life because working hard and showing that one is very busy is a way of attaining status. It may mean carrying a pager or a cell phone or simply handing out one's home phone number to important clients. If a crisis occurs over the weekend, it means dropping everything to head for the office. In-low-status attainment cultures, you have or don't have status because of who you are. Moreover, work hours are shorter and weekends are spent relaxing with friends and family. A call from a manager may evoke feelings of anger and intrusion, since leisure time is considered sacred.

Furthermore, in high-status-attainment cultures, people are comfortable with informal introductions at social events. Parties consist of eclectic groups of people that cross social strata. Attendees often discuss business, even at social events. In low-status-attainment cultures, formal introductions take place at social events, and parties tend to be more homogeneous. It's likely that everyone will know everyone else or have the same sorts of backgrounds or connections. Since achievement is a secondary concern compared with family and background, discussing business would be in poor taste at a social occasion.

Table 10-1 illustrates the challenges you'll face when crossing cultures. Use the table to help tailor your expectations and business behavior.

TABLE 10-1   CROSSING CULTURES: MOTIVATION/ WORK-LIFE BALANCE

Status to Balance	Balance to Status
• Don't expect work to interfere with people's personal lives. People are less likely to relocate for a promotion.	• Expect work to be of primary importance to your employees and colleagues. People will relocate readily if it means a promotion.
• Don't expect people to work on weekends or late into the evenings. The organization cannot interfere in the private lives of individuals easily.	• People are willing to work on weekends or late in the evenings. It is expected that business demands sometimes overlap with personal lives.

(continued)

TABLE 10-1   CROSSING CULTURES: MOTIVATION/ WORK-LIFE BALANCE (CONT'D)

Status to Balance

- Don't expect people who come for interviews to discuss everything they have achieved. It is immodest to brag about personal achievement.
- Don't expect people to define success only in terms of task performance or accomplishments. They focus more on quality of life and job satisfaction.
- Think beyond individual achievement in structuring jobs. Integration of personal and family life and a positive working environment are related to satisfactory job structures.
- Focus on win-win negotiations.

- Organizational goals may not be articulated clearly. Your effectiveness is evaluated relative to your organizational compatibility and affiliations.
- Being a "fast-tracker" is not as important as having influential connections.

Balance to Status

- People will provide details about their work successes enthusiastically. Don't consider them immodest or overestimate their abilities.
- Don't expect broad definitions of success. Achievement, perform ance, and profits often define the success of an operation.

- Individual achievement is the key to structuring jobs. Motivation for high performance relates to increased earnings, promotion, recognition, or intellectual stimulation.
- Focus more on aggressive negotiations that provide you with the optimal market position.
- Respect for organizational goals is highly valued.Success is evaluated against your ability to meet these goals.

- Having proper connections is not as important as working hard and setting and reaching goals.

DEFINITION FOR THIS CHAPTER

Work-life balance: The degree to which people negotiate the competing demands of job and personal lives.

Lessons Learned to Develop Your Cultural Skills

- How motivation/work-life balance is reflected in society

- The impact of motivation/work-life balance in business

- Why some people are motivated by achievement and others are motivated by personal time

Questions to Ponder

1. You're an American expatriate who has just moved to Spain. You work late into the night, long after everyone else has left. You can't understand why people don't comment on your strong work ethic. What do you think is happening?
   Directions: Go to http://book.culturewizard.com and join the discussion.

2. Your American boss is not all that amenable to allowing long vacations for employees. You want to take a three-week vacation in several months. How will you approach the situation?
   Directions: Go to http://book.culturewizard.com and join the discussion.

What Do You Think?

You have had your own experiences. Share them. Go to http://book .culturewizard.com and join the discussion.

PART

IV

DOING BUSINESS WITH A GLOBAL MINDSET

Creating a Global Mindset in Business

What you'll learn in this chapter:

- Integreon: The Global Mindset in Knowledge Outsourcing

- What Is a Global Mindset?

- What Do You Need to Know to Have a Global Mindset?

Integreon: The Global Mindset in Knowledge Outsourcing

Liam Brown strides into the conference room in Los Angeles, preparing to open his weekly executive management team "weekly tactical" team conference call. Already on the projected computer screen are the faces of the members of his executive team, who hail from: Mumbai; New York; Manila; Delhi; Fargo, North Dakota; Washington, D.C.; and London, ready for the call. Despite the early hour, his British-accented "Let's get started" is delivered enthusiastically. This is a high-energy, take-charge guy who is comfortable anywhere in the world. In fact, Liam was born and educated in the United Kingdom, was trained as a physician, lived and worked in major cities around the world, studied culture, and is the embodiment of a person with a global mindset.

These meetings are part of the regular management structure that Liam has established for Integreon. The weekly meetings last 90 minutes, during which time each executive participates at his or her desk with a webcam-enabled computer. They are fast-paced, information-rich meetings in which everyone updates the other members and responds to them with active forthright suggestions and constructive candid questioning. It's obvious that the team has built a strong bond and a trusting relationship, sharing information readily. Liam feels that the webcam video and shared desktops enhance the quality of the communication in these virtual global meetings. This meeting is an illustration of the global mindset with which Liam manages Integreon.

Integreon is a knowledge and legal process outsourcing (KPO and LPO) company serving lawyers, bankers, management consultants, and accounting professionals. Its customers include U.S. and U.K. law firms, investment banks, hedge funds, and many Fortune 100 and FTSE 100 corporations. The company has about 2,000 employees, including

MBAs and lawyers educated at leading universities. Liam is the president and CEO of the company, having taken it from a start-up in 2001 to its current position as one of the leaders in its field in 2008.

What gives Liam a global mindset? He has an unusual ability to grasp the gestalt of a global organization—the business strategy and tactics as well as the entire employee life cycle (hiring, training, and retaining)—and translate it into a unique corporate culture that embraces national cultural differences as a marketplace advantage. As if he were playing three-dimensional chess, Liam saw that he would need to create a company that integrated global best practices in its operations from the inception. With extremely assertive clients who expect high quality and major cost efficiencies, he knew that Integreon would have to: hire the best talent around the world; train those skilled people in intercultural communications and cross-cultural understanding so that they could interact effectively with one another as well as with the clients; offer them development opportunities so that they would remain with Integreon as long as possible, since their knowledge and domain expertise is extremely valuable; and create a robust virtual environment that would support the weight of a rapidly growing organization in a burgeoning industry.

Headquartered in Los Angeles with offices in New York City, Mumbai, Delhi, London, Manila, and Fargo, North Dakota, Integreon's mission is to provide high-quality research, legal publishing, and accounting support services to the top firms in the world at dramatically lower costs than they could get elsewhere. Integreon's talent comes from the United States, the United Kingdom, India, and the Philippines. This posed enormous challenges from the outset that required all of Liam's skills as a business leader with a global mindset. He realized that the company would have to overcome the distances between people—both physical and cultural—if it was to succeed. If the firm was to capitalize on the intellectual talent of people from around the world, it was obvious to him that cultural differences would be a positive part of the equation because Integreon's "product" is the brainpower of its culturally diverse employees.

Liam read everything he could get his hands on about how successful multinational corporations created culture and managed and sustained their corporate success. He grappled with the issue of where to hire from and where to locate the executive team. He pondered what kind of framework to build so that his global executive management team could manage locally and at the same time function globally. Team members would be virtual but would need to develop close working relationships. Should they be located in one place so that they could interact face to face daily, or should they be dispersed so that Integreon could get the best people from around the world? He opted for the best talent in the world operating from various locations.

Liam knew that to make that strategy work, the team members needed to develop rapport and trust with one another. If the vision was to succeed, especially within the virtual constraints of a global company, people needed to develop strong ongoing relationships with one another. In fact, Liam was infusing the corporate culture with his global mindset. It followed that the company invested heavily early on in trust-building face-to-face meetings among members of the team, supported by more frequent, brief virtual meetings so that everyone could keep abreast of what the others were thinking and doing. Thus, the huge investment of time and money in the face-to-face meetings would yield a considerable return on investment over time. The team has these in-person meetings twice annually.

These gatherings aren't blue-sky, what-if exercises; instead they are a matter of rolling up one's sleeves, getting passionate, and trying to solve business problems. "You really have to dig in and debate and argue. We did that together—in person," Liam said. "The only way we could build trust with each other was to argue and say, 'I don't agree with you,' and get past that to where we could trust the other person. We focused on trying to get it right instead of being right."

Meetings are a key discipline in the organization. In addition to the weekly tactical meetings, the executive management team has daily 5-minute "water cooler" conference calls to check in with one another. They adhere strictly to those timelines and agendas. They use technology—video, telephony, instant messaging, e-mail and intranet—as easily as if they were opening the door to the office next door. Liam refers to "rhythm" a lot, and the meetings have a kind of rhythmic regularity. He admits that it took the team some time to embrace a strict rhythm, and new executives initially find it intrusive until they realize the efficiency benefits.

Liam used his global mindset intuitively when building the team. He knew that for the cultures on the team, trust was going to be critical. He knew that he would have to create a direct, open communication culture in which people weren't afraid of conflict because the organization's success depended on that trust. He would have to overcome specific cultural barriers to do that. He also brought in technology to enable a relationship culture.

He instituted wide-ranging professional development training programs to create a strong corporate culture and prepare employees throughout the organization to be effective members of global teams. Liam understood that cultural training affects the bottom line, especially in this field. If Integreon's employees didn't understand culture, they couldn't deal with clients—or with one another. Joyce Thorne, Integreon's director of training and professional development, said, "Training is critical for a global knowledge and legal process organization because it enables our associates to work effectively with our clients and each other." She went on to say, "We approach training with a global vision, but with a local touch, recognizing that the professional development required for associates in Fargo, North Dakota, is different from that needed in Mumbai, India." Not only does the firm teach culture, but it also teaches important interpersonal skills such as assertiveness training and conflict resolution (see Chapter 13 for details).

For example, the company has off-site workshops where employees learn interpersonal skills, human behavior, general communication, conflict resolution, and assertiveness and build professional leadership skills.

Liam was intent on building relationships with and among the management team that would create the underlying trust that was necessary for a global organization. He was building a corporate culture that mirrored his global mindset and in that process creating the relationships that Integreon would require to succeed.

Integreon's professional development training supports the corporate culture and teaches employees how to work with one another and with demanding corporate clients. The training teaches culturally based expectations in regard to the clients and attempts to acknowledge but temper the individual's cultural preferences so that the employees can respond to a customer's demands and one another's needs with fewer barriers that might prevent the mission from being accomplished.

Through working in a company with a global mindset, Integreon employees around the world have come to realize that the demands of their U.S. and U.K. clients are not an assault on their personal values, that harmony isn't always going to be maintained, and that candor—however difficult—is critical for the success of the business outcome. All of this is part of Integreon's global mindset. It's not only reflective of its CEO but is embedded in its corporate culture and is an inextricable component of its success.

What Is a Global Mindset?

A global mindset is the ability to integrate everything you've learned about culture into your attitude and behaviors reflexively. It's about having the ability to read the visible clues of behavior so that you understand what may be going on under the surface and make use of those cues in your actions and thoughts. You're able to interpret behavior and know what it means. Thus, when your French colleague gives a shrug of the shoulders to a statement you make or your Jordanian host takes you by the hand, you know what it means without having to think or at least know enough to put it into cultural context and move on regardless of how foreign it may seem.

In other words, it is like learning a new language. For a while you need to translate sentence by sentence, and then you start to think in the language in which you're speaking instead of consciously translating your thoughts. Having a global mindset is not necessarily new, but it has become increasingly important.

Most of us know people who seem to have a knack for working effectively across cultures and managing effectively in multicultural settings. They seem to be able to address colleagues and situations appropriately, retaining cultural sensitivity without sacrificing their personal values and styles. In spite of being multicultural, they're congruent with their own belief systems and are consistent with others' expectations of the way they will behave.

In a globally connected world, this kind of skill is one to which all global managers aspire. Throughout this book, we've talked about the cultural dimensions: the values they represent and how important they are. We've described the seven cultural dimensions as keys for understanding the behaviors you'll encounter. To gain a global mindset, you need to meld your understanding of these seven dimensions with an ongoing process of learning about the history, mythology, and heroes of the specific countries you're working with because, like dialects in a language, each country is unique and has its own way of expressing the seven dimensions.

Although the seven dimensions will give you a guide, to have a global mindset, you need to understand the individual country because that will affect those values and behaviors profoundly. For example, the cultural dimensions won't tell you why you can make jokes about the queen in England and why it is very bad manners to joke about the monarch in Thailand. It won't explain why you can make a self-deprecating joke with your colleague in Japan but should not do that in China. It won't explain why cows are in the streets in India or why it's difficult to find a cheeseburger in Israel. Thus, specific information about a country is very important to learn to develop a truly global mindset.

Having a global mindset means that you:

- Have the ability to be effective in interpersonal relations

- Understand local markets and take advantage of business opportunities

- Recognize talent regardless of the "package" in which it comes

- Adjust your personal strategies and plans in a foreign culture

Effective managers develop a strategy and a plan, know what the objectives are and move toward those objectives, and continually fine-tune tactics to match the realities that are encountered. That's tough in a domestic setting, but a manager with a global mindset is able to do it with the enormous added complexity of different cultures

Another example of developing a global mindset is the story of Microsoft in China.[1] Bill Gates's first trip to China took place when he was CEO of Microsoft in 1980, when the company was already a $60 billion enterprise. The story goes that Gates got off the airplane in blue jeans and a sweater, carrying only a backpack, and made a perfunctory visit without paying his respects to the political and governmental hierarchy. For the visiting head of a corporation, that was seen as a significant affront to the Chinese.

It took Gates and Microsoft Corporation many more visits to create the very successful relationship they now have with China. In the meantime, Microsoft suffered mightily in that country. Without question, the software was being used in huge numbers, but not much of the money was going to Microsoft. The software was pirated, and Microsoft and China developed a contentious relationship as the company tried to protect its intellectual property and get the Chinese government to support a crackdown on the counterfeiting.

In spite of huge efforts and huge legal costs, the company got minimal satisfaction until it recognized that its true potential in China would be achieved by partnering with that country. It began building significant local research and development labs, hiring Chinese research engineers in large numbers for its global (as well as Chinese) operations, and promoting China as a research and development (R&D) partner. At that point, the equation changed and the Chinese government, seeing this as a partnership, began to support a crackdown on pirating. For China, the relationship had to be a win-win situation with mutual respect and trust. It wasn't until Gates and the Microsoft Corporation developed a global mindset that they realized the opportunity China presented and began to build a hugely profitable, mutually beneficial relationship.

As a manager with a global mindset, you see cultural differences for what they are and are able to develop strategies that take on-the-ground realities into account without losing effectiveness and momentum. In effect, having a global mindset means that the tools in your kit have universal fittings and can work everywhere in the world.

Finally, you realize that it doesn't matter how it's done "at home." People with a global mindset see culture's potential impact on endeavors, recognize culture's influences, and integrate them into the plan.

What Do You Need to Know to Have a Global Mindset?

The requirements for achieving a global mindset are illustrated in Figure 11-1.

How do you gain and maintain this critical asset? You already know that culture is learnable and know the seven keys to learning culture

Figure 11-1   Gaining a global mindset

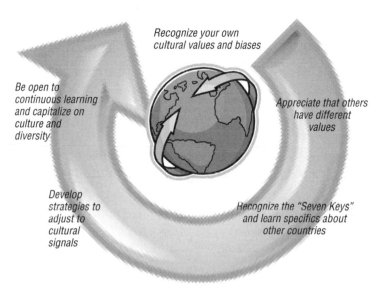

Recognize your own
cultural values and biases

Be open to
continuous learning
and capitalize on
culture and
diversity

Appreciate that others
have different
values

Develop
strategies to
adjust to
cultural
signals

Recognize the "Seven Keys"
and learn specifics about
other countries

and the importance of integrating them with country knowledge. To gain a global mindset you need to do the following:

- Recognize your cultural values and biases

- Understand that others are a product of their cultures

- See the manifestations of the seven keys and learn about the specific cultures of the countries in which you work

- Develop personal strategies to adjust to signals in other cultures

- Be a continuous learner

Recognize Your Cultural Values and Biases

Until you know how profoundly your personal cultural values are defined by your culture, you may think that everyone thinks the same way you do. However, your personal values are not universal. Until you viscerally realize that your values are a product of your upbringing, you can't appreciate the depth of others' experiences.

To gain a global mindset, you begin with an appreciation that we're all a product of our own cultures. Our values and behaviors are a result of our backgrounds and what we've been exposed to since earliest childhood. These things are reinforced throughout our lives, starting with children's stories and the heroes of our youth.

American children are told heroic tales of George Washington, the father of the United States, the leader in the Revolutionary War, and the first president. They are also told the fable of George Washington and the cherry tree in which young George chops down the tree and is confronted by his angry father. George says, "I cannot tell a lie," and confesses.

"I cannot tell a lie" has worked its way into American culture. It is seen in the legal system when people are convicted of perjury rather than the crime itself and in the way the notion of not lying is a deeply held national value. People become outraged when someone lies to them. It also speaks to the sense of individual responsibility and accountability. However, you would be in error if you assumed that *all* societies have the same sense of personal accountability. In some cultures, for example, this is a nonissue because the group determines how you are to behave and imposes restrictions that would make lying unnecessary or inconsequential. In other words, a profound aversion to lying is not necessarily a universal value.

American optimism is another example. The United States is an enormous landmass with generous natural resources; the egalitarian nature of the political structure allows for social mobility and the notion that one can move up in status through achievement and hard work. It follows, then, that as a generalization, Americans are supremely optimistic and believe that "tomorrow will be a better day." That's not a universal truth either.

British children recite "Humpty Dumpty"[2]; they're schooled in the knowledge of the shrinking empire. They went from "the sun never sets on the British Empire" to today's reality. Thus, although the British and American cultures are extremely close, they don't have the same degree of optimism. Again, optimism is not a universal value.

You are making a mistake if you believe that because your worldview appears to be universal, it is shared by other nations. In addition, as we've mentioned all along, your personal background (your location, ethnicity, age, level of education, and personal experiences) affects the way you filter your country's values. It follows that you need to understand where your preferences lie.

Setting Aside Prejudices and Assumptions but Remaining Genuine

Managing people and projects and meeting business objectives require a clear sense of mission and purpose and a passion for accomplishment without imposing one's cultural values on others. This is accomplished by learning from the environment and managing with its constructs, as opposed to against them. However, it does not require compromising one's inner values.

Fred Hassan, chairman and CEO of Schering-Plough, who was born in Pakistan, says, "Having a global attitude is not the same as being able to imitate local styles. It's just as important for managers to be themselves. . . . Being yourself while also showing interest and openness is at the heart of a global attitude."[3]

This is a good time to go back to Chapter 3 (Figure 3-5) and review your personal cultural style. (It's also a good time to fill out your scores in your Personal Cultural Profile (Figure 11-2). Your attitudes are a combination of the influences of your society and your personal experiences.

Figure 11-2 has spaces for you to fill out your Personal Cultural Profile scores.

Figure 11-2

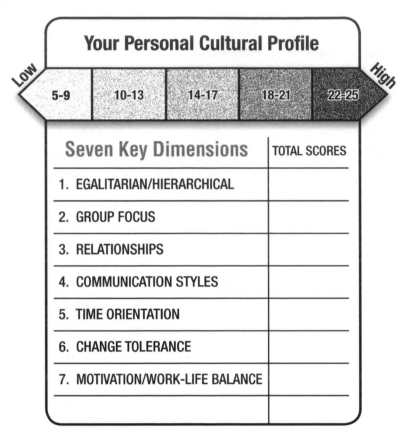

Take a good look at your Personal Cultural Profile and try to commit it to memory. That shouldn't be difficult to do because it's a reflection of your personal style with which you're already very familiar. Now that you can see your cultural preferences in black and white, you can use it as a personal compass. When you encounter different values, whether subtle or strongly visible, knowing who you are helps you refrain from making value judgments and enables you to more effectively manage perplexing situations to achieve your desired outcomes.

Once you fully grasp how your own culture has programmed your value system, it's easier to take the next step in gaining a global mindset. That step consists of appreciating the fact that people in other parts of the world have had similar exposure to another set of values and hold their beliefs as dearly as you hold yours.

Understand That Others Are a Product of Their Cultures

To have a global mindset, you now need to apply the same recognition that you did about yourself when you learned that your values are programmed by your culture. These values, though different, are neither good nor bad in and of themselves. They are the result of the "the collective programming of the mind."[4] The important point here is that others hold their beliefs as unquestioningly as you hold yours and also tend to assume that their values are universal.

In some cases the values others have been exposed to are similar; in others they're dramatically different.

There was an Austrian manager who was put in charge of a French business unit in Paris. When he called his first general staff meeting for 9 a.m., he was astounded to see people strolling in casually for the first 15 minutes of the meeting. He advised the team that this behavior was not going to be tolerated; from that day forward, the door to the conference room would be locked at one minute past nine, and those who weren't there by that time would be barred from the meeting.

He was satisfied because at the next meeting no one was late. In fact, no one ever came late to any of his meetings. However, his tenure as manager of the business unit was short-lived because his accomplishments were few, and he was never able to engage the loyalty and enthusiasm of the workers.

This episode illustrates the fact that the first task of an effective global manager is to learn how things get done in a culture and find a way to achieve the business objectives that is culturally consistent.

In this case, the manager was so intent on his own value system that he compromised the business mission.

Recognize the Manifestations of the Seven Keys and Learn about the Specific Cultures of the Countries with Which You're Dealing

You've already spent a lot of time learning about the seven dimensions of culture and how those dimensions are the reflections of deeply held beliefs. Nevertheless, this is a good time to think back to those seven keys and focus on the importance of learning and appreciating the unique histories, religious ideals, mythologies, and other influences that have created the national cultures with which you are dealing. Learning about holidays, traditions, and everyday behaviors will be different in every society, and although the seven cultural dimensions reflect those values, you need to know the unique country stories if you're going to be effective with people from a specific country.

Develop Personal Strategies to Adjust to Signals in Other Cultures

Fundamentally, you need to be real—to be yourself—so that you can adjust to different cultural challenges while remaining authentic. Developing cultural dexterity does not mean compromising your personal values. It does mean that you recognize the signals and adapt your behavior to them. Of course, to be able to do that, you have to suspend your prejudices and adjust your tactics while keeping the goal clearly in mind. You don't compromise the objective; you try alternative culturally adaptive methods to meet it.

How do you do that? It's not easy, but it's well worth the effort. For instance, if you're finding that a decision is taking too long to be made and instinctively want to impose an end to the discussion, be mindful that the culture you're with has its own decision-making process. It may make you feel uncomfortable because the process isn't what you're accustomed to, yet you know it's unwise to short-circuit the effort. Your challenge is to look at the reality of the situation and assess how the outcome of the local process is likely to affect your objectives. Then you must figure out how to accomplish the business task.

By all means, remember that under pressure we all tend to revert to our traditional styles. Keep in mind that forcing people to do things your way would lead to the least productive outcome.

Ed Hannibal, a senior vice president of ORC Worldwide, was working to design and implement human resources policies to apply to a newly merged organization. The companies were American and northern European. The teams from both organizations met for three days, wrote the policies, and decided on an implementation scheme.

Ed was not quite comfortable that the plan had been bought into fully, but the head of the American team had to return to the United States and was convinced that they had drafted a fully actionable program. The Americans proceeded to implement the new plan, but as it turned out, the Swedes did not.

A few months later the group reconvened to examine some snafus that had occurred because the Swedes had never implemented the plan. Ed asked the Swedes why they hadn't gone forward.

"They explained that they really had never finished discussing the plan and understanding how it would work with their employees," Ed said. "So rather than implement a policy they weren't comfortable with, they stayed with the old one." It's clear that neither the Americans nor the Swedes had adapted to the other's culturally based decision-making process.

Be in a Continuous Learning State

Throughout this book, we've been encouraging you to be mindful of your own culturally based behavioral style and preferences. As you were reading about each of the seven key cultural dimensions, we hope you were thinking about how you would respond in those situations. That is an introduction to the continuous learning state, which is critical to developing a global mindset. Continuous learners use the flood of information and experiences they're surrounded by to enhance and refine their understanding of the world.

Peter Senge, whose work is renowned in this field and whose 1990 book *The Fifth Discipline* coined the phrase "the learning organization," explains that continual learning is interwoven with personal mastery. Continuous learners:

1. Recognize priorities or overall values about themselves and how they want to live and work—they have a personal vision.

2. Take an active role in the world and work.

3. Continue to reflect on their experiences in the world and work.

4. Seek ongoing feedback about the world (including work) and their activities in it.

5. Remain as open as possible to feedback.

6. Make ongoing adjustments, based on ongoing feedback, to the way they live their lives and conduct their work to meet their priorities and values.[5]

There is no greater application of continuous learning than building a global mindset. You get it by training yourself to recognize culturally based behaviors so that you adjust to the signals you're getting. You learn enough about the history, religion, customs, and values of the country you're dealing with so that you have the context and background to understand what motivates people. The global mindset requires the ability to take your penchant for accomplishment and achievement and find a way to make it work.

Integreon's Liam Brown is a good example of how continuous learning leads to a global mindset and why it is so valuable in building a successful enterprise in the twenty-first century. Integreon managers participate in continuous training that involves the following:

- Building the trust required by his high-relationship managers so that they are effective when working virtually

- Using the brevity of communication required by his American colleagues so that they get concise feedback reports from far-flung operations

- Creating an atmosphere in which direct and blunt dialogue is acceptable

- Developing the ability to deal with demanding global clients who have little regard for saving face and avoiding conflict by providing assertiveness and other training

Nobody gave Liam a road map for this structure. It came as a result of his background, his personal style, and the continuous integration of the feedback his global experiences had given him.

Having a global mindset *doesn't* mean changing your core values. On the contrary, the stronger and clearer you are about your core values, the easier it is for you to integrate a continuous stream of new information, some of which will not be congruent with your assumptions and beliefs. No doubt, being able to do that requires a great deal of self-confidence, and that self-confidence needs to be rooted in wisdom and understanding. Even with the best intentions and a flexible disposition, the wisdom of a global mindset can come only from a continuous effort of building on learning experiences and the continuous integration of those experiences into a personal knowledge base.

DEFINITIONS FOR THIS CHAPTER

Global mindset: The ability to recognize and adapt to cultural signals so that you intuitively see global opportunities and are effective in dealing with people from different backgrounds around the world. A global mindset is the ability to integrate the seven cultural dimensions into personal behavior and management styles without compromising your authenticity.

Continuous learning state: Simply put, the ability to learn from the information and signals you receive. This is somewhat more complex than it appears since it requires continuing openness to acquiring new information and using newly learned techniques.

Outsourcing: "At its most basic, outsourcing is simply the farming out of services to a third party. With regard to information technology, outsourcing can include anything from outsourcing all management of IT . . . to outsourcing a very small and easily defined service, such as disaster recovery or data storage, and everything in between."[6]

KPO (knowledge process outsourcing): This involves processes that demand advanced research and analytical, technical, and decision-making skills. Less mature than the business process outsourcing industry, KPO work includes pharmaceutical R&D, legal work, data mining, and patent research. The KPO industry is just beginning to gain acceptance in corporate America.[7]

Lessons Learned to Develop Your Cultural Skills

- The elements of a global mindset and how you acquire one
  - The importance of continuously learning about culture and the behaviors and values of the countries in which you're working

Questions to Ponder

1. You're going on a business trip in which you're going to five different countries to make a presentation, visiting one country a day. How do you make sure your presentation will be appropriate in each country?
Directions: Go to http://book.culturewizard.com and join the discussion.

2. You spent three days in meetings and it's time to return home, yet you can't seem to get the meeting participants to agree on the plan you've been discussing. You decide to return home and reconvene the group virtually. Was that the right decision? What other options did you have?
Directions: Go to http://book.culturewizard.com and join the discussion.

What Do You Think?

You have had your own experiences. Share them. Go to http://book .culturewizard.com and join the discussion.

Notes

[1] Robert Buderi and Gregory T. Huang, *Guanxi (The Art of Relationships): Microsoft, China, and Bill Gates's Plan to Win the Road Ahead*, Simon & Schuster, 2006.

[2] Humpty Dumpty sat on a wall / Humpty Dumpty had a great fall / All the king's horses and all the king's men / couldn't put Humpty together again.

[3] Fred Hassan (chairman and CEO, Schering-Plough), "In Search of Global Leaders," *Harvard Business Review*, Perspectives: A Changed World issue, August 2003, p. 41.

[4] Geert Hofstede and Gert Jan Hofstede, *Cultures and Organizations: Software of the Mind*, McGraw-Hill, 2005.

5 Carter McNamara, Authenticity Consulting, Copyright 1997–2008. http://www.managementhelp
   .org/trng_dev/design/cont_lrn.htm#anchor440098; Peter M. Senge, *The Fifth Discipline: The
   Art and Practice of the Learning Organization*, oubleday/Currency, 2006.

6 Stephanie Overby, "ABC: An Introduction to Outsourcing," CIO, March 9, 2007, available at
   http://www.cio.com/article/40380/ABC_An_Introduction_to_Outsourcing#1.

7 Ibid.

CHAPTER

12

Creating Effective Global Teams and Working with Diverse Colleagues

> *What you'll learn in this chapter:*
>
> • Putting It All Together on Global Teams
>
> • What Are Global (Virtual) Teams and What Makes Them So Challenging?
>
> • Learning How Cultural Diversity Affects Global Teams
>
> • The Manager's Role—Recognizing and Correcting the Difficulties: Structuring for Success, Using Technology to Work across Time Zones, and Addressing the Bane of Multitasking
>
> • Creating Effective Strategies for Teamwork

Putting It All Together on Global Teams

Remember Jeri Hawthorne in Chapter 5 and the meeting in which her group-oriented Danish colleagues expected that everyone would be included in the discussion? Remember Anke Puscher (in Chapter 6), the straight-talking transactional Dutch manager whose Chinese team relied on its network of relationships instead of her suggestion that cold calls could be effective? Do you recall the Australian Paul Grogan (in Chapter 7) whose Texan colleague found himself holding hands with a youthful Saudi Arabian because it was the appropriate nonverbal gesture to show him respect? How about Joyce Thorne (Chapter 8), whose Indian colleagues have a different sense of time and are reluctant to acknowledge missed deadlines?

Remember their issues? Now imagine all of these people on a single global team. You have Americans, Australians, Danes, Dutch, Chinese, and Indians; this is not implausible. You have team members who are group-oriented and those who are individualistic (see Figure 12-1), those who are transactional along with those who are relationship-oriented (see Figure 12-2), those who are direct communicators and those who are indirect (see Figure 12-3), and members who have wide-ranging attitudes toward time (see Figure 12-4). It's clear to see how challenging it would be to make these people an effective and efficient working unit. That would be quite a feat!

Can you imagine the difficulties when this team approaches a business challenge, even something as simple as structuring a meeting? Who feels comfortable speaking? Is everyone in agreement about the agenda? What do you do to ensure that everyone understands the language? It's very complex.

To complicate things further, put all your team members on a conference call from their respective offices around the world. Remove the advantages of a face-to-face meeting in which all can see one another. Now you've got your global virtual team!

Figure 12-1 Your global team members: group-oriented and individualistic

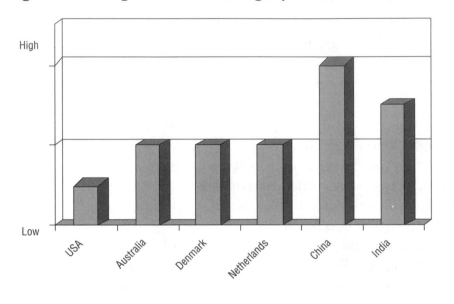

Figure 12-2 Your global team members: transactional and relationship-oriented

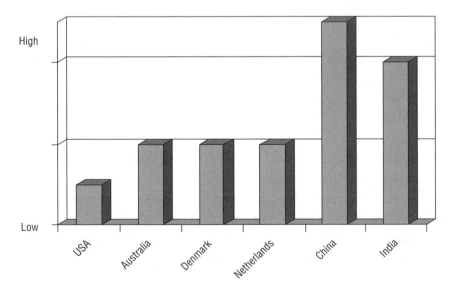

Figure 12-3   Your global team members: direct and indirect communicators

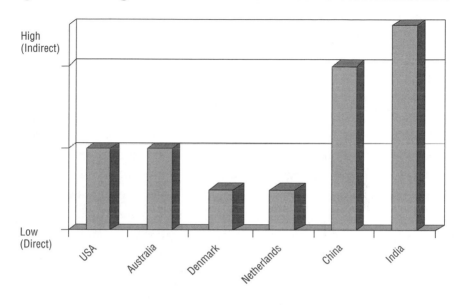

Figure 12-4   Your global team members: wide-ranging attitudes toward time

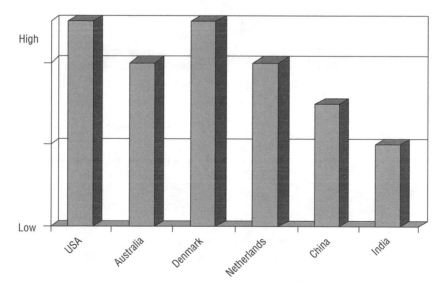

How do you cope with such challenges? More than that, how do you use the diversity of backgrounds and skills in the group and become an effective team? That's what this chapter will teach you.

What Are Global (Virtual) Teams* and What Makes Them So Challenging?

One way or another, if you're in a multinational organization, you're already on a global team, though you may not realize it. You may think of your team members as Tony in Athens and Christine in Oslo, but if you work on a short-term project or in a standing work group with people from other countries, you're on a global team, and depending on the number of members and the variety of nationalities, you'll have more or less difficulty.

Figure 12-5 shows the advantages and disadvantages of multicultural teams.

Figure 12-5   Advantages and disadvantages of multicultural teams

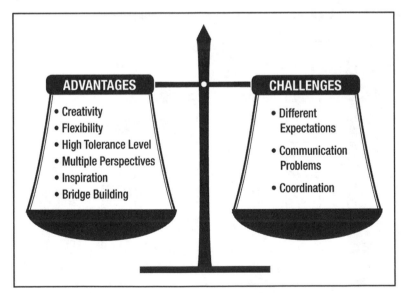

* We use the term *global teams* to include global virtual teams since we've never encountered a global team that didn't have virtual aspects. (See the definition above.)

HOW THE SEVEN CULTURAL DIMENSIONS AFFECT TEAM BEHAVIOR

Think about how the cultural attitudes and values you've learned shape team behaviors, expectations, and decisions:

- Hierarchy/egalitarianism dictates how meetings will be run.

- Group focus dictates the need for agreement and consensus.

- Relationships dictate the importance of trust and small talk.

- Communication style dictates how messages are sent and received.

- Time orientation dictates how deadlines will be established.

- Change tolerance dictates how risk will be addressed and how much detail will be required in a plan.

- Motivation/work-life balance will suffer if meetings are conducted outside normal work hours.

Global teams are a complex mixture of individual personalities and skills, cultural values and diverse work style. In today's corporate world, teams are responsible for everything from day-to-day operations to new business initiatives. Making these teams effective is an important and highly visible corporate objective in most organizations. Of course, global teams have been made possible by technology: collaborative software, telephone conference lines, and mobile computing. With the growth of these teams and the increasingly complex challenges they face, the opportunity for failure lurks around every corner. To be effective, talented individuals have to find mutually agreeable ways to work together to meet their common goals.

Although technology makes the creation of global teams possible, cultural diversity makes them both the vital component in a global organization and the difficult cultural challenge they have proved to be. If you've served on a global team, you know how complicated it can get. Although you may share technology platforms, work simultaneously, and develop strategies and tactics online as if you were in the same room together, you and your team members may have radically different attitudes about adhering to deadlines, scheduling meetings, and even the definition of teamwork. You may have different levels of proficiency with the language, and once you compound that by replacing some of the face-to-face interaction with technology, you don't have visual clues. It's a wonder that global virtual teams are ever effective!

In light of the need for global teams and the frequency with which they come together, it's no surprise that they are ever-present in contemporary organizations. According to Yang Zhang and Johanna Johnson, Ph.D. researchers from Rutgers and Penn State Universities who are currently conducting a study on the effectiveness of virtual global teams, more than half of all organizations with more than 5,000 employees have virtual teams.[1] If you've ever worked in one, you know how difficult it is for a team like this to be productive. With the complexity of working with people who live in different countries, come from various cultures, have different notions of collaboration, and use technology to communicate, it's no wonder that the failure rate can be very high. Research suggests rates upward of 50 percent of these kinds of teams fail to meet their potential.[2]

Take heart. The very diversity that makes global teams challenging also makes them potentially more creative and effective. When global teams work, researchers say they're not only productive but can be more innovative. This makes sense when you read what noted researcher and writer Nancy Adler has to say: "Cultural diversity enables an increase in creativity due to a wider range of perspectives, more and better ideas, and less groupthink, and for these reasons, diversity has the potential to increase performance." In addition, successful global teams have an understanding and appreciation of the role of culture and diversity, as an "imperative for survival," Adler says.[3]

Learning How Cultural Diversity Affects Global Teams

You can't underestimate the challenges of diversity: Cultures have different ways of doing things, different manners, different work styles, and different definitions of what makes a good team member. Dr. Adler goes on to say that while the potential is great, the risk is also great. "Misunderstanding creates mistrust and miscommunication among team members and increases stereotyping," says Adler. "This may make it more difficult to gain consensus and reach decisions."[4]

Let's look to some of the experts for advice.

According to Jon R. Katzenbach and Douglas K. Smith, acknowledged gurus on team behavior, the essence of a team is its shared goals, common commitment, complementary skills, and mutual accountability. This sense of accountability, which is judged on performance standards, is what makes teams potentially much more effective than the separate individual efforts of all the members of a team.[5]

Successful teams have the following elements:

- Clear goals and objectives that are accepted by all the members

- Rules, role definitions, and clear procedures

- Active participation of each team member

- Clear discipline and consequences

- Clear communication channels

It stands to reason that you want to maximize the characteristics of successful teams while considering the challenges that cultural diversity presents. The primary challenges are:

1. Overcoming differences in language and culture

2. Developing trust and relationships despite distance

3. Overcoming logistical challenges

4. Developing a common context for decision making[6]

Let's look at this in more detail. Language is one of the most profound hurdles for a global team. It involves how proficient all team members are with the language being used (most often English). It goes both ways. Let's say that English is the common language. Those who speak it as a second language have to contend with their ability to express their ideas clearly and with all the subtlety needed. Unless they are extremely proficient, expressing thoughts in English will challenge their confidence and may limit their contribution. The speed with which native English speakers talk and the variety of accents pose other potential issues for understanding. First-language English speakers have to interpret accents and sometimes difficult-to-understand pronunciation and restrain their tendency to speak in "shorthand" with idioms and cultural references (such as "hitting a home run" and "all the rage").

You don't have to read a lot of research to understand that those who are most comfortable with the language can be more articulate and persuasive and thus tend to have more power in the group than those who aren't. Imagine a conference call with eager Americans and Australians who have trouble with silence and thus don't explore the thoughts of Japanese team members who are slower to answer because they're considering their responses or are reluctant to express their views because they may be interpreted as critical. To the Americans, silence is interpreted as acquiescence, whereas to the Asians, silence may mean that there is a negative reaction and the participants are reluctant to express it.

Another key cultural issue is the ability to develop a relationship among the group members. Zhang and Johnson point to psychological research that says that people establish relationships more easily and quickly when they see each other.[7] This makes sense and is complicated not only by the distance between team members in global virtual teams but also by the cultural attitudes of the members about doing work with total strangers. In transactional cultures this is possible. In high-relationship cultures it is extremely difficult and can exacerbate misunderstandings that might arise not through personalities but through the cold media of e-mail, online chats, and texting. Terse messages can be misinterpreted as rude. Humor in e-mails can be mistaken as insulting, sarcastic, culturally insensitive, or cruel. If you don't have a backlog of trust, you're apt to ascribe attitudes to other team members and make potentially damaging assumptions.

What about the logistical problems? The first one is time zones.

Make no mistake, this is not a small issue. In fact, Nazma Muhammad-Rosado explains that Genentech tries to rotate the time for its conference calls. This is not done just to be nice; it is done so that everyone experiences and appreciates the handicap of calling into a meeting at 8 p.m. when your family is waiting for you or at 6 a.m. when you're looking forward to your first cup of coffee. It's not only respectful; it's a way of sensitizing all team members to the difficulties of operating globally.

There are also the challenges of proficiency with technology and how that may be affected by age and background as well as the constraints of family responsibility, which can be an element of both age and cultural disposition.

Finally, decision making is a key function that can go awry on a global team because team members differ in their assumptions about how to approach consensus, the degree of decision-making authority each person believes he or she has, and their attitudes about the best way to make decisions.

Decision Making

There has been little research on the decision-making process on global teams, perhaps because it is subsumed in other aspects of intercultural activities. However, making workable, durable decisions is one of the most difficult aspects of teams working across cultures.

Several cultural dimensions come into play during the process. For instance, egalitarian members assume that they will be able to speak and express opinions freely, whereas members from hierarchical societies look to the leadership for decisions, despite being actively involved in the discussion. Some group cultures require consensus, while others are satisfied to go along with the majority. Some risk-averse cultures are leery about making decisions before a full implementation plan is worked out, while risk-taking cultures may be comfortable with a plan that still has missing details because they assume that they can make mid-course modifications.

How does a manager help a global team make effective decisions? Ed Hannibal, senior vice president at ORC Worldwide, tells about a particularly astute manager who was implementing a new process with an aggressive schedule. "She took the opportunity to really make the group feel that they were one unified team, and she did it in a variety of ways:"

- She allowed plenty of time for team members to develop trust with each other and to create a comfortable familiarity.

- She included social events during the business process. Group dinners following meetings and social receptions were held regularly.

- She got a commitment and buy-in from members of the team, where all team members agreed to its strategic and tactical importance.

- She solicited opinions from the less verbal members of the group, both publicly and privately.

- After announcing the aggressive timeline for the team project, she still encouraged team members to thoroughly express themselves, to question, challenge, and perfect the plan.

- In order to accommodate the more high-context team members, each breakout group had note takers who reported back to the entire team with detailed flip charts and conclusions.

As Ed's experience illustrates, managing the decision-making process is an opportunity to implement the cultural skills you gain and to use the cultural dimensions to help understand and manage the challenges that your teams are facing. We've referred to the dimensions as a template for understanding and overcoming global business obstacles, and nowhere are these seven keys more important than in decision making on a team.

PRACTICAL GUIDE TO ENHANCING THE EFFECTIVENESS OF GLOBAL VIRTUAL TEAMS

The following material is adapted from the work of academics Yang Zhang and Johanna Johnson:

Global virtual team members face many complex challenges, such as those described earlier in this chapter. Effective teams have a synergy of unique talents and, more important, diverse backgrounds in approaching problems and decisions. Ineffective teams, in contrast, not only create interpersonal tension among team members but also undermine the benefits of these types of arrangements.

For individual members, global virtual teamwork provides a unique environment for developing the potential to collaborate with others across geographic distances and time zones. For team members to have an optimal learning experience and achieve maximum gain from this developmental opportunity, they should be prepared to enter the environment with self-awareness as well as recognition of another person's perspective on the crucial aspects of individual differences. Research on the ways to manage global teams suggests the following four methods to improve the functioning of global teams.

(continued)

PRACTICAL GUIDE TO ENHANCING THE EFFECTIVENESS OF GLOBAL VIRTUAL TEAMS (CONT'D)

Culture and Language

1. Increase each individual team member's knowledge of his or her own cultural values. This can be accomplished through suggested readings and online resources.

2. Increase the team's collective knowledge of the range of cultural differences in the group. It is important for people to review details of the cultures present in their team and think about where they might face challenges.

3. Encourage people to assess their own personal cultural styles and how those styles may affect the group.

4. Establish conversational rules from the beginning. Acknowledge differences in accents and encourage team members to be mindful of them. Remind team members to refrain from using words with multiple meanings, idioms, or slang.

5. Create multiple channels of communication, especially ones that allow opinions and ideas to be communicated less publicly. Give team members time to consider the options being laid out and allow them to express their opinions in writing or even anonymously.

Developing Trust and Relationships

1. Encourage face-to-face interactions if possible, especially at the beginning of a project.

2. Give team members opportunities to engage in informal conversations if they are comfortable. It is important to keep in mind that not everyone is equally comfortable with or open about talking about his or her nonwork life. Therefore, use this strategy only when team members are receptive to it.

PRACTICAL GUIDE TO ENHANCING THE EFFECTIVENESS OF GLOBAL VIRTUAL TEAMS (CONT'D)

3. Trust often develops when members establish credibility by demonstrating their abilities and competence.[8] Give team members the opportunity early on to engage in tasks that demonstrate their skills or introduce team members to each other by highlighting their past experiences and current expertise with the matters at hand.

Logistical Challenges

1. Have the team work through process and logistical challenges before starting to work together as a team.

2. If it is possible and if the nature of the task does not require much interaction, schedule and coordinate activities in a way that maximizes the "availability" of team members.[9] For example, take advantage of time zone differences by arranging work in a way that allows team members in "earlier" and "later" time zones to finish a piece of work sequentially.

3. If the nature of the task requires interaction and discussion, plan and conduct online meetings or online collaborative tasks with techniques suitable to the group situation.[10] For example, using a facilitator can help make open-ended problem-solving sessions more organized and efficient.

4. Synchronize the pace of working across team members. Specify the amount of time to be spent on each task if possible.

Developing a Context for Decision Making

1. Make conscious choices about the people who will be involved in each decision. Although the project may be collective, it is not necessary that everyone be copied on an e-mail and asked his or her opinion. Explicitly defining these guidelines may be helpful.[11]

(continued)

**PRACTICAL GUIDE TO ENHANCING THE EFFECTIVENESS
OF GLOBAL VIRTUAL TEAMS (CONT'D)**

2. The distributed nature of a virtual team's work sometimes calls for "distributed leadership." The formal leader of the group should oversee and monitor the core activities of the group, but she or he should allow flexibility for subgroups to make decisions on their own in their specific situations.[12]

In other words, as we've mentioned frequently throughout this book, although culture is learnable, it isn't necessarily intuitive. It can affect your team in different ways, and so you want to pay attention to the way it expresses itself and develop a plan for managing diversity on the team. Interestingly, although research can provide a template for creating an effective diverse team, each team has to make it work in its own environment. Obviously, you're dealing not only with different cultures but also with the complexity of different work styles and sometimes different corporate cultural values that create unique situations.

Table 12-1 shows how the seven dimensions affect diversity on teams.

The Manager's Role

The leader of a global team plays a very sensitive and pivotal role in its success. Clearly, different cultures have different expectations of leadership, and an effective global team leader needs to find a way to bridge those different expectations. As Table 12-1 illustrates, some cultures expect a team leader to be an authoritative decision maker, while others expect him or her to be a facilitating coach. Some cultures expect active participation of the leader on the team, while others look for the manager only to facilitiate organizationwide interactions and to be the

TABLE 12-1   THE SEVEN DIMENSIONS AND HOW
THEY AFFECT DIVERSITY ON TEAMS

Hierarchy versus Egalitarian

Characteristics	Team Manifestations
• How do we perceive and deal with people in power?	• Criteria and expectation of leadership
• Are all people equal?	• Role of team members vis-á-vis one another
• Who makes decisions, and who is entitled to an opinion?	• Allocation of roles and responsibilities
• Are people empowered to act and do they feel capable of acting?	• Nature of interaction and discussion in meetings
• How do people with power act, dress, and speak? • Do people assume leadership or wait to be anointed?	• Ability to challenge and question anyone

(continued)

Group Focus

Characteristics	Team Manifestations
• Comfort in acting alone or with a group • The source of an identity and loyalty • Value of individual contributions versus teamwork • Roles and responsibilities of individuals • Comfort with praise and self-promotion • Are individuals or groups more productive?	• How are decisions made? • How much discussion and agreement is necessary? • Is consensus or unanimity necessary? • How much individual initiative is acceptable? • Rewards and recognition • How is conflict addressed?

Relationships

Characteristics	Team Manifestations
• How important is it to have a relationship with the people with whom you work? • Are people more important than schedules? • Is trust assumed or earned? • Is competence more important than trusting or liking one's colleagues? • Is harmony important? • Is saving and giving face important? • Are people comfortable with praise and self-promotion • Are individuals or groups more productive?	• The impact of working with people you don't see or know • The need for informal social interaction • Should a process be created to allow for trust building? • Balancing the need for personal interactions with task-driven personalities

(continued)

Communication Style	
Characteristics	**Team Manifestations**
• The directness or subtleness of language • Importance of verbal versus nonverbal messages • Amount of information people need to receive or share • Is brevity or eloquence valued? • The need to save face and maintain harmony through language • Liking your colleagues • Is harmony important? • Is saving and giving face important? • Are people comfortable with praise and self-promotion? • Are individuals or groups more productive?	• What will protocol and etiquette be? • Ensure that all team members can express themselves • How much background information will need to be shared? • Format for sharing information • What are criteria of respectful interactions? • How to accommodate/ benefit nonverbal communicators and nonnative English speakers

(*continued*)

Time Orientation	
Characteristics	**Team Manifestations**
• Amount of control people feel they have over time • Importance of relationships versus schedules • Attitudes toward punctuality • Comfort with short-range versus longer-term planning • Ability to make and meet deadlines	• Establishing criteria for meeting schedules and adhering to deadlines • Establishing comfort with controlling time • Maintaining balance between schedules and people needs • Some flexibility to allow for negotiating tasks and deadlines • Checkpoints at different stages of project
Change Tolerance	
Characteristics	**Team Manifestations**
• Openness to change and innovation • Willingness to take risks • Who controls destiny? • Preference for rules and structure • How the organization encourages and rewards initiative and permits failure	• How is change accepted? • Attitude toward risk and innovation • What does planning mean? • What is mutually acceptable risk/exposure? • How much direction and supervision is needed without stifling creativity?

(*continued*)

Motivation/Work-Life Balance	
Characteristics	**Team Manifestations**
• How people identify the way they gain status: through achievement or personal life? • How one's work influences one's self-image and self-perception • Motivation for success—why people work and what it means • How much work-life balance is valued • Which is more motivating: time off or a promotion?	• How team members regard one another's aspirations • How each team member feels about himself or herself and brings that into the group • How people work to complete the team goals • What is the responsibility of the member to the team when the work of the team conflicts with outside duties? • How do team members mesh in their attitudes about work?

liaison between the team and the company. Whatever the leader's intuitive management style is, it is important to be aware of the impact of his or her behavior on team members and to adjust the management style to be effective across cultures.

Once the leader makes the expectations clear to the team, it becomes every team member's responsibility to make that team succeed. Some of the tools available include: structuring for success, using technology to work across time zones, and addressing the bane of multitasking.

Structuring for Success

Remember that the essence of a team is that it is judged as a unit on the basis of its collective output. In other words, you can't be a winner if you're on a losing team. Since the entire team shares the responsibility for success, it is incumbent on every member to learn how to be effective on an intercultural team. There are five steps teams should follow in order to become effective:

1. Confirm goals and objectives.

2. Learn about team members: Determine what you know about the lives of your team members when they are away from work (relationship building)?

3. Learn and appreciate the role of culture on your team.

4. Learn about the style preferences of your team members:
   a. Expect to affect behavior, not values.
   b. Respect culture.
   c. Respect styles.
   d. Value one another's contributions.
   e. Express needs.
   f. Understand that success depends on the contributions you're getting from everyone.

5. Define the norms and behavior styles you want for your team: rules, roles, and metrics and establish standards for constructive dialogue.

Using Technology to Work across Time Zones

In 2000, professors Martha L. Maznevski of the University of Virginia and Katherine M. Chudoba of Florida State University decided that they wanted to see what makes global virtual teams work. Like many other researchers, they were fascinated by the growth and complexity of global virtual teams and wanted to explore what made one team more effective than another.[13] They spent 21 months investigating, and, like those who had gone before them, they discovered that some teams are high performers and extremely innovative, whereas others never reach their potential. They were particularly interested in the way technology and communication techniques affect the strength of teams. They examined three teams within one multinational company so that they could isolate some of the specific issues.

What they discovered was that the most successful of the three teams had created a strong and distinct rhythm of regular face-to-face meetings at which the team members experienced "intense interaction" punctuated by monthly hour-long conference calls and only brief interactive contact to complete day-to-day work, usually by telephone. Although the team members were from several different countries, including the highly individualistic United States, they shared a strong sense that the primary loyalty should be to the group and believed in careful planning before embarking on any change.

Think back to Liam's sense of rhythm (Chapter 11) and his formation of different team experiences that ranged from intense face-to-face gatherings to regular daily five-minute water cooler meetings and biweekly discussions. That's exactly what the research bore out as being effective. The face-to-face meetings were packed with important and complex activities, interspersed with regular contact that was focused on more tactical processes.

"This rhythm seemed to be as critical to effectiveness as the incidents themselves. While the individual ... meetings helped in decision making and relationship building, the rhythm of meetings over time provided continuity and long-term stability," said Maznevski and Chudoba. "They reduced ambiguity in the task by structuring expectations and making response times predictable. It was this sense of rhythm that enabled members to work efficiently and confidently alone or in ever-changing subgroups between coordination meetings."[14] The researchers suggested that global virtual teams must schedule rhythms rather than let them develop spontaneously. A predictable rhythm allows team members to develop social ties and relationships and gives them an opportunity to use the face-to-face meetings for their most complex, difficult communication challenges and decision-making tasks.

Addressing the Bane of Multitasking

One of the activities that frequently occurs in virtual collaboration on global teams is multitasking. "Multitasking refers to simultaneously participating in the meeting and engaging in at least one other activity unrelated to the meeting."[15] There has been a great deal of discussion among researchers about both the benefits and the disadvantages of doing more than one thing at a time, as well as anecdotal data showing that it can have both positive and negative effects.

The reality is, however, that when people are on virtual teams, they frequently multitask; they may be sorting papers or answering e-mails, but they often do not give 100 percent of their attention to what's going on during a virtual team meeting. One way to avoid this is to have visual contact using webcams, but often that's not possible.

Researcher Christina Wasson studied people in virtual groups and came away with the idea that multitasking was not all bad. In fact, she believes it enhances employee productivity because, as she says, employees "are usually putting in an extra level of effort, not wasting time." She offers guidelines to the topics and types of meetings in which multitasking doesn't cause a problem as well as meetings in which it does cause problems. She also offers a variety of solutions to the problems when they arise.

For example, sometimes people forget to put their phones on mute and other team members hear background activities, which can be very distracting. Another problem is that people may overestimate their ability to track the meeting as well as do other activities and thus don't follow the meeting. She suggests that if the team leader suspects this is happening, it's a good idea to talk with the person offline and indicate that the team is losing out on the person's participation. Furthermore, if multitasking results in team members not being engaged in the process, Wasson encourages team leaders to create a more interactive environment.[16]

Anthropologist Edward T. Hall points out that some cultures are more comfortable than others with multitasking. According to Hall, polychronic cultures will do several things at one time. Obviously, individuals from polychronic (often low time) cultures will be more able to multitask than individuals from monochronic (high time) cultures.[17]

Creating Effective Strategies for Teamwork

Communication must be conducted in a way that always conveys respectful interaction. Consequently, it's a good idea to set guidelines for communicating when people don't see each other face-to-face.

Remember, cultures vary in formality, respect for rank, and levels of politeness, and it's a good idea to err on the side of formality. As with other areas of cross-cultural communication, when in doubt, ask a colleague who may have more information about that culture.

E-Mail Issues

Although people tend to sigh with frustration and fatigue when they think about e-mail, it actually reduces many of the risks of miscommunication on virtual teams.[18] Guidelines for e-mail are extremely important.

Set guidelines for the expected urgency and turnaround time for answering e-mails. When is a receipt required? What kind of tone should the group create? Who should be copied on e-mails? When is a phone call preferable? When is a follow-up call advisable?

Phone Communication and Conference Calls

When your team has people with different levels of proficiency in the dominant language, try to give everyone time to speak. Some cultures, such as the United States, have a difficult time with silence. This tends to cut people off if they need time to formulate their thoughts. Allow a little time for contemplation.

It's also a good idea to circulate an agenda before a communication or conference call. This serves several purposes. First, it defines a structure for the phone conversation and avoids a freewheeling chaotic experience. Second, it allows people to prepare their thoughts.

Also, be careful about using idioms and slang. Hold off on the humor until you know the other members. Finally, follow up with written communications to be sure everyone understands. Don't be afraid to take certain conversations offline and fill in the rest of the team with only the pertinent information.

Whenever feasible, think about webcams and visuals—either video so that people can see each other and engage more actively or with visual material on their computer screens so that they have a fuller idea of what the speaker is talking about. Consider Web meetings and other collaborative software.

Additional Resources and Activities

Consider the following questions:

- How does your attitude about hierarchy and egalitarian structures affect the following?

    ○ Decision making

    ○ Implementation of decisions

    ○ Relationships (boss/subordinate)

    ○ Communications

AVOID EIGHT COMMON LAND MINES

This section is adapted from the work of academic Nancy Settle-Murphy.

Mistake 1: **Assuming that everyone has more or less the same proficiency in writing, reading, and speaking English.** Even if your company requires that everyone speak English fluently, some people will be more at ease communicating, whether orally or through writing, than others. *Success Strategy*: Make sure that you provide multiple communication channels to allow for these differences. For example, if you have a conference call, build in the use of a Web conferencing tool to enable more people to participate in different ways with confidence and comfort. In general, allocate at least 30 percent more time for conference calls to allow for mental translations.

Mistake 2: **Arranging meeting times and tasks that require occasional work on weekends, vacations, and late evenings.** Although some Americans may forgo personal time willingly for the greater good of their companies, in many other cultures personal time is sacrosanct. *Success Strategy*: When scheduling work, plan around vacation time and local holidays rather than asking people to sacrifice private time. Do the same thing with scheduling team meetings: If some people have to keep very early or late hours to join calls, rotate meeting times so that everyone takes turns being inconvenienced. Also consider using asynchronous means to gather input and ideas from those who may not need to be on the call at 3 a.m. local time.

Mistake 3: **Believing that everyone will be equally willing and able to speak candidly.** In some cultures, criticizing others' ideas is considered unacceptably rude, whereas other cultures relish a vigorous debate. *Success Strategy*: Find ways to enable all members to speak their minds safely even if it means speaking to them one to one or offering them an anonymous means of making contributions. Above all, avoid using the "silence is consensus" rule. Otherwise you may imagine you have agreement when in fact you have no idea how certain people really feel or what they think.

(continued)

AVOID EIGHT COMMON LAND MINES (CONT'D)

Mistake 4: Thinking that all cultures assess trust the same way. Some cultures may place greater value on one's credibility (such as a college degree, related experience, expertise, or seniority), whereas others may place greater emphasis on reliability (e.g., willingness and ability to follow through on commitments) as a cornerstone of trust. *Success Strategy*: Take the time to discover how different members assess trust, and as a team consciously create operating principles designed to encourage attitudes and behavior that will do the most to build and cultivate trust.

Mistake 5: Creating a one-size-fits-all team communications plan. Just as individuals may favor certain communication styles, different cultures tend to have different ways of taking in, processing, and sharing information. For example, some cultures require explicit details about tasks before they start work, whereas others want only a general framework so that they can determine what their tasks should be. *Success Strategy*: Learn enough about all the cultures represented on your team so that you can make some first best guesses about communication preferences. As a team, create some agreed-on team communication norms that work well for most, if not for all.

Mistake 6: Designing a project plan that requires some members to take on multiple jobs. Before you assume that team members will volunteer eagerly when another member is unable to fulfill stated commitments, validate that each member is able and willing to substitute when needed. Some cultures need roles and tasks to be carved out clearly and feel uncomfortable and at times resentful if they are asked to slide into another role, even temporarily. Other cultures value group harmony over individual achievements and are more likely to jump in when and where needed. *Success Strategy*: Create a team environment in which it's okay to say no to make sure that people don't overcommit to please you or team members.

(continued)

AVOID EIGHT COMMON LAND MINES (CONT'D)

Mistake 7: Imagining that everyone has the same definition of ASAP (as soon as possible). Cultures have different notions about time. Americans tend to value immediate gratification and expect that everyone on the team wants to move as quickly as they do. Some other cultures are more deliberate and circumspect before moving ahead and bristle at being rushed. Whereas some cultures value punctuality, others may regard timeliness as less important. *Success Strategy*: Make sure that everyone regards the milestones and deadlines as realistic and achievable and be explicit when mapping out deliverables and associated dates. For example, instead of stating that a certain report is due next week, indicate that all reports need to be submitted by 5 p.m. (specifying which time zone if necessary) on which day.

Mistake 8: Requiring that team decisions be made instantly. Many cultures need to assess input from stakeholders before weighing in. Others prefer making decisions on the fly, often with only partial information. Cultures that value formality may feel disempowered from making decisions without the sanction of their upper management, whereas others may demand an equal vote regardless of their position. *Success Strategy*: Be explicit about how and when decisions will be made, based on whose input and subject to whose approval. Prepare to build in extra time to allow some members to conduct the due diligence they need to make decisions if you expect them to follow through later.[19]

CRITICAL STEPS FOR ENHANCING GLOBAL VIRTUAL TEAM SUCCESS

1. Discuss the impact of culture with all team members.

2. Solicit feedback from all team members: written and oral.

3. Give nonnative English speakers adequate time to express their ideas.

4. Avoid slang.

5. Check often for understanding.

6. Confirm and double-check schedule and time agreements.

7. Define a process for decision making.

8. Define a process for disagreement and debate.

9. Review important decisions in writing and solicit confirmation.

10. Help each other understand and avoid potential cultural misunderstandings.

**DEFINITIONS FOR THIS
CHAPTER**

Global teams: "Groups of people of different nationalities working together on a common project across cultures and time zones for extended periods of time."[20]

Global virtual teams: Teams with individuals who work together from various locations around the world and who may—or may never—meet in person. They use technology to enable collaboration and teamwork. In this book, we use the term *global teams* to include global virtual teams because we believe that using technology (and virtuality) is part and parcel of conducting business with team members from around the world.

Monochronic and polychronic: See the definitions for these terms in Chapter 8 on page 183.

Multitasking: Simultaneously participating in the (virtual) meeting[21] and engaging in at least one other activity unrelated to the meeting.

- How does your attitude about relationship styles (transactional or interpersonal) affect the following?

  o Communication

  o Implementation of decisions

  o Relationships (boss/subordinate)

- How does your attitude about change (risk) tolerance affect the following?

  o Communication styles

  o Timeliness of working

  o Implementation of decisions

  o Presentation styles

- How does your preference for communication styles (direct versus indirect) affect the following?

  ◦ Correspondence

  ◦ Phone conversations and conferences

  ◦ Timeliness of working

  ◦ Presentation styles

Go to http://book.culturewizard.com and join the discussion.

Practice writing an e-mail correspondence to a colleague, using one of these scenarios:

1. Explain to an internal colleague that there is a problem in providing an expatriate with his or her draft contract.

2. Follow up about why an important document is delayed.

3. Explain a new human resources process that has to be shared with all colleagues throughout the organization.

4. Make a complaint to management regarding someone's timeliness in responding to your requests.

Go to http://book.culturewizard.com and join the discussion.

Further Reading

Duarte, Deborah L., and Nancy Tennant Snyder, *Mastering Virtual Teams*, Jossey-Bass, 1999.

Gratton, Lynda, "Working Together . . . When Apart," *Wall Street Journal*, June 16, 2007 (available online at www.wsj.com).

Katzenbach, Jon R., and Douglas K. Smith, "The Discipline of Teams," *The Best of HBR*, 1993.

Marquard, Michael J., and Lisa Horvath, *Global Teams*, Davies-Black, 2001.

Maznevski, Martha L., and Katherine M. Chudoba, "Bridging Space over Time: Global Virtual Team Dynamics and Effectiveness," *Organization Science* 11(5), September–October 2000, pp. 473–492.

O'Hara-Devereaux, M., and R. Johansen, *Globalwork: Bridging Distance, Culture, and Time*, Jossey-Bass, 1994.

Lessons Learned to Develop Your Cultural Skills

- What are teams?

- What makes global (virtual) teams so challenging?

- Learning how cultural diversity affects global teams*

- The manager's challenge—recognizing and correcting the difficulties: structuring for success, using technology to work across time zones, and addressing the curse of multitasking

- Creating effective strategies for teamwork

What Do You Think?

You have had your own experiences. Share them. Go to http://book.culturewizard.com and join the discussion.

Notes

[1] Yang Zhang and Johanna Johnson, *Building Effective Global Virtual Teams: Challenges and Guidelines*, RW[3] LLC. info@rw-3llc.com.

[2] Jenny Goodbody, "Critical Success Factors for Global Virtual Teams," *Strategic Communication Management*, February 1, 2005. http://www.allbusiness.com/human-resources/workforce-management/1045913-1.html.

[3] Nancy J. Adler, *International Dimensions of Organizational Behavior*, South Western, 1997.

[4] Ibid.

5 Jon R. Katzenbach and Douglas K. Smith, "The Discipline of Teams," *The Best of HBR*, 1993.

6 Zhang and Johnson, *Building Effective Global Virtual Teams*.

7 Ibid.

8 S. L. Jarvenpaa and D. E. Leidner, "Communication and Trust in Global Virtual Teams," *Journal of Computer Mediated Communication* 3(4), 1998. http://jcmc.indiana.edu/vol3/issue4/jarvenpaa.html.

9 C. D. Cramton, "The Mutual Knowledge Problem and Its Consequences for Dispersed Collaboration, *Organization Science* 12(3), 2001, pp. 346–371.

10 Jarvenpaa and Leidner, "Communication and Trust."

11 J. E. McGrath, "Time, Interaction, and Performance (TIP): A Theory of Groups," *Small Group Research* 22(2), 1991, pp. 147–174.

12 J. R. Katzenbach and D. K. Smith, *The Discipline of Teams: A Mindbook-Workbook for Delivering Small Group Performance*, Wiley, 2001.

13 Martha L. Maznevski and Katherine M. Chudoba, "Bridging Space over Time: Global Virtual Team Dynamics and Effectiveness," *Organization Science* 11(5), September–October 2000, pp. 473–492. They are with the McIntire School of Commerce, University of Virginia, Charlottesville, VA 22903, Martha@virginia.edu, and the College of Business, Florida State University, Tallahassee, FL 32306, kchudoba@cob.fsu.edu.

14 Ibid., p. 487.

15 Christina Wasson, "Multitasking during Virtual Meetings," *Human Resource Planning* 27(4), 2004, p. 4.

16 Ibid.

17 Edward T. Hall, *The Dance of Life: The Other Dimension of Time*, Anchor Books, 1989.

18 Jarvenpaa and Leidner, "Communication and Trust."

19 Nancy Settle-Murphy is a facilitator of remote and face-to-face meetings, trainer, presenter, and author of many articles and white papers aimed at getting the most out of remote teams, especially those that span cultures and time zones. See "Mobilize Global Virtual Teams by Avoiding 8 Common Landmines," http://www.ittoday.info/ITPerformanceImprovement/Articles/Landmines.htm.

20 Michael J. Marquard and Lisa Horvath. *Global Teams*, Davies-Black, 2001.

21 Wasson, "Multitasking," p. 47.

CHAPTER 13

Effective Leadership: Managing Talent Across Cultures—Hiring, Training, and Retaining

> ### *What you'll learn in this chapter:*
>
> - Intel Corporate Culture Helps Managers Cross Cultures
>
> - Hiring and Selection in a Global Environment
>
> - Guidelines for Selection
>
> - Steps for the Hiring Manager
>
> - People Make the Difference
>
> - Training for Excellence
>
> - Integreon Designs Training for a Global Mindset
>
> - Performance Appraisal in a Global Environment
>
> - Global Leadership

Intel's Corporate Culture Helps Managers Cross Cultures

You've learned the seven dimensions and know how to recognize and begin to acquire a global mindset. As a result, you're aware that culture affects almost every management activity you'll encounter: the way you hire and select, the way you train, and the way you promote, recognize, and lead employees.

The next step is to look at how to apply a global mindset to these daily activities. How do you go about your everyday work life actively using a global mindset? Dale A. Welcome, human resources global workforce mobility group manager for Intel Corporation, is a manager you can learn from. At Intel, he's fortunate to have a strong, cohesive corporate culture to help him transcend national cultural differences by establishing a uniform, corporatewide value system that all employees share, even when those values may be somewhat different from the national norm. Because of that, the definition of work is the same, the definition of commitment is the same, and the definition of the corporate values is shared around the world.

Walk into any Intel office in the world and you'll see a very similar environment. If you're in Vietnam or Israel, China or the United States, you can go to an Intel facility and it will be familiar. You know where the bathrooms are, know how to find people in their cubicles, and know what the protocol is regarding conference rooms. As soon as you walk in, the uniform facilities reinforce the message that there are the same standards of behavior no matter where you are. Indeed, Intel takes its global corporate culture seriously enough to build it literally from the ground up.

The strong corporate culture is reinforced by its consistent human resources policies and practices, which give managers the luxury of a corporate framework as they tackle cultural differences in their daily work. Dale said, "This is reinforced at every turn. We have educational classes that teach and support our corporate values while they teach respect for the local culture."

Employees learn the Intel culture from the moment they join the company. All the new hires start on a Monday, and before they go to their desks, they attend a new employee orientation and are taught corporate values as they're completing their new-hire paperwork.

Even after an employee joins the company, his or her ongoing training includes reinforcement of the cultural values. "Everything focuses on these consistent values: management training courses, the way you talk to people in their performance reviews, the way you agree and disagree with each other," Dale explained.

The corporate culture supports managers when certain issues run counter to the national culture. For example, from its earlier days, Intel's CEO, Andy Grove, stressed the importance of constructive confrontation. The belief was (and still is) that for a culture of excellence to thrive, the company needs an open, candid environment at all levels of the organization. He and the company leadership recognized that this idea of constructive confrontation would have to overcome some national cultural reticence, but they considered it important enough to train people in and reinforce it.

When you think about cultures that value harmony and are very hierarchical, you can see the challenge of instituting such an idea. How do you undo the teaching of deference and respect for senior managers or older colleagues? How do you overcome the distinct discomfort that cultures that value harmony have with confrontation? It's done through training and reinforced with a consistent message. If you do it effectively, you can create a corporate culture that may differ from national values.

In Vietnam, Intel faced the challenge of instituting this ideal in a culture in which harmony and saving face are core values of the society. Dale explained that in factories—from the perspective of both construction and day-to-day operations—safety is the number one issue. It is visible wherever you go. In some buildings there is a yellow stripe down the middle of the stairs with arrows on one side to go down and arrows on the other to go up; there are signs to hold the handrail. You're supposed to stay on the correct side of the line. "I have seen somebody say, 'Hey, you're on the wrong side and you need to hold the handrail,'" Dale said.

It gets to the notion of constructive confrontation. As Dale explained, "It doesn't matter what level of the company I'm at or they're at, but they have the right to enforce that safety rule—and tell me if I'm doing something wrong."

Being in a company with a strong corporate culture and having a global mindset enable Dale to recognize that it is sometimes difficult for people from hierarchical and group-oriented cultures to be assertive and forthcoming with criticism. For example, it can be difficult to have a discussion on a challenging topic on the phone or face to face because many Asians will not speak up at a meeting since they don't want to speak in opposition to their boss. "In that case," said Dale, "the workaround, if you will, is to say to yourself, 'Okay' and have that discussion. Then go off and have ad hoc one on ones with certain people on the side and say, 'Tell me what you really think; I'd really like to hear your opinions, and let's talk about it.' They'll begin to open up and share their ideas," he said. "Then you can come back into a meeting and say, 'Okay, here's some different approaches to it.' That way it's not coming from one person who is speaking in opposition to the boss in a public setting. Instead, you're bringing it back into the meeting in a nonthreatening way."

However, effective global managers need more than just a strong, cohesive corporate culture. You need to appreciate how the day-to-day business tasks differ between cultures. The way you hire, train, and promote people from other cultures requires you to apply all the cultural dexterity you've gained. It's not easy, but using the guidelines you have already and applying them to your everyday business activities puts you on track for being effective.

Let's look at the general tasks of business management. They include hiring and selecting, training, rewarding, and promoting employees.

Hiring and Selecting in a Global Environment

Let's assume you're in the middle of hiring a new general manager for your offices in Tokyo. You've narrowed down the selections from the local recruiting firm to two excellent candidates with good experience and credentials. One of them is assured and self-confident and responds to your questions about her background by listing her accomplishments and successes. You're sure that the management team in Chicago will like her very much. The other candidate is a gentleman who is soft-spoken and extremely deferential and never interrupts. He speaks at length about his understanding of the role but not about his individual accomplishments and focuses on the importance of establishing a good team rather than the leadership of it. Who would you hire?

If you identified the man, you are probably right, and you would do so because Japan is a hierarchical culture in which respect and deference are valued credentials. It is also a group-oriented culture, and aggrandizing oneself is out of place in that culture. If you were staffing the position in Chicago, you might have been right to choose the woman, but since you were staffing the Tokyo office, the less self-promoting person would be the better choice.

Now imagine you're interviewing several candidates in Shanghai for a plant manager's position. You are dismayed by the lack of eye contact and the weak handshake of most of the candidates. You're challenged about whether to hire any of them, concerned about the poor impression all of them would make on Western visitors to the facility. You check with a couple of local colleagues. What do you think they will tell you?

You're pleased when your Chinese counterparts explain that the candidates are acceptable and you can choose from among the most qualified. They elaborate by saying that it would be arrogant, even rude, for the candidates to maintain prolonged direct eye contact considering the hierarchical deference they need to be giving you. Their body language is completely appropriate.

How do you know how to hire someone from another culture?

Guidelines for Selection

Yang Zhang, Ph.D., is a Chinese national researcher who has studied cross-cultural selection and hiring techniques. She offers the following guidelines.

Culture influences various elements of the selection process. First, be aware that this is a situation in which people may be self-conscious and even anxious during the process. When stressed, people revert to their cultural roots, so allow some leeway for the candidates' behaviors as they embark on the interview process. Second, set the stage for optimum success. In other words, try to create an environment that enables the candidates to be at their best so that you can assess their real qualities. In some situations this may mean being aware of hierarchical levels; in others you may be better off with a group interview.

Culture affects the way you conduct an interview as well as the behaviors of the people being interviewed. Consider the following:

THE INTERVIEWER'S ATTITUDE, BEHAVIOR, AND METHODS

- How appropriate (from the cultural and legal perspective) the personal questions you ask are about age and marital status.

- How formal or casual you are and how that appears to the interviewee.

- How you ask about previous company experience. (If you're hiring a shop floor manager, in the United States you could ask about the previous

(continued)

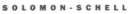

THE INTERVIEWER'S ATTITUDE, BEHAVIOR, AND METHODS (CONT'D)

employer's quality management processes, but you could not ask that question in China because in a hierarchical group culture, that would be perceived as violating social norms.)

- Are you using language that is understandable, and are you careful not to use idioms and colloquialisms?

THE INTERVIEWER'S INTERPRETATION OF THE CANDIDATE

- In light of the customs of the country, how do the candidates believe they should behave in an interview? Should they talk about themselves? Should they ask questions about the position and its opportunities?

- How should they talk about their previous experience?

- Should they make or avoid eye contact?

- Should they be formal and deferential or informal and comfortable?

Steps for the Hiring Manager

Step 1: Identify the Success Factors of the Position for Which You're Hiring in That Culture

What constitutes successful traits in that position? Is gregariousness important for a successful sales executive? In the United States, for example, salespeople believe that they need to "sell themselves" to sell their product. In Germany, in contrast, the personality of the salesperson isn't as important as the credentials of the product. Low-key salespeople could be more effective because they wouldn't put their personalities into the buying decision.

Do some background research. Gather information about the position and its responsibilities in that country. For example, what does a software engineer in the Czech Republic believe constitutes his or her job? Be clear about what the job description entails in the country in which the job resides. This will help you develop a competitive position description and design and articulate the position to attract the most qualified and best suited candidates. Do the software engineers expect close supervision or freedom to write code as they see fit?

Step 2: Prepare for the Interviews

Develop questions that are based on the information you gathered in step 1. For instance, if you identify that consistency is an important success factor, you might think about developing questions that explore how a candidate values that behavior.

Plan a culturally appropriate interview. If there are certain questions that shouldn't be asked, try to find another way to gather the information.

Step 3: Validate Your Assumptions with Local Colleagues

Getting a diversity of opinion and local expertise will help prevent hiring errors. For instance, if you're hiring a program manager in Australia, was the candidate's reference to you as "mate" a personality issue or a culturally acceptable behavior? To what extent would it affect that person's job performance?

People Make the Difference

As we've pointed out often, the success of a global business depends on the ability of the company to attract and recruit the best talent wherever in the world it does business. It's also important for managers who are hiring around the world to extol the corporate culture of the organization: You want to explain why working for your company is good for the candidate's career and lifestyle.

As Jeffrey Immelt, chairman and CEO of General Electric, put it, "The ultimate evidence that a business has become a global people company is the talent it attracts; it matters to us that we get the best talent. We try very hard to provide a company, a set of values and a culture that employees can be proud of whether it be in Pittsfield, Paris, Shanghai or London."[1]

Training for Excellence

In a world in which intellectual contribution is critical, training is an integral part of day-to-day activities. Managers with a global mindset such as Dale Welcome of Intel understand that adults around the world learn differently and need culturally appropriate training methods. For instance, in most Western cultures adults thrive on interactive learning. People learn by articulating and sharing ideas and want to be involved in discussions to frame unformed thoughts and gain understanding. They ask questions and need to be engaged constantly as part of the learning experience. In African and Asian societies, in contrast, learning can take place without that kind of active interaction. In fact, expecting all individuals to behave the same way when they're learning is a culturally bound assumption.

Geremie Sawadogo, program manager for global mobility at the World Bank, points out in a widely cited paper that in African culture, learning is a passive process, as opposed to "a Western context where passivity connotes a lack of energy, a lack of direction and leadership." For this reason, a Western manager avoids being seen as a "passive person," whereas in an African culture being passive "is a sign that one is wise and has self-control." He quotes an African proverb: "Only the fool rushes."[2]

In actuality, passivity is a "valued and cultivated" trait. In the African context, knowledge is so respected and even revered that asking questions often is considered disrespectful. Students believe it is respectful to allow the teacher to present all the material before questioning it. Learners expect to listen, observe, reflect, and then act. Therefore, there's very little interaction between the presenter or teacher and the participants.

In many cultures, if you want interaction among the participants, you will get the best results if you have small, homogeneous groups. This tends to be true in Latin cultures (which are hierarchical) because people are more comfortable expressing themselves among peers. They are "reluctant to express opinions that they believe should be delivered by more senior managers."[3]

According to Peter Bregman of Bregman Partners, Americans, Canadians, and Australians are not intimidated by large groups. As a matter of fact, unlike people from many Asian cultures who prefer small homogeneous group interactions, in many cases Westerners would rather participate in a large, heterogeneous group so that they "don't miss anything." By contrast, Asian cultures that value face rarely ask questions for fear of embarrassing the teacher and prefer to work in small groups in which people are of the same status so that they don't risk contradicting a more senior colleague. Asians prefer to learn by listening. By definition, this is an entirely different group dynamic.

Of course, in a global company, training and education often involve participants from different cultures. Training is often part of a manager's job whether it's introducing a small work group to a new process or a larger group presentation for which you've called together global colleagues to develop a solution for a companywide problem. You need to be aware of the different learning styles of your participants and discover the best way to gain their participation.

Integreon Designs Training for a Global Mindset

Joyce Thorne, Integreon's director of training and professional development (see Chapter 11 for Integreon's story), explains that preparing high-level knowledge workers to be effective requires ongoing training. Integreon's 2,000-plus employees are all involved in the company's training programs, and even though the turnover in the company's Indian employee base is lower than the industry average, a significant ongoing training component continuously takes place. It is organized to build skills as well as address behavioral issues that might become problematic.

The training curriculum in general can be divided between job-related training, which focuses on job process and content—what's expected, how to conduct research, and how to address what one does not know—and communication/interaction training, which focuses on assertiveness training, conflict resolution, and other interpersonal skills. In whatever way the curriculum is divided, it needs to be culturally appropriate for Indians, Filipinos, Americans, and English people.

The bulk of Integreon's clients are American and British professional firms. The individuals in those firms tend to be demanding, outspoken, and direct, characteristics that are challenging for the Asian and Indian employees. "Our goal is to create a safe and comfortable work environment where people want to come to work," Joyce said. "Your ability to communicate with other people effectively and to reduce and resolve conflicts rather than avoid them or meet them in a passive-aggressive manner actually helps people. It also fills a gap in terms of being able to interface in a cross-cultural team."

Throughout the training, Integreon addresses issues of cultural perceptions and cultural differences. They keep people aware that working with different sorts of people shouldn't be frightening but should be an interesting challenge in which the employees can apply their communication skills and effectively work with people with a totally different frame of reference.

Joyce explained, "We work with our teams in India to understand that just because someone speaks in a particular tone of voice doesn't mean that they're levying criticism. It may simply be their interaction style. So one of the biggest things we face is having our Indian employees not being fearful or resentful of the New York and London customers or coworkers who may come across as overly aggressive when in fact they believe they're simply being candid and expressing their needs."

Since Integreon is the embodiment of an organization with a global mindset, the creation of the training curricula recognizes that communication is a two-way street. For example, employees in Fargo, North Dakota, need to learn that if they don't understand what the Indian colleague is saying, it doesn't mean that the Indian isn't saying something of value.

"Everyone in a global company needs to be trained. Everyone is responsible for understanding the challenge of a global organization," Joyce said.

The training needs to be ongoing and comprehensive. Kishore Velankar, who oversees Integreon's human resources function in India, agrees. Although Indians have a difficult time saying no and will say yes about their ability to meet a deadline even if they are aware that they may not be able to make it, managers need to understand what is going on under the surface.

"You can train Indians to learn to say no to impossible requests, but that's not enough," Joyce explained. American and Western companies will expect them to say, "No, I cannot do it on Friday, but I will have it to you the middle of the following week." Thus, as you're developing curricula, it's important to recognize and honor the cultural basis of an individual's response. Thus, an Indian's reluctance to say no and thus disappoint someone is the same cultural barrier that inhibits Indians from feeling empowered to suggest an alternative. Therefore, you need to address the full range of issues and get to the cultural core as you're training people for effective business interaction.

Cross-Cultural Training

Although culture is learnable, it is not intuitive. Learning culture is a critical aspect of creating a global mindset, and being able to assess or develop an effective cultural training course is crucial. Cultural training courses begin with teaching recognition of what culture is and where it comes from and how to recognize cultural behaviors. They go on to define the values and beliefs that underlie the visible actions.

Garnering an appreciation of culture enables the participants in a cross-cultural training program to appreciate more fully the culture of a specific country or countries and further enables them to identify a context and alternatives for what might be assumed to be insurmountable cultural challenges.

In the author's view, everyone in the workplace needs cultural training, and enlightened managers make sure that this type of training is available for the whole workforce. Online culture courses are the most effective way to reach the entire organization because they are available at any time. Blended learning programs that use online tools and some face-to-face learning sessions enrich the process and address the learning styles of individuals and cultures that thrive on interactive, more personal learning. Some organizations also provide a culture coach; this is especially helpful for managers who are trying to unravel the cultural puzzles they often confront.

Components of Cross-Cultural Training Programs

The fundamental challenge to the training program is the participants' desire to learn international tactics (such as etiquette) before fully understanding the basics of culture—what it is, where it comes from, and how it manifests itself—in other words, before understanding a cultural model. This is critical. Think about how difficult it would be to learn about culture on a country-by-country basis. You'd have no context in which to put the new information and very quickly would become confused about which behaviors are appropriate to which country.

An effective intercultural program must begin by providing a basis for understanding culture and an ability to practice recognizing and adjusting to culturally based behaviors.

The basics of culture need to be the cornerstone of a cross-cultural training program. The other elements are built in to achieve specific tactical objectives either in the foreign country or with global teams. These specific modules are based on the first element.

Performance Appraisal in a Global Environment

Global companies establish certain uniform cultural practices, and employee management and recognition practices. Although establishing uniform standards globally is often a good idea, applying global standards for performance appraisals often is not. John Kovach, the transitional HR manager who was to bring Nuovo Pignone into the General Electric family (see Chapter 9 for the full story of Nuovo Pignone), experienced that challenge when he attempted to introduce GE's 360-degree feedback method into the Italian company.

The 360-degree feedback technique is employed to evaluate performance. It is used to get performance evaluation reports from the full circle of contacts with which an employee interacts, including that employee's managers, colleagues, subordinates, and sometimes even outside vendors.

During his tenure with Nuovo Pignone in Italy, Kovach was told to introduce a 360-degree feedback program that the company wanted deployed globally. By the time John was asked to deploy this program, he was well enough steeped in Italian management processes to realize how difficult it would be to institute such a program in a relatively hierarchical environment. He wasn't sure it could be done at all.

John began the process (as he did in many other instances) by letting the U.S. management know how difficult it would be because of the local hierarchical culture.

John approached one of the most senior members of the Nuovo Pignone management team and explained the importance of the process. The Italian acknowledged that he could see how it would be useful in the United States but stressed how difficult it would be in Italy. He was incredulous when asked to pilot the program and complete an evaluation of his own boss.

"It not only seemed inappropriate to him, but he also thought it was unthinkable to do a performance evaluation on his boss," John explained. John said this was a company standard and asked the senior executive to do what he could. The executive said he would try and asked to be given a few days with the forms so that he could think about how to complete the evaluation.

John broached the idea with other Italian colleagues and found that none of them were able to do an evaluation of their own managers. It was only with great pain that they were able to evaluate their peers. "They could not bring themselves to be so disrespectful as to critique their supervisor's performance and couldn't understand why the company would want them to," John said.

It turned out that despite their best efforts, there was no way the senior managers at Nuovo Pignone could bring themselves to do performance evaluations of their own bosses. That incident proved how difficult it is to institute globally uniform HR practices, especially when they run counter to deeply held local cultural values. Although in a global organization it's important to create standard management practices, what works in one culture does not always work in another.

Performance evaluations, as with other kinds of feedback, are highly charged communications and have to be handled with a great deal of cultural sensitivity. Imagine the potential for doing serious damage when a Danish manager who values blunt, straightforward messages shares negative feedback with an indirect, subtle communicator from Thailand. A comment as simple as, "I was unhappy with the way you did this," would have one meaning to the Danish manager but would be heard by the Thai recipient as a devastating condemnation. Unfortunately, a good and dedicated employee could be demotivated by feedback that was intended to motivate change and improve performance.

At the other extreme, a Dutch employee from an Anglo-Dutch company who reported to a British supervisor felt confused by the feedback he was getting. The British "sandwich" criticism. Before anything negative was said, the supervisor said something positive, quickly followed by the negative comment and then another positive comment. The employee wasn't sure where his manager was happy with his work and where he was not. For him, the message was lost in its tactful delivery.

Performance evaluations are one of the activities that call on you to make use of all the cultural skills at your disposal. They need to be approached with understanding, wisdom, and appreciation of the cultural message.

Culture complicates the already difficult interaction around performance issues.[4] Research indicates that managers as well as employees are uncomfortable during this process. During stressful moments, we all revert to our accustomed ways of doing things. Thus, differences in cultural communication styles between manager and employee could add to the already significant anxiety and potential for miscommunication.

Part of the typical appraisal process in Western culture is to engage employees in establishing their own performance objectives so that they take ownership of their responsibilities and development. This works well with empowered employees in egalitarian societies, but you can see the potential difficulty with employees from hierarchical cultures. This can be confusing to those employees, and the appraisal process that is so successful in an egalitarian culture could undermine the respect of a worker for his or her boss in a more hierarchical one.

Global Leadership

Leadership values are formed in earliest childhood by one's heroes, teachers, and parents. Imagine if all of your life the leadership models you had were males who dressed, acted, and spoke in a manner befitting their station. This is what you would come to expect from a leader. What if your teachers wore ties and were stern disciplinarians and your boss at work gave specific instructions on how you were to do everything?

Imagine that you're in a new position in which your new boss is a female who is friendly and engaging. She asks your opinion, invites your ideas, and expects you to structure your day to accomplish your tasks. How would you expect to react? It would certainly require you to adjust your expectations.

This happens all the time when people cross cultures.

Leadership styles, like all other behaviors, are a reflection of culture. In some societies, leadership is created most effectively through the establishment of collegial relationships. In others, leadership is authoritative and the leader overtly displays power. Obviously, what works in one culture can be extremely counterproductive in others.

For example, an effective American leader who solicits opinions from subordinates, values them openly, and credits those opinions and looks to subordinates for recommendations and input in everyday activity is considered an inclusive, empowering manager. Employees in egalitarian societies appreciate such leadership and function most effectively with it.

Now assume that that leader is managing a team in Mexico, a hierarchical society in which employees are accustomed to authoritative leadership in which the boss tells them what to do in detailed step-by-step instructions and formality is expected. How effective will that boss be unless there's acknowledgment that the employees need different management techniques? How will employees and colleagues react to such a foreign influence?

What are the characteristics of a global leader? What are the behavioral preferences that a global leader displays? Can you evaluate how ready you are to take on that role? Paula Caligiuri, Ph.D.,[5] has studied and conducted significant research on the attributes of global leadership and has created an online tool to assess and develop global leadership skills.[6] She identifies five characteristics: goal-oriented tenacity, managing complexity, cultural sensitivity, emotional resilience, and ability to form relationships. These are the foundation of a strong leader.

GLOBAL BUSINESS LEADER ATTRIBUTES[7]

Why are the following characteristics important?
- *Goal-oriented tenacity*. Successful global business leaders tend to have a strong commitment to achieve their goals even when presented with difficult and culturally nuanced challenges. Compared with their domestic counterparts, global leaders need to be more focused and even at times seem tireless. (Imagine being jet-lagged and having a long meeting to discuss complex business challenges while speaking a second language.) In light of the higher level of complexity required in global leadership tasks (e.g., managing foreign suppliers or vendors), they require more effort than do comparable tasks in the domestic context (e.g., managing domestically based suppliers or vendors).
- *Managing complexity*. International responsibilities are more complex than similar responsibilities in the domestic context. Working in foreign cultures with unfamiliar and ambiguous cues makes decision making more challenging. Effective global leaders need to acquire information and skills to help them navigate the cultural nuances of working in cross-cultural situations.

  Intellectually curious business leaders take the time to learn about potential cross-national challenges and acquire the knowledge, skills, and abilities needed to execute their global business responsibilities effectively. These leaders thrive in complex cross-national business situations and are more inclined to view globally oriented activities as opportunities.

(continued)

GLOBAL BUSINESS LEADER
ATTRIBUTES (CONT'D)

These responsibilities can be especially frustrating for people who do not have the cognitive skills to manage the challenges embedded in cross-national situations. People who lack both the cognitive skill and desire to learn often become frustrated with situations they are unable to predict and people they cannot read accurately.

- *Cultural sensitivity.* Global leadership activities require a nonjudgmental and open-minded approach to the attitudes and behaviors of people from other cultures. Research has identified this as one of the most critical personality characteristics related to successful global leaders, enabling them to respect cultural differences. They believe that values, norms, and behaviors are as justified as their own even when they are vastly different. People who are open to the differences in others have less rigid views of what is right and wrong, or appropriate and inappropriate, and are less likely to treat people from different cultures as inferior.

    Cultural sensitivity gives leaders an opportunity to grow as they allow their own assumptions to be challenged. Similarly, they develop global business skills by seeing the world through different eyes.

    Cultural sensitivity also enables global leaders to work effectively in host environments without holding any preconceived notions (i.e., stereotypes) about different cultures. Often stereotyping leads to business problems because the situation is not being assessed correctly. Cultural sensitivity gives global leaders an advantage as they are more likely to take the time to assess the real situation in a culturally nuanced context. Research has found that those with greater cultural sensitivity are able to form better social alliances with colleagues from diverse cultures. Leaders who are more culturally sensitive are better able to manage cross-cultural conflict collaboratively, are more likely to strive for mutual understanding, and are likely to have greater success in global leadership tasks involving collaboration (e.g., working with colleagues from other countries).

- *Emotional resilience.* Many global leadership activities can produce anxiety because of the ambiguity of cross-national situations and the

(continued)

GLOBAL BUSINESS LEADER
ATTRIBUTES (CONT'D)

complexity embedded in most multicultural activities. These ambiguities can range from not knowing another country's business practices to not understanding how to negotiate effectively. For example, when there is a language difference and leaders are unable to express their thoughts clearly, they can feel frustrated and embarrassed. In other cases, leaders may not have their desired outcomes when engaging in familiar leadership behaviors (e.g., not receiving a completed work product by the deadline or not receiving feedback from subordinates despite the leader's request). Emotional stability is a universal adaptive mechanism that enables people to cope with stress in their environment.

Even people who have normal stability find themselves pushed to their limits when they engage in some global leadership activities. Most successful global business leaders are very even-tempered, calm, and emotionally resilient. People with high degrees of emotional resiliency are able to adjust their behaviors without becoming overly stressed, embarrassed, or frustrated.

- *Ability to form relationships.* People who are more sociable tend to be more successful as global leaders, especially if they know the culturally appropriate behaviors for developing interpersonal professional relationships. Social people, those most able to form positive interpersonal relationships, are more likely to learn from their environment through the people with whom they interact. This exposure makes them more comfortable with the culture, better adjusted to the nuances of work life, and more satisfied, and this ultimately affects their success at work. (As you learned in Chapter 6, the ability to form relationships is often a requirement for doing business.)

Related to sociability is extroversion. People who possess a more extroverted personality tend to have the ability or desire to establish interpersonal relationships. In light of the many uncertainties of the multicultural context, global leaders must have a social orientation and a desire to communicate with people from many cultures to learn how to be most effective in those cultures. They are able to build their global network of trusted colleagues and business associates and put more energy into maintaining those relationships and building a support system that spans boundaries.

DEFINITIONS FOR THIS CHAPTER

360-degree feedback: Performance appraisal feedback that comes from above, below, and around the employee. In other words, it comes from the supervisor, the subordinates, and peers. Typically the individual also will rate his or her own performance.

Lessons Learned to Develop Your Cultural Skills

- How to hire for excellence with a global mindset
- Training for different cultural learning styles
- How to enhance performance
- Developing global leadership skills

Questions to Ponder

1. You're presenting a program regarding a rollout of a new production process. Your audience is multicultural, including Latin Americans, Africans, and Asians. How might you approach the session?
   Directions: Go to http://book.culturewizard.com and join the discussion.

2. Your company believes that 360-degree feedback is very valuable. Could you introduce it to your Japanese division?
   Directions: Go to http://book.culturewizard.com and join the discussion.

What Do You Think?

You have had your own experiences. Share them. Go to http://book.culturewizard.com and join the discussion.

Notes

[1] Jeffrey Immelt, "Perspectives: In Search of Global Leaders," *Harvard Business Review*, http://harvardbusinessonline.hbsp.harvard.edu/hbsp/hbr/articles/article.jsp?articleID=R0308B&ml_action=get-article&print=true&ml_issueid=null.

[2] Geremie Sawadogo, "Training for the African Mind," *International Journal of Intercultural Relations* 19(2), 1995, pp. 281–293.

[3] Ibid.

[4] John F. Kikoski, "Effective Communication in the Performance Appraisal Interview: Face-to-Face Communication for Public Managers in the Culturally Diverse Workplace," *Public Personnel Management* 28, 1999, p. 491.

[5] Paula Caligiuri, Ph.D., director, Center for Human Resource Strategy, Rutgers University School of Management and Labor Relations. Creator of SAGE (self-assessment for global effectiveness) and SAGE for global business leaders.

[6] SAGE for global business leaders on CultureWizard Web site, created by Paula Caligiuri, 2008.

[7] Ibid, edited for use in this text.

CHAPTER 14

Women Crossing Cultures

What you'll learn in this chapter:

- Unique Challenges Women Face

- The Path Isn't Always Smooth

- Women in Hierarchical Cultures Must Work Harder to Achieve Credibility

- Women Can Be Successful in Muslim Countries

- Women May Face Unwanted Attention Because of Their Gender

- Women Face Greater Security Issues

- Women Face a Challenge with Alcoholic Beverages

- Expatriate Women Are More Visible

Unique Challenges Women Face

Carolyn Gould scours the globe as a principal at Pricewaterhouse-Coopers LLC. She's been consulting internationally in human resources services for over 20 years. She's seen it all and views her experiences as a woman as simply part of the panoply of experiences she has. In other words, her gender is just part of the multicultural diversity with which she and her colleagues interact.

Carolyn is just one of the many successful global women executives and managers who are dynamic, strong individuals, working hard and finding creative alternatives to cultural barriers they may encounter. In some cases, they've done so extraordinarily well, and they view their gender as an advantage.

In some ways, women may be more apt to develop strong relationships. They may also be more unfamiliar to their global colleagues (who may be more accustomed to dealing with men), and may benefit as a result. It's what Nancy J. Adler of McGill University[1] referred to several years ago as, "the Gaijin syndrome." In her terms, foreign businesswomen may be seen as "foreigners" first, who are governed by different codes of conduct than are local women. As business travelers or expat managers, women like Carolyn also know that it is crucial to establish credibility and authority (based on skills and expertise), and to do so, they must be culturally aware and capable.

"I think it may be even more important that a women understand the culture of a country before she goes," says Carolyn. "In some places in the world, women may not be on equal footing with their male colleagues, and they need to understand how to work within that culture and context." It could be said that while intercultural skills are important for everyone, they may be particularly crucial for women because they often confront taboos, prejudices, and particularly restrictive stereotypes in many societies that are still male-dominated.

A Chinese saying is that women hold up half the sky. Statistics show that the number of women business travelers and expats is increasing. The *International Herald Tribune*[2] reports that 40 percent of all business travelers are female. A Mercer survey of more than 100 multinational companies, with 17,000 expatriates, found that there are 16 times more females on assignment than there were in 2001.[3] The GMAC 2008 Global Relocation Trends Survey found that 19 percent of the expats were women.

As the number of women working internationally increases, they often face unique challenges because of their gender. This means that it is more important for them to understand culture and prepare themselves for working in an environment where the rules of accepted behavior may be different.

The Path Isn't Always Smooth

Carrie Shearer, currently content director for the author's firm, RW[3], is a veteran international business traveler and expatriate. By her own admission, her path was not always smooth: "Every trip I made and every assignment taught me how important it is to understand the local culture, especially the way they view women." She faced several cultural and gender challenges on a business trip to Egypt with Caltex Petroleum.

"Muslim countries can be emotionally draining because you have to be so conscious of not offending people. You're in a culture where the rules governing appropriate behavior for women are radically different from what you experience at home. Consequently, you're always operating outside your comfort zone," she said.

Egyptian women are protected by their male relations. They don't go out unescorted and aren't spoken to by men outside the family unless they have been formally introduced and are in the presence of an older, preferably male relative. Since Carrie had worked in the Middle East for years, she was not surprised when the Egyptian office assigned someone to take her to dinner each night, since it would have been unthinkable for a respectable woman to go to a restaurant alone. The office was protecting her. By Egyptian custom, the dinners were scheduled late in the evening, generally between 9:30 and 10:00 p.m. This would have been fine if Carrie could have gone home from the office and taken a nap before dinner, as her dinner companions had been able to do.

Egyptians are proud of their cultural heritage and want to share it with visitors. The local office organized sightseeing tours each afternoon and each weekend sent Carrie to visit other sights with the wife of the country manager. Although she wanted to turn down trips to museums and weekend jaunts to Luxor and Aswan, the savvy business professional understood that that would insult the Egyptians who were being gracious hosts, a prized cultural value. If she had been male, the company would have arranged weekend group tours, but because she was a woman, the wife of a senior executive had to accompany her and the private tour guide. By traveling with a private tour guide, both women were afforded status because it demonstrated that they were under someone's care and protection.

At the end of three weeks Carrie was exhausted. The office staff had left her at the door to the terminal since only ticketed passengers were allowed inside. Carrie searched for the premium-class check-in counter and waited in line. As she looked around, she quickly noticed she was the only woman who was not accompanied by a man. When her suitcase was put on the scale, the clerk informed her that it was overweight. She leaned over to check the weight, and he quickly removed her suitcase from the scale.

She knew that her suitcase was within the limit. If she had been at home, she would have asked for the supervisor and requested that another scale be used. "I was a woman alone: I had no voice and no one to protect me," she explained. In essence, she had no status. Seeing a credit card machine, she took her company card from her wallet.

The man shook his head and explained that there was no paper for the machine. "The situation was clear. If I wanted to get on my flight, I'd have to pay *baksheesh*. One hundred dollars seemed pretty steep, but I had no idea what would happen if I made a scene. More importantly, I didn't want to find out." She opened her wallet and gave the clerk the money.

This story shows the importance of understanding both the culture and the way women are viewed within the culture. Although it is important for any foreigner to understand the culture, it is especially important for women, who often face prejudices or restrictions that are based on their gender. While a male expatriate might have been asked to pay *baksheesh*, he would have had sufficient status to challenge the situation, whereas a woman alone had no status.

Women in Hierarchical Cultures Must Work Harder to Achieve Credibility

In some hierarchical cultures in which age equals status, younger women often have to prove their credibility. When Carrie made her first visit to Indonesia, she traveled with a male colleague who was retiring and turning over the liaison with the Indonesian operation to her. Although her company did not offer cross-cultural training, Carrie had read extensively about the Indonesian culture. She knew they respected age and position, neither of which she had. The only Indonesian women working in the operation were in secretarial or support positions.

When the Indonesian staff members had questions, they addressed them to the male colleague. If he wasn't available, they wouldn't discuss the problem with Carrie. After a week, she cornered her colleague over dinner and asked for his help. She suggested that he think of her as his legacy. He had spent 30 years working with the Indonesians, and they respected him. If he treated her as a knowledgeable expert despite her age and gender, the local staff would follow his lead. They agreed that during meetings he would refer certain questions to her and stress her academic credentials and background. The fact that she was a graduate of Cornell would let the local staff see her as someone with status even though she was not a gray-haired male.

The next year, when she was assigned to Indonesia, Carrie spent the first three months observing how things were done. When she saw something she did not understand, she made a note and put it in a file folder she labeled the Tomorrow file.

The night Carrie took the file home, she discarded all but 10 percent of the notes. She studied the remaining ones and then worked out how best to approach the Indonesian staff. "By then, my coworkers and I had developed a relationship, and I'd earned the right to make suggestions. Even then, diplomacy was the order of the day. Things worked better if I approached an issue by saying, 'Have you ever considered?' rather than telling them there was a better way. The three months had taught me how sensitive Indonesians were to criticism, even when it's only implied. Had I tried to insert my opinion when I arrived, I'd have been cut off and treated as if I didn't exist," she explained.

Helena Deal, a British expatriate in her middle thirties, has worked internationally in the petroleum industry for the last 10 years in Thailand, Japan, and Malaysia. "The best thing I have found is that you have to demonstrate that you can deliver consistently and over a sustained period of time. I have found people to be much more accepting of a woman from outside if they see you to be a harder worker, competent at the job, do what you say you will do, and add value. Once you have done this, it also helps if you can demonstrate that you will help them achieve more and enable them to grow and develop. Regardless of the culture, I have found these to be the principles by which I have operated," she said.

Young women must learn to highlight any part of their background that allows the local staff to give them status. Attending a prestigious university often helps (Helena went to the London School of Economics), as does previous international experience or proven success dealing with a similar problem. By offering something tangible that can offset their age, women can gain credibility and status. It may take time and they may have to be patient, but over time they will be accepted.

In some cultures, however, such as in Japan, being a foreigner is the foremost difference, and everything else is secondary. Ruth Stevens, a veteran marketer whose work has taken her around the globe, concurs: "When I was in Japan, I was a foreigner. The fact that I was also a tall woman was a rounding error; it wasn't an issue."

Women Can Be Successful in Muslim Countries

When working in Muslim countries, women must be careful about the way they dress; they must understand the role gender plays in the culture. The status of women changes with each country in the Middle East, along with what is culturally acceptable behavior. Women can be effective if they assert their authority in a subtle and nonthreatening manner. The local staff generally accepts the idea that the woman must be an expert for the company to have sent her rather than a man. At the same time, they have clear cultural biases that must be handled diplomatically.

Relationships are crucial when one is conducting business in the Middle East. Since entertaining often involves men only, women must develop their relationships in the office. They will not have a chance to do that in social situations. Thus, it is vital that they do all they can to develop a rapport.

When she was on a short assignment to Bahrain, Carrie was told that there were no extra cars in the pool. Since every expat in the compound worked at the refinery, it was easy to get a ride to and from the office. After the first weekend, when it felt like the walls of her room were closing in on her, she knew she had to do something. She approached the managing director and suggested that the problem was that the Muslim staff members were uncomfortable giving a company car to her and that it might be easier to rent a car for her from an agency in Manama. The result was that she got the car she needed for her independence, and everyone retained face. Like most Muslim countries, Bahrain relies on relationships. If Carrie had made an issue of the car, she would have been given one but would have destroyed her chance of a developing a relationship.

On a business trip to Bahrain, Jan Sullivan-Chalmers, who worked in the travel services industry, was told to wait in a chair to the side when clearing customs. She was carrying a bottle of gin for a friend and thought that might be the reason. By the time everyone on her flight had been through customs, several men were waiting with her. Since flights to Bahrain arrive late in the evening, travelers are tired, jet-lagged, and eager to get to their hotel rooms. When the customs official came over to where the foreigners were sitting, he dealt with the men first even though Jan had been waiting the longest. Understanding that women, especially women traveling alone, are considered less important than men, she did not make an issue or demand her proper spot in the queue. When the man looked at her passport again, he pointed out that her visa had expired the day before. There was no problem, and a new one was issued quickly.

Since Jan was a veteran traveler as well as an expat, she understood that, as a guest in a foreign country, she had to abide by the local rules for appropriate behavior. By waiting patiently, she demonstrated that she understood the local culture.

Since family is important to Muslims, it is a good idea to demonstrate that you have strong family ties. Women should carry photos of their families. If they don't have children, photos of nieces and nephews prove that they have strong ties to their families. This is a plus in a culture in which family and business are linked.

Women May Face Unwanted Attention Because of Their Gender

It's important for women to know before arriving if they are going to a country where machismo is prevalent. If that is the case, businessmen may believe that making comments about what a woman is wearing or her hairstyle is a sincere form of flattery. This can be disconcerting to some women even when they are aware of it in advance.

Jacqueline Barr spent a summer in Italy and Spain. "You'd feel men's eyes on you as you walked down the street. That was fine. I'm not sure I'd have been as happy if they made catcalls," she said.

Women working in Latin American or Mediterranean countries should know that they may face comments in the office that would be unthinkable at home. If a woman knows in advance that this may happen, she can prepare responses to defuse the situation. It's sometimes acceptable, depending upon your relationship, to use gentle humor as a way to relieve any tension. However, there may be situations where that doesn't work. Over the years, Carolyn has witnessed situations that became tense. "I think if someone kept talking to me or treating me in a way I felt uncomfortable with—different culture or not—I would figure out a way to talk about the behavior.

"Just as I feel that on the one-hand you need to be sensitive to others culture and not alienate everybody by forcing your own values, others also need to respect your values." She suggests first talking with a colleague that you trust from the other culture to find out how best to approach the individual so as to make the point but to allow the other person to maintain *face*.

Susie Inwood of BG International handles expatriate matters and is a frequent business traveler who has spent time in these countries. She isn't certain that you ever get comfortable with the comments, but you learn to accept them. Knowing that this will be an issue can help prepare you. You may never be able to flirt in the office the way local women do, but expat women can learn to smile at a comment about their dress and hairstyle and accept it as a cultural nuance. And, don't be surprised if a male colleague puts his hand on you or makes an otherwise unwanted advance. Many women experience that situation. In such instances, a firm "no" is usually sufficient to end the problem.

Women Face Greater Security Issues

When Jan worked in England, she made twice-monthly business trips to Rome. During those trips, she frequented the same restaurant regularly. One evening, the waiter came over and told her that when a gentleman had asked to buy her a drink, the waiter had told him that she wouldn't be interested. True, Italian culture reveres women, because she was a regular customer, and the Italian waiter afforded her the same protection he would have offered a female relative.

Valerie Greenly, director of global client services of RW³ LLC reported an experience with the Sheraton Hotel in Chennai. When she checked in, she received a letter from the hotel's general manager. It said that he realized she was a woman traveling alone and that the hotel would offer security for screening phone calls so that she didn't get inappropriate calls. Valerie had not known this was an issue in India until it happened to her later in New Delhi. Again, the practice of protecting women was extended to the expat.

Many hotels are attempting to woo the increasing number of women business travelers by offering secure floors for women only, lighter meals in their restaurants and on room service menus, and providing special services and amenities.[4]

When Bev Belisle, a Canadian expatriate, was on a business trip to Peru, she was provided with a car and driver and a security guard to protect her. She always felt scrutinized, and that made her uncomfortable. It was obvious that she traveled with a guard, and that made her stand out.

Susie Inwood remembers a trip to Rio de Janeiro. After a day of meetings, she wanted to go for a walk before dinner. The cultural briefing she had received before leaving England had discussed the frequent robberies of tourists and ways to avoid being targeted. She removed her jewelry, did not take a purse, and did not carry a map. "It was important that I not call attention to myself," she explained.

In some countries, expat women stand out. Smart women quickly learn to blend in with the local culture by dressing more conservatively and not wearing a great deal of jewelry. Others learn to wear dark sunglasses in public so that no one can make eye contact with them. Some go as far as to wear headphones and listen to music so that they don't hear the comments.

Women Face a Challenge with Alcoholic Beverages

There are some cultures in which drinking is an integral part of doing business. Teetotalers face the fewest problems since most cultures understand that some people simply don't imbibe. How do other women handle the situation? Some, like Brenda, an American expatriate in Hong Kong for a life insurance company, do what they would at home: "I'm not a drinker, so when dinner was over, I'd say, "I enjoyed myself," and not go to a bar, even if everyone else was."

In some cultures, such as Japan and Korea, drinking is expected but women are excluded. How do women handle this? Ruth said, "I was happy I wasn't asked to go out drinking into the early morning hours. I was rested in the morning." Carla was equally philosophical: "Over time I realized it was preferable to the lads playing golf after a meeting. Since drinking was their primary focus, they weren't discussing business, which they often did at sports."

Expatriate Women Are More Visible

Since they are rarities in many cultures and stand out, expat women can have an easier time gaining access to higher-level executives. "At company functions, our local managing director in Indonesia, an American expat, would seek me out," Carrie claimed. "My boss, who was Indonesian, would probably have mumbled incoherently if the doctor asked him a question, because it was unthinkable in their hierarchical culture for the top man to speak with a manager." Having the ear of someone can be enticing, but it is a card successful women learn not to play unless it is absolutely necessary. "No matter what I was asked, I said things were great. Then I sought out my Indonesian boss and told him what I had been asked and what I said," Carrie said.

Carrie understood that in a culture that relies on relationships, it was imperative that her boss not think that she was going over his head or reporting on him: "My local boss was skeptical the first time. But when nothing untoward happened to him at the office on Monday, he believed me. Later, he tried to use my 'relationship' with the doctor to get me to feed him information. I said no, and we had a tense couple of days."

This heightened visibility can be a double-edged sword. Since they are more easily remembered, women business travelers often discover that people they've met once will come up to them and start talking the next time they visit the same company. Noreen, an Australian regional director for the Pacific Rim, handles this by keeping extensive notes on everyone she meets during a trip. If it is permissible in the culture, she takes digital photos of the people she deals with. Before returning to the country, she reviews the pictures and makes notes so that she can greet everyone with a personal comment or question.

In summary, women face unique challenges when traveling or working globally. It is important to understand both the culture you're going into and that culture's view of women. Armed with this knowledge, women managers can avoid behaviors that could be misinterpreted or perceived as indicators of low status. Learning as much as you can about the culture before arriving prepares you to be able to respond appropriately to gender-biased behavior. Table 14.1 provides tips for women.

TABLE 14-1   TIPS FOR WOMEN

General Tips

- Learn what you can about the culture before arriving.
- Network with other women who have been there.
- Follow the lead of local women and dress accordingly.
- In less developed countries, do not wear excessive jewelry or display wealth.
- Plan ways to deal with situations before they occur.

Business Tips

- Present yourself as sincere, confident, and professional.
- Act in a reserved manner with business colleagues. Being overly friendly can be misinterpreted.
- If possible, be introduced by a higher-ranking person who knows the people with whom you will be dealing. The person handling the introduction can explain your qualifications in a way you could not.

If There Is Culturally Based Sexism

- Expect to be asked questions about your marital status and whether you have children.
- Prepare stock answers in advance so that you can handle the questions with grace and aplomb.
- In macho cultures, accept that it may be culturally insensitive to offer to pay for drinks or a meal.
- If it is important that your company play host, make payment arrangements in advance.
- Invite the spouse of a male colleague to join you for dinner.

If the Culture Is More Hierarchical

- Ensure that your business card title says manager or a higher title even if this is not your title at home.
- Find a way to introduce your education and qualifications into the conversation or send a business bio in advance.
- Demonstrate respect for the hierarchy.

Some of the same traits once thought to preclude women from international assignment may in fact be their greatest strengths. Women are generally more inclusive and adept at developing and maintaining personal relationships. They also pay greater attention to nonverbal clues and are sensitive to the points of view of others.

Questions to Ponder

1. Women who are technical experts face fewer challenges being credible in hierarchical cultures than do nontechnical businesswomen. How can women develop credibility in relationship-driven cultures? Why do you think this is happening?
   Directions: Go to http://book.culturewizard.com and join the discussion.

2. Women are often more skilled at mirroring the behavior of a culture than are men. What behaviors have you learned to mirror in order to get the results you want?
   Directions: Go to http://book.culturewizard.com and join the discussion.

What Do You Think?

You have your own experiences. Share them. Go to http://book .culurewizard.com and join the discussion.

Notes

[1] http://www.iht.com/articles/2007/04/19/travel/trfreq20.php; Nancy J. Adler, "Pacific Basin Managers: A Gaijin, Not a Woman," *Human Resource Management* 26, 1987, pp. 169–192. (For additional reading on this topic see Nancy Adler and Dafna Izraeli, *Competitive Frontiers: Women Managers in a Global Economy*, Blackwell Business Press, 1994).

2 http://www.management-issues.com/2006/10/12/research/big-rise-in-number-of-female-expats.asp.

3 http://www.gmacglobalrelocation.com/insight_support/grts/2008_GRTS.pdf.

4 http://www.4hoteliers.com/4hots_nshw.php?mwi=3228.

Creating Cultural Competence: The International Assignee Experience

What you'll learn in this chapter:

- Colgate-Palmolive: The Corporation with Global DNA

- Making a Global Mindset Operational

- The Global Mindset in Marketing

- International Assignments Lead to Cultural Wisdom

- The Expatriate Adjustment Cycle, or Culture Shock

- Culture Shock Helps Build Your Skills

Colgate-Palmolive: The Corporation with Global DNA

Some twenty-first-century companies were launched as international firms, with a multicultural workforce and global ideas. Almost two centuries ago, the Colgate-Palmolive Company, one of today's most culturally astute global powerhouses, began as a quintessentially American company. Selling soaps and detergents, toothpaste and toothbrushes, deodorants and specialty pet food, Colgate had revenues of $13.8 billion in 2007, with only 20 percent coming from North America.[1]

Colgate-Palmolive Company lives or dies by how well it intuits and predicts the needs, wishes, and aspirations of its diverse consumer base in over 200 countries. Understanding cultural behavior is at the very core of the company. To create and market products, the people at Colgate who make decisions need to know that Latin Americans prefer stronger flavors and fragrances than do North Americans, Europeans use cold water to wash their clothes, and consumers in rural Asia prefer to buy small sizes of products such as shampoo, because they cannot afford more. They need to observe those preferences and creatively apply them to shape other global consumer buying habits and develop manufacturing and distribution efficiencies.

Moreover, if the company wants to attract and retain the best talent—both international and local—its management must know what will entice workers to apply for jobs and what will make employees remain with the company. The answers may be as commonplace as compensation schemes or as unusual as providing private buses so that workers from areas with poor infrastructure have a way to get to work.

Consequently, cultural understanding is woven into the DNA of the organization, and a global mindset permeates the way the employees think and interact. Warren Heaps is currently a partner with the Birches Group, a human resources consulting firm headquartered in New York, and previously was the international assignment manager at Colgate.

Heaps said, "The company hires from everywhere in the world; it moves people everywhere around the world, and we do become 'homogeneously' global. We borrow from each other's cultures." Warren should know. He was the international assignment manager for 10 years and spent 6 years in other international HR positions with Colgate.

It goes without saying that this global mindset didn't happen by itself. Many people credit the visionary strategic thinking of Reuben Mark, chief executive officer of Colgate-Palmolive from 1984 to July 2007. His quest was to have an organization in which global thinking would be pervasive and the best talent from all over the world would be available. There was a lot of work to do if Mark was going to enable Colgate to create a team of leaders who would develop and implement global standards and criteria for excellence that would catapult the company into the ranks of global best practices.

"Colgate people around the world form a similar culture even though we come from everywhere around the word. It permeates the way we interact with each other and feeds into Colgate's culture as a global company," said Philip Durocher, head of long-term innovation for oral care. "There is actually a general belief that by tapping into the international perspectives of the individuals we meet from so many backgrounds, we'll get the best solutions."

That happens quite frequently through the international assignment process and succession planning.[2] "Someone who is identified as a high potential must complete their full development cycle by working in a developing country and one that's already developed. They have to get multiple categories in international business," explained Warren, who was responsible for hundreds of expatriate assignments during his tenure. Philip, for example, was born a Canadian and worked for Colgate in Switzerland, the United States, Mexico, and France.

The origins of Colgate-Palmolive go back about 200 years when William Colgate started his soap and candle business in New York City in 1806. In 1864, the company that would become Palmolive was started in Milwaukee, Wisconsin, and the two merged in 1928. In 1914,

Colgate launched its first subsidiary in Canada, and it expanded into Europe, Asia, Latin America, and Africa in the 1920s. Today it sells products in over 200 countries.

International assignments are at its core. The company actually guides its employees through different experiences: operations, strategy, and then overseas and domestic. "There are few boomerang assignments," Warren explained. "They keep you moving and keep you learning and expanding."

Making a Global Mindset Operational

Perhaps the best example of how the vision permeates the company is its system for international assignments. In many companies an expatriate assignment is a "boomerang" experience. People are sent out and back with a specific function in mind for their assignment. They are sent out to introduce a new technology, find a local replacement, or fill a position for which there is no local person available; an expatriate assignment may serve as an investment in which a high-potential individual gains the requisite international experience. Colgate employees go on a global track, moving from one location to another to get both multicultural experience and multifunctional business experience. They'll go from a manufacturing plant in Brazil to one in Russia. The international employee grows both culturally and functionally as a result of that global track.

Of course, Colgate isn't the only company that follows this idea. Companies such as HSBC Bank and Shell Oil use global career tracks. However, what makes the Colgate experience unique is that unlike global organizations that haven't figured out how to enable the returning employees to enrich the organization with their global experience, at Colgate it is the essence of the business.

"The expat assignments at Colgate were so successful because they were critical to the core strategy of the organization. They were vital to appreciating how local markets used and valued Colgate products,"

Heaps said. "In other words, the expats were not only fulfilling their job functions but maintaining the information flow throughout the company."

One HR example would be the way the company sets out to develop compensation and bonus plans. Once you have a deep understanding of the cultures your employees come from, you ask smarter questions; for example, should the company develop bonus plans that are applicable worldwide, or should salary grades and bonus plans be tailored to the local marketplace? You develop an understanding of the compensation and reward plans that are effective in local cultures. For example, if you're developing a compensation plan in a group-oriented culture, you have to know if you should reward the head of the group with a bonus or only the people involved in the customer service portion or the entire team. Which approach will best achieve what the plan is intended to accomplish?

The Global Mindset in Marketing

Philip Durocher has been with Colgate for over 17 years, during which time he worked in a number of locations including Canada and Europe as well as in New York where he is head of oral care long term innovation. "We see similarities rather than difference," he said.

To do that, he refers to the strong Colgate corporate culture that includes the way people do PowerPoint presentations all the way through to their fact-based decision making.

One of Philip's assignments was with the global toothbrush group. He was charged with introducing a $3 toothbrush to the Brazilian market. At that time, the typical toothbrush was selling in Brazil for 50 cents, and although the $3 toothbrush was significantly better, everyone feared that its price point would take it out of the market. Philip and the sales team were aware that there was a wealthier class in Brazil that would pay for the more expensive toothbrush. They also knew that if they marketed the product to that class, it could become an aspirational product for the wider Brazilian marketplace. Thus, they knew there was a market.

Colgate developed a regional campaign as an upscale, much improved "high-class" product by using the marketing vehicles that wealthier Brazilians read and watch. It took a long time and a lot of convincing, even within his own sales force, before they believed it could work. To the doubters' surprise, the new toothbrush captured a 10 percent market share within an 18-month time frame.

Another assignment of Philip's was to help to grow Russia's toothbrush business, which also demonstrates his cultural dexterity as well as Colgate's dedication to learning about what its diverse consumers need. The toothbrush group wanted to introduce a new toothbrush into Russia. The question was: Would the Russians buy an improved but more expensive toothbrush? Again, the team members looked at the Russian cultural environment and quickly realized that the aspirational strategy that had been used so effectively in Brazil would not work in Russia.

What their culturally based market research told them was that selling to Russians required a fact-based approach. The company proceeded to launch a consumer research campaign designed to demonstrate how the new toothbrush was a significant improvement over the current ones. After seeing the consumer data, the Russians accepted the fact that this was an improvement and became ambassadors for the product.

From a succession planning perspective, people who are identified as having high potential need to go on multiple international assignments in both developing and developed countries. They need to get multiple experiences in positions in which they manage people and positions in which they don't have to directly manage people but have to influence them remotely. There is a series of sequential steps for each area of the company to groom leaders who can thrive in a global environment. It's not just a matter of sending Americans to London for some international exposure. Said H. R. consultant Heaps, "You need to go to some dusty places too and understand what you're observing and learning."[3]

Understanding culture enabled the company not only to address the needs of its employees and customers effectively but also to develop products and market its products effectively in different countries. For Colgate's global reach to become pervasive, the company needed to integrate a global mindset and global skills into every part of its business operations. Whether you're in product development or sales and marketing, whether you work in one of the labs or in a factory, the notion of Colgate's global marketplace never leaves your consciousness. The international assignees coming and going around the world—whether on short-term or long-term assignments—nourish the company's DNA.

International Assignments Lead to Cultural Wisdom

RW[3] LLC and ORC Worldwide conducted a survey in 2008 called "The Importance of Cultural Skills in Senior Managers." Over 100 companies responded. According to the survey, most global managers gained international experience through an expat assignment. This implies that international assignments are a critical way to attain the necessary global exposure that is so important for leadership.

What makes these assignments such a valuable experience? Of course, living and working in other cultures does, but perhaps the phenomenon we call culture shock helps subconsciously to build an appreciation of culture that will become second nature.

Here's what happens during culture shock. After getting through the honeymoon stage (see page 322) and the excitement of being in a foreign country and living in it for a while, the constant exposure to slightly different mores, behaviors, and values tends to wear people out. They get somewhat depressed from the process of finding that they have to do things a little differently everywhere. You have to speak differently, act differently, and talk differently. You have to maintain a consciousness that the way people behave here is a little different from the way they behave at home. As opposed to finding the differences cute and exciting during the early stages, the expatriates tend to get depressed. Let's look at the expatriate adjustment cycle more closely.

The Expatriate Adjustment Cycle, or Culture Shock[4]

An international transfer is a major life event that presents the same mix of excitement and stress, exhilaration and exhaustion, that you may face during other periods of drastic change. It can take a toll physically, emotionally, and psychologically, and it usually does. Research and experience have shown a typical pattern of ups and downs that affects most expatriates. We call this the *expatriate adjustment cycle*. It starts when you and your family leave home and ends with your eventual repatriation.

The stages in the first half of this cycle are preparation, honeymoon, culture shock, and adaptation. Since the assignment isn't complete until you're back home again, the cycle comes full circle with repatriation, which is when you can experience reverse culture shock. You may not experience all these stages in the same order or in the way we present them here—people are different—but these are fairly common events, and it's likely you'll experience them to some degree. If you're aware of them, you can be proactive and find ways to smooth the transition. It's important to remember that it's not just you who will be affected by the move. All the family members who go with you will encounter unique challenges at different times. Children will look at the experience differently from the way adults do. The partner with a job may not face the same issues as the partner focused on setting up a household.

Preparation

This is a time of mixed emotions. You're excited about your new life, but at the same time you have to deal with leaving friends and family behind, and you're probably apprehensive about living and working in a different culture. If you're the expat employee, you find yourself pulled in different directions, forced to make decisions about the new job while you're still wrapping up the loose ends in your current position. If you have to move quickly, your family may be split between those who've gone ahead and those left behind to handle the move.

Don't let the logistics overwhelm you. During this exciting and stressful time, try to focus on the positives, not just the work you need to accomplish to move. Get everyone involved in planning the move. Set regular family discussion times to talk about your feelings and report back on research and planning. It's vital that you keep your family talking. This is true throughout the assignment. Each family member has feelings about the relocation, and it's important to identify and address the concerns.

Honeymoon

You're excited by the possibilities that await you. The environment around you is exhilarating. There's a whole new world to explore just outside your door. Everybody is welcoming and pleasant. People make you feel special. Even if the customs and protocol take a little getting used to, it's all very interesting and provides an opportunity to apply what you've learned about the culture.

These positive feelings of excitement and discovery can last several weeks. You're too busy getting to know your new life to think about what you miss from your old life. Different ways of doing things are enchanting and exotic. You haven't had time to find them frustrating. Indeed, you begin to think that all the stories you've heard about culture shock and depression were exaggerations. That's clearly not going to happen to you!

The next stage in the expatriate adjustment cycle is culture shock, and you'll learn all about it. The thing to know now is that this is the time to prepare for it. Focus on resting, regrouping, and building a support system of local friends and activities. One of the most important things you can do is set some goals for your assignment. Create a wish list: Where do you want to go? What do you want to see? What do you want to learn before it's time to go home? If you use your positive energy in the honeymoon stage to get ready, you'll minimize the impact of the next stage and get into a routine.

Culture Shock

All of a sudden you're tired of trying so hard. Why does everything have to be so different and take so much effort? Culture shock has hit you. Everyone can tolerate cultural differences for a few weeks—the length of an extended vacation—and psychologically, that's what you've done so far. But now weeks of unfamiliar stimuli begin to get under your skin. Culture shock stings when you realize that you're going be there a while and that all those differences you've been tolerating because they were so fascinating and exotic are now part of your daily life. You're not going home; this *is* your home.

This is the hardest part of the adjustment cycle. It may result in homesickness and depression. It could be manifested in physical ways, with symptoms of stress such as headaches, lack of energy, and digestive problems. What makes culture shock particularly hard is that it doesn't affect you alone. Don't be surprised if your partner or children are also irritable and unhappy. They could be dealing with their own disillusionment with their new surroundings. It takes all your coping skills to navigate these murky waters. What should you do?

First, expect culture shock and recognize it for what it is whether you get it in month one or month six or both. Remind yourself that you're not alone. It's a common experience in the life of an expatri-ate, as you will discover by talking with others. Second, expect culture shock to end. Experience shows that this phase is temporary. Generally, it lasts only a few weeks, although every individual's experience is different. Thus, you can look forward to getting past it. That's not to say that certain aspects of your new home won't continue to present challenges, but with time you should find yourself better equipped to deal with them. Third and most important, you can prepare for culture shock. It's very much a reaction—sometimes an overreaction—to the "romance" of the honeymoon stage. That's why we suggest that you use the honeymoon stage to get ready for the rest of your time abroad.

For example, if you alleviate stress by going to a gym, it's good to have joined one before culture shock sets in. You may not have the motivation to find one afterward. Because of the groundwork you laid during the honeymoon, you now have a routine, a set of goals, and a whole list of planned activities ready and waiting to carry you through this difficult time.

Take good care of your support system. Who are the people you turn to when you're unhappy? If you've moved with family members, you have a built-in network. However, you may have a group of people all facing culture shock at the same time and feeling more in need of support than being supportive. By understanding the root causes of cultural differences, you're already prepared to face the strangeness of your new surroundings. Continue to do research, learn the language, and enjoy your new friends. These activities will help you build cultural fluency. See if you can identify a "cultural mentor": either a local national or a fellow expatriate who can interpret some of the cultural nuances for you. That extra knowledge will make things seem less strange and speed your passage through the culture shock phase.

Here are two things to avoid. First, don't retreat into an expatriate bubble. By all means, compare notes with your fellow expatriates, especially those from your home country. Let them know how you feel and listen to their suggestions for ways to cope. But avoid withdrawing completely from the culture around you. Don't spend all your time with expatriates, using their company as a buffer between you and the world outside your door. Certainly don't fall into the habit of disparaging what you see around you. This will only delay your recovery from culture shock. Second, don't go home—to your old home, that is—even for a short visit. A trip back to your home country while you're in the culture shock phase will unsettle you and may send you back to square one. This may sound discouraging, but if you prepare well and hold onto the knowledge that culture shock is normal and transient, you'll soon reach the next phase of the adjustment cycle.

Adaptation

The adaptation phase lasts for the entire length of your stay in the host country. You'll continue to learn and continue to grow, and by the time you return home you will be proficient, maybe even expert, at living in the host country. In cultural terms, you'll become bilingual.

One day culture shock will abate. You won't forget that much of the world around you is different from your home country, but the differences will stop irritating you, and you will feel less frustrated and isolated. Even if you still miss your favorite foods or newspapers, you can put up with the substitutes you've found. You're facing your everyday activities with growing expertise. You realize you can accept different outlooks and see their merits even if you never will adopt the local values.

Adaptation is a continuing process. It begins as you feel a measure of confidence in your abilities to live and work in the new culture. There may still be puzzles and pitfalls, but you're now certain you can continue. You may even admit to yourself that you prefer some of the new ways of doing things to your old, ingrained habits. However, beware of the occasional relapse into culture shock, especially after a trip home or a particularly challenging event. These relapses will be minor, but they mean you shouldn't abandon your coping strategies the moment you reach the adaptation stage.

Repatriation

The second half of the cycle—repatriation—is in many ways a mirror image of the first. This means that you should remember the lessons and coping strategies you've just learned so that you can apply them again later. It's also helpful to remember that a successful repatriation depends very much on how well you and your family stay in touch with people and events back home during the first half of the adjustment cycle.

You may be surprised to discover that going home can be just as challenging as starting the assignment, perhaps even more so. Perhaps the most significant reason for the difficulty is this: It's not just your home country that has changed while you've been away; you've changed too. You now have a new perspective, and as a result, you see your home country and local community through a new set of cultural lenses. Your worldview will set you apart from those with less global experience, and for a time this will make you feel isolated and uncomfortable.

To some extent, as your repatriation date looms, your preparations for the return home are the same as those for the outward voyage, only now you're collecting e-mail addresses and saying your goodbyes to your friends in the host country. You also should accept the fact that you'll be saying goodbye to a way of life you may not be able to re-create back home. For example, while living abroad, you may have become accustomed to having household staff or easy access to social clubs. These things may be unaffordable without an expat compensation package or in a location with a higher cost of living.

The first thing you need to do is reconnect with old friends and family members you haven't seen in a while. How about a party?

Be sure to include your children's friends in your reunion plans. If you were the working partner, you're probably returning to your old company, maybe even to your old job. Reactivate your network. If you haven't done it already, identify a mentor in the organization who can brief you on the changes that have taken place.

If you accompanied your partner on the assignment, you may be looking for work now. Bear in mind that you're not the person you were when you left. Your experiences with a different culture may have changed your outlook on life, and you've undoubtedly broadened your skill base. Look for a new career, professional development, or volunteer opportunities to stay with the interests you developed overseas and use your new qualifications.

Reverse culture shock will hit you when the excitement of your homecoming dies down: You're not special anymore. Back home you're a local, just like everyone else. Your friends and family are delighted you're back, but they can hear your traveler's tales only so many times. Your skill at juggling two cultures, which you were awfully proud of, isn't needed anymore.

You're surprised at how much you have forgotten about daily life in your home country. You wonder where you will find the time to mow the lawn, do the laundry, and prepare your taxes now that you don't have someone to do those things for you. It's typical for expatriates to go through a period of alienation on their return, feeling like strangers in a not so strange land. During reverse culture shock, when the difficulties of repatriation seem to outweigh the pleasures of the assignment, it's common to wonder whether it was all worth it. The answer, of course, is a resounding yes. Your time in another country was rich and life-enhancing. You feel that life at home is different from the way it was before because *you* are different from the way you were before, and that's a powerful advantage. The way to survive reverse culture shock is to remind yourself of this.

Culture Shock Helps Build Your Skills

Integrating the idea that you have to behave differently, that you have to adjust to different cultures because people around you have different values and belief systems that generate different manners, is critical to building a global mindset. Once you integrate that and come out of culture shock, you understand that you've really got it. You've got it in an intuitive, reflexive way. It's almost integrated into your DNA. That's why an expatriate assignment is so critical to career development and to the success of management growth. You learn intuitively how to adjust to the signals you get from the culture around you and adjust your behavior to them.

Lessons Learned to Develop Your Cultural Skills

- The importance of international assignments

- How corporate values help expats do their jobs

- The expat adjustment cycle

Questions to Ponder

1. What are some of your ideas about strong leadership in the global marketplace?
   Directions: Go to http://book.culturewizard.com and join the discussion.

2. You're very happy in your new country, but you have some extra time and know that you should be preparing for the inevitable culture shock. What should you start to do?
   Directions: Go to http://book.culturewizard.com and join the discussion.

What Do You Think?

You have had your own experiences. Share them. Go to http://book
.culturewizard.com and join the discussion.

Notes

[1] Colgate-Palmolive Company 2007 annual report, available at http://investor.colgate.com/
downloads/2007AR.pdf.

[2] Charlene Solomon, "Staff Selection Impacts Global Success," *Personnel Journal* 73(1),
January 1994, pp. 88–101.

[3] For more details, see, "Colgate Palmolive: Managing International Careers," Harvard
Business School Case 9-394-184, May 24, 1994.

[4] This section was adapted from CultureWizard Expatriate Adjustment Cycle.

Further Reading and Additional Resources

Adler, Nancy J., *International Dimensions of Organizational Behavior*, Cincinnati: South-Western, 1997.

Adler, Nancy J., and Dafna N. Izraeli. *Competitive Frontiers: Women Managers in a Global Economy,* Cambridge, MA: Blackwell, 1994.

Ancona, Deborah, and Henrik Bresman. *X-Team: How to Build Teams That Lead, Innovate, and Succeed,* Cambridge, MA: Harvard Business School Press, 2007.

Austin, Clyde N., Ph.D. *Cross-Cultural Reentry: A Book of Readings*, Abilene, TX: Abilene Christian University Press, 1986.

Axtell, Roger E., *Gestures: The Do's and Taboos of Body Language around the World*, New York: John Wiley & Sons Inc., 1998.

Bartlet, Christopher A., and Sumantra Ghoshal, *Managing across Borders: The Transnational Solution,* Cambridge, MA: Harvard Business School Press, 1991.

Caligiuri, P. M., 2006, "Developing Global Leaders," *Human Resource Management Review* 16:219–228.

Caligiuri, P. M., and V. DiSanto, 2001, "Global Competence: What Is It—and Can It Be Developed through Global Assignments?" *Human Resource Planning Journal* 24(3):27–38.

Caligiuri, P. M., and M. Lazarova, "Work-Life Balance and the Effective Management of Global Assignees," refereed book chapter in S. Poelmans, ed., *Work and Family:* An *International Research Perspective*, Mahwah, NJ: Lawrence Erlbaum Associates, 2005.

Coppola, N. W., S. R. Hiltz, and N. G. Rotter, 2004, "Building Trust in Virtual Teams," *IEEE Transactions on Professional Communication*, 47:95–104.

Dalton, Maxine, Chris Ernst, Jennifer Deal, and Jean Leslie, *Success for the New Global Manager*, San Francisco: Jossey-Bass and Greensboro, NC: Center for Creative Leadership, 2002.

David, Thomas C., and Kerr Inkston, *Cultural Intelligence: People Skills for Global Business*, San Francisco: Berrett-Koehler Publishers, Inc., 2003.

Duarte, Deborah L., and Nancy Tennant Snyder, *Mastering Virtual Teams: Strategies, Tools, and Techniques That Succeed*, San Francisco: Jossey-Bass, 1999.

Ferraro, Gary P., *The Cultural Dimension of International Business*, Charlotte, NC: Pearson, 2006.

Friedman, Thomas L. *The World Is Flat: A Brief History of the Twenty-First Century*, New York: Farrar, Straus and Giroux, 2005.

Gladwell, Malcolm, *Blink: The Power of Thinking Without Thinking*, New York: Little, Brown, 2005.

Goleman, Daniel, *Emotional Intelligence: Why It Can Matter More Than IQ*, New York: Scientific American, 1994.

Hall, Edward T., *Anthropology of Everyday Life*, New York: Doubleday, 1993.

Hall, Edward T., *Dance of Life*, Garden City, NY: Doubleday, 1984.

Hall, Edward T., *The Hidden Dimension*, Garden City, NY: Doubleday, 1966.

Hall, Edward T., and Mildred Reed Hall, *Understanding Cultural Differences: Germans, French, and Americans*, Yarmouth, ME: Intercultural Press, 1990.

Hamel, Gary, and C.K. Prahalad, *Competing for the Future*, Cambridge, MA: Harvard Business School Press, 1994.

Hampden-Turner, Charles, and Fons Trompenaars, *Riding the Waves of Culture: Understanding Diversity in Global Business*, New York: McGraw-Hill, 1997.

Harrison, E. Lawrence, and Samuel P. Huntington, *Culture Matters: How Values Shape Human Progress*, New York: Basic Books, 2000.

Hofstede, Geert, *Culture's Consequences: Comparing Values, Behavior, Institutions, and Organizations Across Nations*, Thousand Oaks, CA: Sage Publications, 2001.

Hofstede, Geert, *Cultures and Organizations: Software of the Mind*, New York: McGraw Hill, 2004.

House, Robert J., Paul J. Hanges, Mansour Javidan, Peter W. Dorfman, and Vipin Gupta, *Culture, Leadership, and Organizations: The GLOBE Study of 62 Societies*, Thousand Oaks, CA: Sage Publications, 2004.

Johnston, William B., and Arnold H. Packer, *Workforce 2000: Work and Workers for the 21st Century*, Indianapolis: Hudson Institute, 1987.

Kalb, Rosalind, and Penelope Welch, *Moving Your Family Overseas,* Yarmouth, ME: Intercultural Press, 1992.

Katzenbach, Jon R., and Douglas K. Smith, "The Discipline of Teams," In *The Best of HBR*, Cambridge, MA: Harvard Business School Press, 1993.

Kayworth, T., and D. E. Leidner, "The Global Virtual Manager: A Perspective for Success," *European Management Journal*, 2000, 18: 183–194.

Kitchen, D., and D. McDougall, "Collaborative Learning on the Internet," *Journal of Educational Technology Systems*, 1999, 27: 245–258.

Kohls, Robert L., *Survival Kit for Overseas Living: For Americans Planning to Live and Work Abroad,* Yarmouth, ME: Intercultural Press, 1996.

Lane, Patty, *A Beginner's Guide to Crossing Cultures: Making Friends in a Multicultural World,* Downers Grove, IL: InterVarsity Press, 2002.

Lipnack, Jessica, and Jeffrey Stamps, *Virtual Teams: Reaching across Space, Time, and Organizations with Technology,* New York: John Wiley & Sons, 1997.

Lipnack, Jessica, and Jeffrey Stamps, *Virtual Teams: People Working Across Boundaries with Technology*, 2nd ed. New York: John Wiley & Sons, 2000.

Marquardt, Michael J., and Nancy O. Berger, *Global Leaders for the 21st Century,* New York: State University of New York Press, 2000.

McCall, Morgan W., Jr., and George P. Hollenbeck, *Developing Global Executives: The Lessons of International Experience*, Cambridge, MA: Harvard Business School Press, 2002.

McGregor, James, *One Billion Customers: Lessons from the Front Lines of Doing Business in China,* New York: Wall Street Journal Books, 2005.

Morrison, Terri, Wayne A. Conaway, and George A. Borden, Ph.D., *Kiss, Bow, or Shake Hands,* Holbrook: Bob Adams, Inc., 1994.

Moynihan, Michael, *Global Manager: Recruiting, Developing, and Keeping World Class Executives*, New York: McGraw-Hill, 1993.

Nath, Kamal, *India's Century: The Age of Entrepreneurship in the World's Biggest Democracy,* New York: McGraw-Hill, 2008.

O'Hara-Devereaux, Mary, and Robert Johansen, *GlobalWork: Bridging Distance, Culture, and Time,* San Francisco: Jossey-Bass, 1994.

Phillips, Nicola, *Managing International Teams,* New York: Irwin Professional Publishing, 1994.

Plafker, Ted, *Doing Business in China: How to Profit in the World's Fastest Growing Economy,* New York: Warner Business Books, 2007.

Rhinesmith, Stephen H., *A Managers Guide to Globalization: Six Skills for Success in a Changing World*, Burr Ridge, IL: Irwin Professional Publishing, 1996.

Ricks, David A., *Blunders in International Business*, Cambridge, U.K.: Blackwell Business, 1993.

Rogers, Jim, *A Bull in China: Investing Profitably in the World's Greatest Market*, New York: Random House, 2007.

Rosen, Robert, Patricia Digh, Marshall Singer, and Carl Phillips, *Global Literacies: Lessons on Business Leadership and National Cultures*, New York: Simon & Schuster, 2000.

Saxon, Mike, M.B.A., *An American's Guide to Doing Business in China*, Avon: Adams Media, 2007.

Scheffler, Axel, *Let Sleeping Dogs Lie and Other Proverbs from around the World*, New York: Barron's Educational Series, 1997.

Schell, Michael S., and Charlene Solomon, *Capitalizing on the Global Workforce*, New York: McGraw-Hill, 1997.

Schell, Michael S., and Charlene Solomon, "Global Culture: Who's the Gatekeeper?" *Workforce*, November 1997, pp. 35–39.

Senge, Peter M. *The Fifth Discipline: The Art and Practice of the Learning Organization*, New York: Doubleday/Currency, 2006.

Solomon, Charlene, "Building Teams Across Borders," *Global Workforce*, November 1998, 3:6, pp. 12–17.

Solomon, Charlene, "Danger Below: Spot Failing Assignments," *Personnel Journal*, November 1996, 75:11, pp. 78–85.

Solomon, Charlene, "Expatriates Say, Make Us Mobile," *Personnel Journal*, July 1996, 75:7, pp. 47–52.

Solomon, Charlene, "How Virtual Teams Bring Real Savings," *Workforce*, June 2001, p. 62.

Solomon, Charlene, "One Assignment, Two Lives," *Personnel Journal*, May 1996, 75: 5, pp. 36–47.

Solomon, Charlene, "Staff Selection Impacts Global Success," *Personnel Journal*, January 1994, 73:1.

Solomon, Charlene, "Women Expats—Shattering the Myths," *Global Workforce*, May 1998, 3:3, pp. 10–14.

Storti, Craig, *The Art of Coming Home,* Yarmouth, ME: Intercultural Press, 1997.

Storti, Craig, *The Art of Crossing Cultures,* Yarmouth, ME: Intercultural Press, 1990.

Storti, Craig, *Figuring Foreigners Out: A Practical Guide,* Yarmouth, ME: Intercultural Press, 1999.

Suchan, J., and G. Hayzak. 2001. "The Communication Characteristics of Virtual Teams: A Case Study." *IEEE Transactions on Professional Communication,* 44:174–186.

Sull, Donald N., and Yong Wang, *Made in China: What Western Managers Can Learn from Trailblazing Chinese Entrepreneurs,* Cambridge, MA: Harvard Business School Press, 2005.

Trompenaars, Fons, *Riding the Waves of Culture: Understanding Diversity in Global Business,* Irwin Professional Publishing, 1993 and 1994.

Williams, Jeremy, *Don't They Know It's Friday? Cross-Cultural Considerations for Business and Life in the Gulf,* Dubai, UAE, Motivate Publishing, 1998.

Diversity Web Sites and Organizations

SHRM Diversity Focus Area. http://www.shrm.org/diversity/
Diversity.com. http://www.diversity.com/
Diversity Inc. http://www.diversityinc.com/
Diversity Central. http://www.diversitycentral.com/
Workplace Diversity. http://www.workplacediversity.com/
Cultural Diversity in the Workplace. http://www.cultural-diversity-in-the-workplace.blogspot.com/
Diversity Matters. http://www.diversity-matters.net/index.html
Diversity Builder. http://www.diversitybuilder.com/index.php

Diversity Articles

"Diversity in the Workplace: Benefits, Challenges, and the Required Managerial Tools." http://edis.ifas.ufl.edu/HR022

"Diversity in the Workplace: Benefits, Challenges and Solutions," http://ezinearticles.com/?Diversity-in-the-Workplace:-Benefits,-Challenges-and-Solutions&id=11053

"Workplace Diversity: Leveraging the Power of Difference for Competitive Advantage." http://findarticles.com/p/articles/mi_m3495/is_6_50/ai_n14702678

"Managing Diversity in the Workplace." http://www.sideroad.com/Diversity_in_the_Workplace/managing-diversity-in-the-workplace.html

"Diversity Can Improve Decision-Making." http://www.vault.com/nr/newsmain.jsp?nr_page=3&ch_id=402&article_id=14805372&cat_id=1102

"Cultural Diversity in the Workplace." www.imi.ie/GetAttachment.aspx?id=bbf9befa-21cb-4372-a3b3-27866645c06c

"Multicultural Is New Workplace Model." http://the-diversity-working-guy.blogspot.com/2007/10/multicultural-is-new-workplace-model.html

Expatriate Web Sites

Expat Social Network. http://www.expats.com/site/ (*Free membership*)
Expat Exchange. http://www.expatexchange.com/
Expatica. http://www.expatica.com/
Expat Blogs. http://expats.totalblogdirectory.com/
Expat Communities. http://www.expatcommunities.com/
Expat Expert. http://expatexpert.com/
Expat Exchange. http://www.expatexchange.com/
Expat Interviews. http://www.expatinterviews.com/belgium
Expat Women. http://www.expatwomen.com/
InterNations. http://www.internations.org/
Just Landed. http://www.justlanded.com/
Moving Away or Coming Home. http://www.movingawayorcominghome.com/
Tales from a Small Planet. http://www.talesmag.com/

Country-Specific Expatriate Web Sites

Living in Argentina. http://www.livinginargentina.com/
Living in Indonesia. http://www.expat.or.id/
Expat Singapore. http://www.expatsingapore.com/

Expats Russia. http://www.expat.ru/
How to Germany. http://www.howtogermany.com/
Korea 4 Expats. http://www.korea4expats.com/

Expat Spouse Web Sites

Federation of American Women's Clubs. http://www.fawco.org/
Newcomers Clubs. http://www.newcomersclub.com/
British Clubs Worldwide. http://www.britishclubworldwide.com/
A Portable Identity. http://www.aportableidentity.com/reso.htm
Trailing Spouses. http://trailing-spouses.blogspot.com/
The Trailing Spouse. http://users.anet.com/~smcnulty/homepage.html

Expatriate Articles Online

"Challenges that Face Expat Spouses." http://www.x-patgeneration.com/
Articles/9290.aspx
"What Do Expat Spouses Need?" http://www.ausmerica.com/blog/2008/
08/what-do-expat-spouses-need-interview-with-dr-nina-cole/
"Surviving Abroad Without a Career." http://www.overseasdigest.com/
expat-spouses-no-career.htm
"How Wives Experience Culture Shock." http://www.telegraph.co.uk/expat/
relocatingabroad/4179183/How-wives-experience-culture-shock.html
"Lost in the Move Abroad." http://www.telegraph.co.uk/expat/4193662/
Lost-in-the-move-abroad.html
"Trailing Spouses in Expat Assignments Get No Respect." http://hragitator.
com/2008/04/trailing-spouses-in-expatriate-assignments-get-no-respect/
"The Male Trailing Spouse." http://myglobalcoach.com/db3/00210/my
globalcoach.com/_download/MaleTSarticle.pdf
"Not Dead Yet." http://chronicle.com/jobs/news/2005/10/2005102401c.htm
"Business Recruiters Focus on Trailing Spouses." http://community.seattle
-times.nwsource.com/archive/?date=20010122&slug=bizrelocate220
"Trials of Trailing Spouses." http://www.economist.com/world/international/
displaystory.cfm?story_id=8781700

Global Virtual Teams Online Articles

"Communication and Trust in Global Virtual Teams." http://jcmc.indiana
.edu/vol3/issue4/jarvenpaa.html

"Trust in Global Virtual Teams." http://www.ariadne.ac.uk/issue43/panteli/

"Global Virtual Team Dynamics and Effectiveness." http://uainfo.arizona
.edu/~weisband/distwork/maznevski.pdf

"Leadership Competencies for Managing Global Virtual Teams—Introduction, Background, Government Leadership Competencies, Future Trends, Conclusion." http://encyclopedia.jrank.org/articles/pages/6654/Leadership-Competencies-for-Managing-Global-Virtual-Teams.html

"Critical Success Factors for Global Virtual Teams." http://www.allbusiness
.com/human-resources/workforce-management/1045913-1.html

"Galvanize Global Virtual Teams with Clear Operating Principles." http://
www.leadergrow.com/Globalremoteteams.pdf

"Leadership Challenges in Global Virtual Teams: Lessons from the Field,"
http://findarticles.com/p/articles/mi_hb6698/is_/ai_n29141193

"Global Teams." http://www.fastcompany.com/blog/fast-company-staff/fast
-company-blog/global-teams

"Multinational Enterprises in Dissimilar Cultural Contexts: The Role of Global Virtual Teams." http://www.ifipwg94.org.br/fullpapers/R0039-1.pdf

"Communication and Collaborative Process in Global Virtual Teams."
http://www.cscw.msu.edu/papers/INTEnD_Summary.pdf

"Working Together Virtually: The Care and Feeding of Global Virtual Teams."
http://www.dodccrp.org/events/5th_ICCRTS/papers/Track4/009.pdf

"Mobilize Global Virtual Teams by Avoiding 8 Common Landmines." http://
www.ittoday.info/ITPerformanceImprovement/Articles/Landmines.htm

"Leadership Challenges in Global Virtual Teams." http://goliath.ecnext.com/
coms2/gi_0199-3573403/Leadership-challenges-in-global-virtual.html

"Working Together Apart? Building a Knowledge-sharing Culture for Global Virtual Teams." http://papers.ssrn.com/sol3/papers.cfm?abstract_id=513397

"Challenges to Staffing Global Virtual Teams." Go to http://www.sciencedirect
and search for this article.

"Leading Global Virtual Teams." http://www.ingentaconnect.com/content/
mcb/037/2006/00000038/00000003/art00001

Index

About the Authors

Charlene Marmer Solomon is an award-winning author who has written seven books, including *Capitalizing on the Global Workforce: A Strategic Guide to Expatriate Management* (McGraw-Hill, 1997, which she coauthored with Michael Schell). She was an editor at both business and consumer magazines, including *Workforce* and *Global Workforce* magazines, and has written hundreds of magazine and journal articles, specializing in human resources, business, dual careers, and interpersonal relationships. She was also a consultant and teacher for several years.

She is currently Executive Vice President of RW^3 LLC, an intercultural consulting and training organization that designs and creates online cultural learning tools for global organizations. CultureWizard.com, its flagship service, is used by dozens of multinational organizations worldwide. Visit the CultureWizard Digest and blog at http://culturewizard.rw-3llc.com.

Ms. Solomon was cofounder of ExpatSpouse.com, an online community helping families with transitions from one country to another, and has been a communications consultant on global management and human resource issues, and issues specifically related to spouse, family, and work-life concerns. She is the recipient of several magazine awards, a Lowell Thomas award, and awards from The American Society of Business Press Editors and The Community Action Network.

Ms. Solomon is a lecturer at UCLA. She has worked with The Conference Board and Catalyst women's think tank on global business issues. She is a frequent speaker and has appeared at conferences for the Society of Human Resource Management, ORC, National Foreign Trade Council, Deloitte & Touche, KPMG, PricewaterhouseCoopers and the American Society of Journalists and Authors. She conducts roundtables, and has been a commentator for NPR's *Marketplace*. She has been featured on radio and television news and feature programs and was the chairperson for the Southern California Committee for the international humanitarian organization CARE.

She lived and worked in Japan for two years, during which time she studied Japanese language and culture. Contact her at charlene.solomon@rw-3.com.

Michael S. Schell is CEO and president of RW³ LLC, an intercultural consulting and training organization, specializing in customized online delivery. CultureWizard.com is one of its primary platforms, used by multinational organizations around the world. Prior to RW³, he was CEO of Windham International, a global intercultural relocation consulting and management firm founded in 1991 and acquired in 1999 by GMAC.

Mr. Schell has written extensively on the subject of intercultural understanding and has designed and conducted intercultural training programs around the world for expatriates, global managers, and intercultural teams. He was a creator of the Windham International Cultural Model, which has become a standard for teaching and understanding cultures.

Mr. Schell has been a leader in the intercultural and relocation industry for over 30 years. Prior to creating Windham International, he was president and founding partner of Moran, Stahl, & Boyer (MS & B), a business location and global relocation consulting company.

He is coauthor of *Capitalizing on the Global Workforce: A Strategic Guide for Expatriate Management* (McGraw-Hill, 1997). He has written many articles related to international mobility. In addition, he is a frequent speaker at human resources and relocation industry events, including the Society of Human Resource Management, the Employee Relocation Council, the National Foreign Trade Council, Deloitte & Touche, KPMG, Pricewaterhouse-Coopers, and ORC. In 1999, he received the Meritorious Service Award of the Employee Relocation Council (ERC). He is a contributor to the monthly CultureWizard Digest and blog (http://culturewizard.rw-3llc.com). He is a member of the Institute of International Human Resources (IIHR) of the Society of Human Resource Management (SHRM), the National Foreign Trade Council (NFTC), ERC, Society of International Education (SIETAR), and several other organizations. You can contact him at michael.schell@rw-3.com